HEAFEY LAW ... RY
W9-CZJ-845 ITY
5053

Victims –
Support and assistance

(2nd edition)

Council of Europe Publishing

French edition:

Soutien et aide aux victimes

ISBN 978-92-871-6376-9

KJC
9799
V53
2007

The opinions expressed in this work are the responsibility of the authors and do not necessarily reflect the official policy of the Council of Europe.

All rights reserved. No part of this publication may be translated, reproduced or transmitted, in any form or by any means, electronic (CD-Rom, Internet, etc.) or mechanical, including photocopying, recording or any information storage or retrieval system, without prior permission in writing from the Public Information and Publications Division, Directorate of Communication (F-67075 Strasbourg Cedex or publishing@coe.int).

For further information, please contact us:
Counter-Terrorism Task Force
Council of Europe
F-67075 Strasbourg Cedex (France)
Tel.: +33 3 88 41 34 79 – Fax: +33 3 90 21 51 31
gmt@coe.int – www.coe.int/gmt

Cover design: Graphic Design Workshop, Council of Europe

Council of Europe Publishing
F-67075 Strasbourg Cedex
http://book.coe.int

ISBN 978-92-871-6377-6
© Council of Europe, December 2007
Printed at the Council of Europe

Table of contents

Foreword

True justice depends not only on States' ability to prosecute the perpetrators of crime, but also on their capacity to restore the situation of victims. For more than 50 years, the Council of Europe has contributed to building a common legal area based on the respect for human rights, the development of democracy and the promotion of the rule of law. The fight against crime has been at the heart of these efforts.

Since the 1980s the Council of Europe has integrated the victim's perspective in its work in this field and has produced and updated a set of legal instruments to assist States in dealing with the needs of victims.

This publication brings together the main Council of Europe standards related to victims. It is intended to provide guidance for those who are dealing with victims as well as tools to increase the level of assistance given to them.

Terry DAVIS
Secretary General of
the Council of Europe

Council of Europe conventions

European Convention on the Compensation of Victims of Violent Crimes (ETS No. 116)

The member states of the Council of Europe, signatory hereto,

Considering that the aim of the Council of Europe is to achieve a greater unity between its members;

Considering that for reasons of equity and social solidarity it is necessary to deal with the situation of victims of intentional crimes of violence who have suffered bodily injury or impairment of health and of dependants of persons who have died as a result of such crimes;

Considering that it is necessary to introduce or develop schemes for the compensation of these victims by the State in whose territory such crimes were committed, in particular when the offender has not been identified or is without resources;

Considering that it is necessary to establish minimum provisions in this field;

Having regard to Resolution (77) 27 of the Committee of Ministers of the Council of Europe on the compensation of victims of crime,

Have agreed as follows:

Part I – Basic principles

Article 1

The Parties undertake to take the necessary steps to give effect to the principles set out in Part I of this Convention.

Article 2

1. When compensation is not fully available from other sources the State shall contribute to compensate:
   a. those who have sustained serious bodily injury or impairment of health directly attributable to an intentional crime of violence;
   b. the dependants of persons who have died as a result of such crime.
2. Compensation shall be awarded in the above cases even if the offender cannot be prosecuted or punished.

Article 3

Compensation shall be paid by the State on whose territory the crime was committed:
a. to nationals of the States party to this Convention;

b. to nationals of all member states of the Council of Europe who are permanent residents in the State on whose territory the crime was committed.

Article 4

Compensation shall cover, according to the case under consideration, at least the following items: loss of earnings, medical and hospitalisation expenses and funeral expenses, and, as regards dependants, loss of maintenance.

Article 5

The compensation scheme may, if necessary, set for any or all elements of compensation an upper limit above which and a minimum threshold below which such compensation shall not be granted.

Article 6

The compensation scheme may specify a period within which any application for compensation must be made.

Article 7

Compensation may be reduced or refused on account of the applicant's financial situation.

Article 8

1. Compensation may be reduced or refused on account of the victim's or the applicant's conduct before, during or after the crime, or in relation to the injury or death.
2. Compensation may also be reduced or refused on account of the victim's or the applicant's involvement in organised crime or his membership of an organisation which engages in crimes of violence.
3. Compensation may also be reduced or refused if an award or a full award would be contrary to a sense of justice or to public policy *(ordre public)*.

Article 9

With a view to avoiding double compensation, the State or the competent authority may deduct from the compensation awarded or reclaim from the person compensated any amount of money received, in consequence of the injury or death, from the offender, social security or insurance, or coming from any other source.

Article 10

The State or the competent authority may be subrogated to the rights of the person compensated for the amount of the compensation paid.

Article 11

Each Party shall take appropriate steps to ensure that information about the scheme is available to potential applicants.

Part II – International co-operation

Article 12

Subject to the application of bilateral or multilateral agreements on mutual assistance concluded between Contracting States, the competent authorities of each Party shall, at the request of the appropriate authorities of any other Party, give the maximum possible assistance in connection with the matters covered by this Convention. To this end, each Contracting State shall designate a central authority to receive, and to take action on, requests for such assistance, and shall inform thereof the Secretary General of the Council of Europe when depositing its instrument of ratification, acceptance, approval or accession.

Article 13

1. The European Committee on Crime Problems (CDPC) of the Council of Europe shall be kept informed regarding the application of the Convention.
2. To this end, each Party shall transmit to the Secretary General of the Council of Europe any relevant information about its legislative or regulatory provisions concerning the matters covered by the Convention.

Part III – Final clauses

Article 14

This Convention shall be open for signature by the member states of the Council of Europe. It is subject to ratification, acceptance or approval. Instruments of ratification, acceptance or approval shall be deposited with the Secretary General of the Council of Europe.

Article 15

1. This Convention shall enter into force on the first day of the month following the expiration of a period of three months after the date on which three member states of the Council of Europe have expressed

their consent to be bound by the Convention in accordance with the provisions of Article 14.

2. In respect of any member state which subsequently expresses its consent to be bound by it, the Convention shall enter into force on the first day of the month following the expiration of a period of three months after the date of the deposit of the instrument of ratification, acceptance or approval.

Article 16

1. After the entry into force of this Convention, the Committee of Ministers of the Council of Europe may invite any State not a member of the Council of Europe to accede to this Convention by a decision taken by the majority provided for in Article 20.d of the Statute of the Council of Europe and by the unanimous vote of the representatives of the Contracting States entitled to sit on the Committee.

2. In respect of any acceding State, the Convention shall enter into force on the first day of the month following the expiration of a period of three months after the date of deposit of the instrument of accession with the Secretary General of the Council of Europe.

Article 17

1. Any State may at the time of signature or when depositing its instrument of ratification, acceptance, approval or accession, specify the territory or territories to which this Convention shall apply.

2. Any State may at any later date, by a declaration addressed to the Secretary General of the Council of Europe, extend the application of this Convention to any other territory specified in the declaration. In respect of such territory the Convention shall enter into force on the first day of the month following the expiration of a period of three months after the date of receipt of such declaration by the Secretary General.

3. Any declaration made under the two preceding paragraphs may, in respect of any territory specified in such declaration, be withdrawn by a notification addressed to the Secretary General. The withdrawal shall become effective on the first day of the month following the expiration of a period of six months after the date of receipt of such notification by the Secretary General.

Article 18

1. Any State may, at the time of signature or when depositing its instrument of ratification, acceptance, approval or accession, declare that it avails itself of one or more reservations.

2. Any Contracting State which has made a reservation under the preceding paragraph may wholly or partly withdraw it by means of a notification addressed to the Secretary General of the Council of Europe. The withdrawal shall take effect on the date of receipt of such notification by the Secretary General.

3. A Party which has made a reservation in respect of a provision of this Convention may not claim the application of that provision by any other Party; it may, however, if its reservation is partial or conditional, claim the application of that provision in so far as it has itself accepted it.

Article 19

1. Any Party may at any time denounce this Convention by means of a notification addressed to the Secretary General of the Council of Europe.
2. Such a denunciation shall become effective on the first day of the month following the expiration of a period of six months after the date of receipt of the notification by the Secretary General.

Article 20

The Secretary General of the Council of Europe shall notify the member States of the Council and any State which has acceded to this Convention, of:

a. any signature;
b. the deposit of any instrument of ratification, acceptance, approval or accession;
c. any date of entry into force of this Convention in accordance with Articles 15, 16 and 17;
d. any other act, notification or communication relating to this Convention.

In witness whereof the undersigned, being duly authorised thereto, have signed this Convention.

Done at Strasbourg, this 24th day of November 1983, in English and French, both texts being equally authentic, in a single copy which shall be deposited in the archives of the Council of Europe. The Secretary General of the Council of Europe shall transmit certified copies to each member State of the Council of Europe and to any State invited to accede to this Convention.

Explanatory Report

I.   The European Convention on the Compensation of Victims of Violent Crimes, drawn up within the Council of Europe by a Committee of Governmental Experts under the authority of the European Committee on Crime Problems (CDPC), was opened for signature by the member states of the Council of Europe on 24 November 1983.

II.   The text of the explanatory report prepared by the committee of experts and submitted the Committee of Ministers of the Council of Europe, as amended and completed by the CCJ, does not constitute an instrument providing an authoritative interpretation of the Convention although it might be of such a nature to facilitate the application of the provisions contained therein.

I.   Introduction

1.   In recent decades, policy makers and criminologists have been particularly concerned with the victim's position in crime and with protecting the victim's interests. They have emphasised that assisting victims must be a constant concern of crime policy, on a par with the penal treatment of offenders. Such assistance includes measures designed to alleviate psychological distress as well as to make reparation for the victim's physical injuries.

One of these concerns is to provide compensation for the victim or his dependants. In principle, the offender should pay the compensation, by order of the civil or - in some countries - criminal courts or by a judicial or extrajudicial arrangement between him and the victim. However, though the victim can obtain satisfaction by this means in theory, full reparation is seldom made in practice, in particular because of the offender's non-apprehension, disappearance or lack of means.

2.   In the 1960s, therefore, various Council of Europe member states started setting up schemes to compensate victims from public funds when compensation was otherwise unavailable. In view of this development, the CEPC (now the CDPC) decided in 1970 to add the compensation of victims of crime to its work programme. This decision was approved by the Committee of Ministers of the Council of Europe at their Deputies' 192nd meeting, but no action was taken on it pending the outcome of relevant work by the International Association of Penal Law (11th International Congress on Penal Law, Budapest, 1974).

Having discussed the compensation of victims of crime, the 9th Conference of European Ministers of Justice (Vienna, 1974) recommended that the Committee of Ministers of the Council of Europe instruct the CEPC to hold an exchange of views and information on the subject.

This was duly held by the CEPC in January 1975.

Finally, a CEPC sub-committee was asked to draw up common principles governing the compensation of victims of crime, with particular reference to compensation from public funds. The subcommittee produced a draft resolution and a report on the subject, which were submitted to the CEPC and approved in 1977.

In September 1977, the Committee of Ministers of the Council of Europe adopted Resolution (77) 27 on the compensation of victims of crime. This recommended that the member states provide for state compensation of victims, or dependants of victims, of intentional violence where compensation could not be ensured by any other means, and set out guidelines.

The CEPC report on the compensation of victims of crime was published in 1978.

3.   In the five years following the adoption of Resolution (77) 27, various Council of Europe member states, guided, *inter alia,* by the said resolution, either introduced state schemes for compensating victims of crime or drafted legislation on the subject.

Various member states soon found, however, that if foreigners moving between member States - notably migrant workers - were to be socially protected, the principles laid down in Resolution (77) 27 (and more particularly in Article 13) needed to be reconsidered and an instrument drawn up which would have binding force.

These considerations are mentioned in the report submitted by Mr Luster on behalf of the European Parliament's Legal Affairs Committee (Doc. 1-464/80). During the European Parliament debate on 12 March 1981, it was stated that the EEC should draw up a directive in this sphere, unless the Council of Europe embarked on producing a convention on the basis of Resolution (77) 27. The Resolution on Compensation for Victims of Acts of Violence, adopted by the European Parliament on 13 March 1981, reflects this view.

4.   At its 30th plenary Session (1981) the CDPC heeded this concern by instructing the Select Committee on the Victim and Criminal and Social Policy to begin its work by drawing up a European convention on compensation of victims of crime on the basis of Resolution (77) 27 on the same subject.

5.   The Select Committee met twice in 1982 (24-26 February and 29 September-1 October) under the chairmanship of Mr J. G. Schätzler (Federal Republic of Germany). Its meetings were attended by experts from France, Iceland, Italy., Luxembourg, the Netherlands, Portugal, Switzerland, Turkey and the United Kingdom, as well as by Mr H.J. Schneider (Federal

Republic of Germany) and Ms J. Shapland (United Kingdom), consultants, and observers from Canada and the IAPL.

An enlarged meeting of the committee took place from 17 to 21 January 1983 under the chairmanship of Mr J. G. Schätzler. The meeting was attended by all the Council of Europe member states, except Belgium, Ireland, Liechtenstein and Malta.

The Select Committee's draft European Convention on the Compensation of Victims of Violent Crimes, as approved after amendment by the enlarged committee, and the draft explanatory report were approved by the CDPC at its 32nd plenary Session (April 1983). At the 361st meeting of the Deputies (June 1983), the Committee of Ministers adopted the Convention and decided to open it for signature on 24 November 1983.

II. General considerations

A. Framework of the Convention

6. The Council of Europe's aim of promoting closer unity between its member states is pursued in particular through the harmonisation of their legislation and agreement among them on common policy.

In this context, the European Committee on Crime Problems has sought, since its inception, to promote joint policy on crime prevention and the treatment of offenders.

Such a policy demands that balanced consideration be given to all the components of the criminal act. Victim studies carried out in various countries in the last few decades have revealed the interaction which may exist between criminal and victim during the commission of a crime. At the same time, they have thrown light on victims' psychological and physical distress after a crime and on the difficulties they often encounter in asserting their rights. These considerations lead one to conclude that as much importance must be attached to the victims, and in particular to the protection of their interests, as to the treatment and social rehabilitation of offenders.

7. This points to the need to compensate the victim, not only to alleviate as far as possible the injury and distress suffered by him, but also to quell the social conflict caused by the offence and make it easier to apply rational, effective crime policy.

8. Various provisions in force in member states are designed to induce the offender to compensate the victim (for example, suspended sentence or probation may depend on payment of compensation, payment of compensation may constitute the main penalty, etc.). In very few cases is

compensation for injury actually paid, however. A State contribution to compensation is accordingly thought necessary.

9. Various arguments for State involvement in compensation have been put forward:

    a. One theory is that the State is bound to compensate the victim because:

        - it has failed to prevent the crime by means of effective criminal policy,

        - it introduced criminal policy measures which have failed,

        - having prohibited personal vengeance, it is bound to appease the victim, or his dependants (principle of State responsibility for crime);

    b. Another theory is that State intervention is justified on grounds of social solidarity and equity: since some citizens are more vulnerable, or unluckier, than others, they must be compensated by the whole community for any injury sustained:

    c. Lastly, it has been suggested that by removing the victim's sense of injustice, State compensation makes it easier to apply a less punitive criminal policy, but one which is more effective.

10. Resolution (77) 27 accepted equity and social solidarity as the basic principles of compensation.

These same principles underlie the European Convention on the Compensation of Victims of Violent Crimes (second preambular paragraph).

The majority view in the committee was, however, that these principles did not mean that the State should intervene only in cases of absolute necessity (that is hardship). Compensation awards may nevertheless take the victim's or victim's dependants' financial position Into account (Article 7).

B. Aims of the Convention

11. The European Convention on the Compensation of Victims of Violent Crimes, based on Resolution (77) 27, pursues the following aims:

a. To harmonise at European level the guidelines (minimum provisions) on the compensation of victims of violent crimes and to give them binding force.

States ratifying the Convention will have to comply with the principles laid down, either by amending existing legislation and administrative arrangements or by introducing these principles to any new legislation or arrangements.

b. To ensure co-operation between the Parties in the compensation of victims of violent crimes, and more particularly to promote:

- the compensation of foreign victims by the State on whose territory the offence was committed;
- mutual assistance between Parties in all matters concerning compensation.

The presence of numerous foreigners on the Parties' territories (migrant workers, tourists, students, etc.) makes such co-operation necessary.

III. Commentary on the articles of the Convention

PART I – Basic principles

Article 1

12. By the terms of Article 1, the Parties undertake to ensure that their present and future legislation and administrative arrangements on the compensation of victims of crimes of violence comply with the Convention. It follows that this Convention is not directly enforceable.

It is for the Contracting States to establish the legal basis, the administrative framework and the methods of operation of the compensation schemes having due regard to these principles.

13. Since several member states have for some years effectively operated schemes for paying compensation from public funds, the committee decided to draw up minimum provisions rather than a model act, whose rigidity might have prevented several member states from ratifying the Convention.

Article 2

14. This article sets out the basic conditions governing State compensation of victims of violent crimes. Since the rules given are minima, more generous compensation arrangements by Parties are not precluded.

The succeeding articles foresee, for specific cases, limitations to the obligations laid down by Article 2.

15. The State pays compensation only where compensation is not fully available from other sources (the offender, social security, etc.).

As is clear from Articles 9 and 10, however, this provision must not be taken to preclude an interim State contribution to compensation of the victim pending decision of an action, judicial or extrajudicial (arbitration), to recover damages. A victim urgently needing help sometimes cannot await the outcome of often complicated proceedings (cf. paragraph 8 of Resolution (77) 27). In such cases, the Parties can provide that the State or the competent authority may subrogate in the rights of the person compensated for the amount of the compensation paid (Article 10) or, if later the person compensated obtains reparation from any other source, may reclaim totally or partially the amount of money awarded (Article g).

16. For compensation to be payable to the victim from public funds, offences must be:
- intentional,
- violent,
- the direct cause of serious bodily injury or damage to health.

17. The Convention applies only to intentional offences, because they are particularly serious and give rise to compensation less often than non-intentional offences, which include the huge range of road traffic offences and are in principle covered by other schemes (private insurance, social security, etc.).

18. The violence inflicted by the offender need not be physical. Compensation may also be payable in cases of psychological violence (for example serious threats) causing serious injury or death.

19. The Convention aims at protecting victims of offences against life, physical integrity and health.

The term health may include, according to the domestic law of each State, mental as well as physical health.

Injury must be serious and directly attributable to the crime, a relationship of cause and effect being proven.

Having regard both to the underlying principle of solidarity, which requires the alleviation of major distress and injury, and to financial constraints, the Convention does not cover:
- slight injury or injury not directly caused by the offence;
- injury to other interests, notably property.

Poisoning, rape and arson are to be treated as intentional violence.

20. The persons eligible for compensation are:

a. The victim

In the event of serious bodily injury or damage to health, compensation is payable to the victim direct. The victim's dependants thus benefit indirectly.

Victims of violent crimes may include anyone injured or killed in trying to prevent an offence, or in helping the police to prevent the offence, apprehend the culprit or help the victim.

b.   The dependants of persons who have died as a result of a violent crime

It is for the Parties to define the term according to the requirements of their domestic law (children, spouse, etc.).

21. Compensation from public funds is payable to the victim irrespective of the offender's prosecution or conviction.

Particular categories of offender specified in national legislation (for example, minors, the mentally ill) may not be subject to prosecution, being regarded as not responsible for their actions.

Offenders prosecuted may escape conviction for other reasons (act arising from necessity, for example).

The State may nonetheless make reparation, even in respect of these acts, if compensation is not fully available from other sources.

Article 3

22. This article regulates international aspects of the compensation of victims of violent crimes.

23. Like Resolution (77) 27 before it, the Convention recognises the principle of "territoriality": compensation is payable by the State in whose territory the offence is committed.

Where different parts of a crime are committed in different States, compensation shall be paid by the State in which the victim or his dependants are permanently resident, provided part of the offence is committed in the territory of this State.

The Convention does not provide for compensation of nationals who fall victim to violent crimes while abroad, but there is nothing to prevent the Parties from recognising the nationality principle in certain cases.

24. Compensation of foreign victims of violent crimes on the same basis as nationals - already provided for in some of the Council of Europe member states - seems necessary for the following main reasons:
- solidarity and equity demand that, on certain conditions, the State contribute to the compensation of other victims in its territory and not just its own nationals;
- foreigners often contribute to a country's economic and social development (for example, as migrant workers); consequently, they are entitled to the same advantages as nationals.

25. The Convention specifies categories of foreigners to be entitled to compensation:

a.   Nationals of Parties to the Convention.

This provision complies with the principle of reciprocity.

b.   Nationals of any Council of Europe member state who are permanently resident in the State in whose territory the offence is committed.

The main purpose of this provision, a departure from the principle of reciprocity, Is to protect migrant workers, a lower-income group which nonetheless contributes to the receiving country's economy and ought not to be penalised where the State of origin is still unable to ratify the Convention.

Compensation of all foreign victims of crime without a reciprocity requirement was also recommended by the 11th International Congress on Penal Law (Budapest, 1974, Conclusions, item A. 7).

26. The concept of permanent residence must be construed in the light of Committee of Ministers Resolution (72) 1 on the standardisation of the legal concepts of "domicile" and of "residence".

27. Though the Convention lays down minimum provisions, this need not prevent Contracting States from compensating:
- nationals of any State (and not just nationals of Council of Europe member states) who are permanently resident in their territory;
- all foreigners (which would enable tourists to be compensated).

Article 4

28. This article specifies as minimum requirements items for which reasonable compensation shall be paid, when the loss is verified in a particular case. These are the following:
- loss of earnings (for example, as a result of immobilisation through injury);
- medical expenses (which may include prescription charges and the cost of dental treatment);
- hospital fees;
- funeral expenses;
- in the case of dependants (children, spouse, etc.), loss of maintenance.

Other possible items, subject to the provisions of national legislation, are, in particular:
- pain and suffering (*pretium doloris*);
- loss of expectation of life;
- additional expenses arising from disablement caused by an offence.

Compensation of these items is to be calculated by the State paying the compensation according to the scales normally applied for social security or private insurance or according to normal practice under civil law.

Article 5

29. This allows the setting of:

- An upper limit to compensation.

As the public funds earmarked for the compensation of victims of violent crimes are not unlimited, a ceiling on such compensation may be necessary in certain circumstances.

- A minimum threshold below which compensation is not payable.

In line with the principle of *de minimis non curat praetor*, this provision narrows the scope of the Convention to exclude minor damage the victim can readily make good.

30. The Convention obviously cannot set rigidly quantified limits, since resources and living standards vary from State to State. These differences will mean that the sum awarded in compensation by different States will vary, and this will be particularly noticeable where foreign victims are compensated. In such cases, it is desirable that due regard should be had to the standard of living in the country where the victim habitually resides. Limits are to be set with particular reference to:
- administrative constraints (for example individual States' resources),
- financial factors (for example, wages, medical or hospital fees, etc.).

These limits may apply either to the total amount of compensation in a particular case or to the Individual elements of compensation, for example for loss of earnings or pain and suffering.

Article 6

31. Applications for compensation of a victim or, if he has died, of his dependants, should be made within a period of time to be laid down by each State according to its own customary practice.

An application must be made as soon as possible after the crime has been committed, so that:
- the victim may be assisted if in physical and psychological distress;
- the damage may be ascertained and assessed without untoward difficulty.

Article 7

32. Since compensation of the victim from public funds is an act of social solidarity, it may be unnecessary where the victim or his dependants are plainly comfortably off. In such a case, the State may reduce or even withhold its contribution to compensation of the victim without being

regarded as discriminating unfairly against a section of the population. However, this provision must not be construed as precluding State compensation where no hardship exists.

Nor need it prevent States from paying compensation regardless of the victim's or his dependants' financial position (on the same basis as war disablement pensions, for example).

Article 8

33. Whereas Article 7 contains an objective criterion for reducing or withholding compensation, Article 8 allows compensation to be reduced or withheld where the victim is at fault.

34. a. *Improper behaviour of the victim in relation to the crime or to the damage suffered*

There is frequent evidence of a degree of interaction between the victim's behaviour and the offender's. The first paragraph of Article 8 refers to cases where the victim triggers the crime, for example by behaving exceptionally provocatively or aggressively, or causes worse violence through criminal retaliation, as well as to cases where the victim by his behaviour contributes to the causation or aggravation of the damage (for example by unreasonably refusing medical treatment).

Refusal to report the offence to the police or to co-operate with the administration of justice may also give grounds for reducing or withholding compensation.

35. b. *Membership of criminal gangs or of organisations which commit acts of violence*

Where the victim belongs to the world of organised crime (for example drug trafficking) or of organisations which commit acts of violence (for example terrorist organisations), he may be regarded as forfeiting the sympathy or solidarity of society as a whole. As a consequence, the victim may be refused compensation or be paid reduced compensation, even if the crime which caused the damage was not directly related to the foregoing activities.

36. c. *Compensation repugnant to the sense of justice or contrary to public policy* (ordre public)

States which introduce compensation schemes usually want to retain some discretion in awarding compensation and to be able to refuse it in certain cases where it is clear that a gesture of solidarity would be contrary to public feeling or interests or would be contrary to the basic principles of the legislation of the State concerned. This being so, a known criminal who was the victim of a crime of violence could be refused compensation even if the crime in question was unrelated to his criminal activities.

37. The principles justifying the withholding or reduction of compensation are valid not only in respect of a victim in person but also in relation to dependants of a victim who has died as a result of a violent crime.

Article 9

38. To avoid double compensation, compensation already received from the offender or other sources maybe deducted from the amount of compensation payable from public funds.

It is for the Parties to specify which sums are so deductible. In some of the member states, for instance, sums paid to the victim under private insurance schemes are not generally deductible from compensation.

39. A State may require any compensation the victim receives from the offender or other sources after being compensated from public funds to be repaid in full or in part (depending on the sum received) to the State or the authority paying compensation from public funds.

This eventuality is liable to arise, for example, where:
-   a victim suffering hardship receives State compensation pending decision of an action brought against an offender or agency;
-   the offender, unknown at the time of compensation from public funds, is subsequently traced and convicted, and has fully or partly made reparation to the victim.

40. Informing the compensating authority of subsequent compensation awards poses obvious problems. In some States, the courts inform the compensating authority of awards made to the victim, thus facilitating restitution of the sums allowed by the compensating authority.

Article 10

41. Where the victim or his dependants receive compensation from public funds, their rights against the offender or other sources of compensation (social security, etc.) may, if the domestic law so provides, pass to the State or the compensating authority, which may then take action to obtain reimbursement on that basis.

Article 11

42. In States with schemes for paying compensation from public funds, it has often been found that they are rarely used. This is mainly due to public ignorance of the existence of compensation schemes and brings home the need to publicise them better.

The main responsibility for informing the victim of his compensation rights should lie with the authorities and agencies dealing with him immediately after the offence (the police, hospitals, the examining judge, the public prosecutor's office, etc.). Information, specially published by the competent authorities, should be available to such agencies who should distribute this, whenever practicable, to the persons concerned.

The mass media (press, radio, television) could also help publicise such arrangements.

PART II – International co-operation

Article 12

43. Various matters relating to the implementation of the Convention may necessitate co-operation between the Parties, particularly:
-   information about compensation available to a foreign victim in his country of origin;
-   facilities whereby a State which compensates a victim can seek reimbursement from the offender resident abroad (or from a foreign agency, such as a social security authority);
-   information from medical authorities or employers.

44. International co-operation here may be helped by Council of Europe conventions, particularly the European Convention on Mutual Assistance in Criminal Matters and its Protocol and the European Convention on the Obtaining Abroad of Information and Evidence in Administrative Matters, and by bilateral and multilateral agreements concluded by the Contracting Parties.

45. As well as recommending that the Contracting Parties assist one another in all matters covered by the Convention, Article 12 also requires that, when depositing its instrument of ratification, acceptance, approval or accession, each State designate a central authority to receive and take action on requests for assistance. This will not prevent a State, with more than one compensation scheme, from designating more than one such authority.

Article 13

46. This article indicates that the European Committee on Crime Problems must be kept informed of the application of the Convention.

47. To this end, the Parties accept the obligation to transmit periodically to the Secretary General of the Council of Europe information about new legislation or regulations on compensation schemes; by this is meant provisions introducing methods of operation for these schemes which are of some interest and not merely internal administrative regulations.

48. This information will:

a.   help the CDPC to collect sufficient documentation for making available to member states who request it (member States who envisage introducing a compensation scheme, for example); and

b.   enable the CDPC to identify any difficulties arising from the application of the Convention and see whether it is necessary to hold meetings to solve such problems or whether protocols to the Convention need to be drawn up.

PART III – Final clauses

Articles 14-20

49. These articles are inspired by the final clauses usual in European conventions.

Council of Europe Convention on the Prevention of Terrorism
(CETS No. 196)

The member States of the Council of Europe and the other Signatories hereto,

Considering that the aim of the Council of Europe is to achieve greater unity between its members;

Recognising the value of reinforcing co-operation with the other Parties to this Convention;

Wishing to take effective measures to prevent terrorism and to counter, in particular, public provocation to commit terrorist offences and recruitment and training for terrorism;

Aware of the grave concern caused by the increase in terrorist offences and the growing terrorist threat;

Aware of the precarious situation faced by those who suffer from terrorism, and in this connection reaffirming their profound solidarity with the victims of terrorism and their families;

Recognising that terrorist offences and the offences set forth in this Convention, by whoever perpetrated, are under no circumstances justifiable by considerations of a political, philosophical, ideological, racial, ethnic, religious or other similar nature, and recalling the obligation of all Parties to prevent such offences and, if not prevented, to prosecute and ensure that they are punishable by penalties which take into account their grave nature;

Recalling the need to strengthen the fight against terrorism and reaffirming that all measures taken to prevent or suppress terrorist offences have to respect the rule of law and democratic values, human rights and fundamental freedoms as well as other provisions of international law, including, where applicable, international humanitarian law;

Recognising that this Convention is not intended to affect established principles relating to freedom of expression and freedom of association;

Recalling that acts of terrorism have the purpose by their nature or context to seriously intimidate a population or unduly compel a government or an international organisation to perform or abstain from performing any act or seriously destabilise or destroy the fundamental political, constitutional, economic or social structures of a country or an international organisation;

Have agreed as follows:

Article 1 – Terminology

1   For the purposes of this Convention, "terrorist offence" means any of the offences within the scope of and as defined in one of the treaties listed in the Appendix.

2   On depositing its instrument of ratification, acceptance, approval or accession, a State or the European Community which is not a party to a treaty listed in the Appendix may declare that, in the application of this Convention to the Party concerned, that treaty shall be deemed not to be included in the Appendix. This declaration shall cease to have effect as soon as the treaty enters into force for the Party having made such a declaration, which shall notify the Secretary General of the Council of Europe of this entry into force.

Article 2 – Purpose

The purpose of the present Convention is to enhance the efforts of Parties in preventing terrorism and its negative effects on the full enjoyment of human rights, in particular the right to life, both by measures to be taken at national level and through international co-operation, with due regard to the existing applicable multilateral or bilateral treaties or agreements between the Parties.

Article 3 – National prevention policies

1   Each Party shall take appropriate measures, particularly in the field of training of law enforcement authorities and other bodies, and in the fields of education, culture, information, media and public awareness raising, with a view to preventing terrorist offences and their negative effects while respecting human rights obligations as set forth in, where applicable to that Party, the Convention for the Protection of Human Rights and Fundamental Freedoms, the International Covenant on Civil and Political Rights, and other obligations under international law.

2   Each Party shall take such measures as may be necessary to improve and develop the co-operation among national authorities with a view to preventing terrorist offences and their negative effects by, *inter alia*:
a   exchanging information;
b   improving the physical protection of persons and facilities;
c   enhancing training and co-ordination plans for civil emergencies.

3   Each Party shall promote tolerance by encouraging inter-religious and cross-cultural dialogue involving, where appropriate, non-governmental organisations and other elements of civil society with a view to preventing tensions that might contribute to the commission of terrorist offences.

4   Each Party shall endeavour to promote public awareness regarding the existence, causes and gravity of and the threat posed by terrorist offences and the offences set forth in this Convention and consider encouraging the public to provide factual, specific help to its competent authorities that may contribute to preventing terrorist offences and offences set forth in this Convention.

Article 4 – International co-operation on prevention

Parties shall, as appropriate and with due regard to their capabilities, assist and support each other with a view to enhancing their capacity to prevent the commission of terrorist offences, including through exchange of information and best practices, as well as through training and other joint efforts of a preventive character.

Article 5 – Public provocation to commit a terrorist offence

1   For the purposes of this Convention, "public provocation to commit a terrorist offence" means the distribution, or otherwise making available, of a message to the public, with the intent to incite the commission of a terrorist offence, where such conduct, whether or not directly advocating terrorist offences, causes a danger that one or more such offences may be committed.

2   Each Party shall adopt such measures as may be necessary to establish public provocation to commit a terrorist offence, as defined in paragraph 1, when committed unlawfully and intentionally, as a criminal offence under its domestic law.

Article 6 – Recruitment for terrorism

1   For the purposes of this Convention, "recruitment for terrorism" means to solicit another person to commit or participate in the commission of a terrorist offence, or to join an association or group, for the purpose of contributing to the commission of one or more terrorist offences by the association or the group.

2   Each Party shall adopt such measures as may be necessary to establish recruitment for terrorism, as defined in paragraph 1, when committed unlawfully and intentionally, as a criminal offence under its domestic law.

Article 7 – Training for terrorism

1   For the purposes of this Convention, "training for terrorism" means to provide instruction in the making or use of explosives, firearms or other weapons or noxious or hazardous substances, or in other specific methods or techniques, for the purpose of carrying out or contributing to

the commission of a terrorist offence, knowing that the skills provided are intended to be used for this purpose.

2 Each Party shall adopt such measures as may be necessary to establish training for terrorism, as defined in paragraph 1, when committed unlawfully and intentionally, as a criminal offence under its domestic law.

Article 8 – Irrelevance of the commission of a terrorist offence

For an act to constitute an offence as set forth in Articles 5 to 7 of this Convention, it shall not be necessary that a terrorist offence be actually committed.

Article 9 – Ancillary offences

1 Each Party shall adopt such measures as may be necessary to establish as a criminal offence under its domestic law:
  a Participating as an accomplice in an offence as set forth in Articles 5 to 7 of this Convention;
  b Organising or directing others to commit an offence as set forth in Articles 5 to 7 of this Convention;
  c Contributing to the commission of one or more offences as set forth in Articles 5 to 7 of this Convention by a group of persons acting with a common purpose. Such contribution shall be intentional and shall either:
    i be made with the aim of furthering the criminal activity or criminal purpose of the group, where such activity or purpose involves the commission of an offence as set forth in Articles 5 to 7 of this Convention; or
    ii be made in the knowledge of the intention of the group to commit an offence as set forth in Articles 5 to 7 of this Convention.

2 Each Party shall also adopt such measures as may be necessary to establish as a criminal offence under, and in accordance with, its domestic law the attempt to commit an offence as set forth in Articles 6 and 7 of this Convention.

Article 10 – Liability of legal entities

1 Each Party shall adopt such measures as may be necessary, in accordance with its legal principles, to establish the liability of legal entities for participation in the offences set forth in Articles 5 to 7 and 9 of this Convention.

2 Subject to the legal principles of the Party, the liability of legal entities may be criminal, civil or administrative.

3   Such liability shall be without prejudice to the criminal liability of the natural persons who have committed the offences.

Article 11 – Sanctions and measures

1   Each Party shall adopt such measures as may be necessary to make the offences set forth in Articles 5 to 7 and 9 of this Convention punishable by effective, proportionate and dissuasive penalties.

2   Previous final convictions pronounced in foreign States for offences set forth in the present Convention may, to the extent permitted by domestic law, be taken into account for the purpose of determining the sentence in accordance with domestic law.

3   Each Party shall ensure that legal entities held liable in accordance with Article 10 are subject to effective, proportionate and dissuasive criminal or non-criminal sanctions, including monetary sanctions.

Article 12 – Conditions and safeguards

1   Each Party shall ensure that the establishment, implementation and application of the criminalisation under Articles 5 to 7 and 9 of this Convention are carried out while respecting human rights obligations, in particular the right to freedom of expression, freedom of association and freedom of religion, as set forth in, where applicable to that Party, the Convention for the Protection of Human Rights and Fundamental Freedoms, the International Covenant on Civil and Political Rights, and other obligations under international law.

2   The establishment, implementation and application of the criminalisation under Articles 5 to 7 and 9 of this Convention should furthermore be subject to the principle of proportionality, with respect to the legitimate aims pursued and to their necessity in a democratic society, and should exclude any form of arbitrariness or discriminatory or racist treatment.

Article 13 – Protection, compensation and support for victims of terrorism

Each Party shall adopt such measures as may be necessary to protect and support the victims of terrorism that has been committed within its own territory. These measures may include, through the appropriate national schemes and subject to domestic legislation, *inter alia*, financial assistance and compensation for victims of terrorism and their close family members.

Article 14 – Jurisdiction

1   Each Party shall take such measures as may be necessary to establish its jurisdiction over the offences set forth in this Convention:
a   when the offence is committed in the territory of that Party;

b   when the offence is committed on board a ship flying the flag of that Party, or on board an aircraft registered under the laws of that Party;

c   when the offence is committed by a national of that Party.

2   Each Party may also establish its jurisdiction over the offences set forth in this Convention:

a   when the offence was directed towards or resulted in the carrying out of an offence referred to in Article 1 of this Convention, in the territory of or against a national of that Party;

b   when the offence was directed towards or resulted in the carrying out of an offence referred to in Article 1 of this Convention, against a State or government facility of that Party abroad, including diplomatic or consular premises of that Party;

c   when the offence was directed towards or resulted in an offence referred to in Article 1 of this Convention, committed in an attempt to compel that Party to do or abstain from doing any act;

d   when the offence is committed by a stateless person who has his or her habitual residence in the territory of that Party;

e   when the offence is committed on board an aircraft which is operated by the Government of that Party.

3   Each Party shall take such measures as may be necessary to establish its jurisdiction over the offences set forth in this Convention in the case where the alleged offender is present in its territory and it does not extradite him or her to a Party whose jurisdiction is based on a rule of jurisdiction existing equally in the law of the requested Party.

4   This Convention does not exclude any criminal jurisdiction exercised in accordance with national law.

5   When more than one Party claims jurisdiction over an alleged offence set forth in this Convention, the Parties involved shall, where appropriate, consult with a view to determining the most appropriate jurisdiction for prosecution.

Article 15 – Duty to investigate

1   Upon receiving information that a person who has committed or who is alleged to have committed an offence set forth in this Convention may be present in its territory, the Party concerned shall take such measures as may be necessary under its domestic law to investigate the facts contained in the information.

2   Upon being satisfied that the circumstances so warrant, the Party in whose territory the offender or alleged offender is present shall take the appropriate measures under its domestic law so as to ensure that person's presence for the purpose of prosecution or extradition.

3   Any person in respect of whom the measures referred to in paragraph 2 are being taken shall be entitled to:

    a   communicate without delay with the nearest appropriate representative of the State of which that person is a national or which is otherwise entitled to protect that person's rights or, if that person is a stateless person, the State in the territory of which that person habitually resides;

    b   be visited by a representative of that State;

    c   be informed of that person's rights under subparagraphs a. and b.

4   The rights referred to in paragraph 3 shall be exercised in conformity with the laws and regulations of the Party in the territory of which the offender or alleged offender is present, subject to the provision that the said laws and regulations must enable full effect to be given to the purposes for which the rights accorded under paragraph 3 are intended.

5   The provisions of paragraphs 3 and 4 shall be without prejudice to the right of any Party having a claim of jurisdiction in accordance with Article 14, paragraphs 1.c and 2.d to invite the International Committee of the Red Cross to communicate with and visit the alleged offender.

Article 16 – Non application of the Convention

This Convention shall not apply where any of the offences established in accordance with Articles 5 to 7 and 9 is committed within a single State, the alleged offender is a national of that State and is present in the territory of that State, and no other State has a basis under Article 14, paragraph 1 or 2 of this Convention, to exercise jurisdiction, it being understood that the provisions of Articles 17 and 20 to 22 of this Convention shall, as appropriate, apply in those cases.

Article 17 – International co-operation in criminal matters

1   Parties shall afford one another the greatest measure of assistance in connection with criminal investigations or criminal or extradition proceedings in respect of the offences set forth in Articles 5 to 7 and 9 of this Convention, including assistance in obtaining evidence in their possession necessary for the proceedings.

2   Parties shall carry out their obligations under paragraph 1 in conformity with any treaties or other agreements on mutual legal assistance that may exist between them. In the absence of such treaties or agreements, Parties shall afford one another assistance in accordance with their domestic law.

3   Parties shall co-operate with each other to the fullest extent possible under relevant law, treaties, agreements and arrangements of the requested Party with respect to criminal investigations or proceedings in

relation to the offences for which a legal entity may be held liable in accordance with Article 10 of this Convention in the requesting Party.

4   Each Party may give consideration to establishing additional mechanisms to share with other Parties information or evidence needed to establish criminal, civil or administrative liability pursuant to Article 10.

Article 18 – Extradite or prosecute

1   The Party in the territory of which the alleged offender is present shall, when it has jurisdiction in accordance with Article 14, if it does not extradite that person, be obliged, without exception whatsoever and whether or not the offence was committed in its territory, to submit the case without undue delay to its competent authorities for the purpose of prosecution, through proceedings in accordance with the laws of that Party. Those authorities shall take their decision in the same manner as in the case of any other offence of a serious nature under the law of that Party.

2   Whenever a Party is permitted under its domestic law to extradite or otherwise surrender one of its nationals only upon the condition that the person will be returned to that Party to serve the sentence imposed as a result of the trial or proceeding for which the extradition or surrender of the person was sought, and this Party and the Party seeking the extradition of the person agree with this option and other terms they may deem appropriate, such a conditional extradition or surrender shall be sufficient to discharge the obligation set forth in paragraph 1.

Article 19 – Extradition

1   The offences set forth in Articles 5 to 7 and 9 of this Convention shall be deemed to be included as extraditable offences in any extradition treaty existing between any of the Parties before the entry into force of this Convention. Parties undertake to include such offences as extraditable offences in every extradition treaty to be subsequently concluded between them.

2   When a Party which makes extradition conditional on the existence of a treaty receives a request for extradition from another Party with which it has no extradition treaty, the requested Party may, if it so decides, consider this Convention as a legal basis for extradition in respect of the offences set forth in Articles 5 to 7 and 9 of this Convention. Extradition shall be subject to the other conditions provided by the law of the requested Party.

3   Parties which do not make extradition conditional on the existence of a treaty shall recognise the offences set forth in Articles 5 to 7 and 9 of this Convention as extraditable offences between themselves, subject to the conditions provided by the law of the requested Party.

4   Where necessary, the offences set forth in Articles 5 to 7 and 9 of this Convention shall be treated, for the purposes of extradition between Parties, as if they had been committed not only in the place in which they occurred but also in the territory of the Parties that have established jurisdiction in accordance with Article 14.

5   The provisions of all extradition treaties and agreements concluded between Parties in respect of offences set forth in Articles 5 to 7 and 9 of this Convention shall be deemed to be modified as between Parties to the extent that they are incompatible with this Convention.

Article 20 – Exclusion of the political exception clause

1   None of the offences referred to in Articles 5 to 7 and 9 of this Convention, shall be regarded, for the purposes of extradition or mutual legal assistance, as a political offence, an offence connected with a political offence, or as an offence inspired by political motives. Accordingly, a request for extradition or for mutual legal assistance based on such an offence may not be refused on the sole ground that it concerns a political offence or an offence connected with a political offence or an offence inspired by political motives.

2   Without prejudice to the application of Articles 19 to 23 of the Vienna Convention on the Law of Treaties of 23 May 1969 to the other Articles of this Convention, any State or the European Community may, at the time of signature or when depositing its instrument of ratification, acceptance, approval or accession of the Convention, declare that it reserves the right to not apply paragraph 1 of this Article as far as extradition in respect of an offence set forth in this Convention is concerned. The Party undertakes to apply this reservation on a case-by-case basis, through a duly reasoned decision.

3   Any Party may wholly or partly withdraw a reservation it has made in accordance with paragraph 2 by means of a declaration addressed to the Secretary General of the Council of Europe which shall become effective as from the date of its receipt.

4   A Party which has made a reservation in accordance with paragraph 2 of this Article may not claim the application of paragraph 1 of this Article by any other Party; it may, however, if its reservation is partial or conditional, claim the application of this Article in so far as it has itself accepted it.

5   The reservation shall be valid for a period of three years from the day of the entry into force of this Convention in respect of the Party concerned. However, such reservation may be renewed for periods of the same duration.

6   Twelve months before the date of expiry of the reservation, the Secretary General of the Council of Europe shall give notice of that expiry to the Party concerned. No later than three months before expiry, the Party shall notify the Secretary General of the Council of Europe that it is upholding, amending or withdrawing its reservation. Where a Party notifies the Secretary General of the Council of Europe that it is upholding its reservation, it shall provide an explanation of the grounds justifying its continuance. In the absence of notification by the Party concerned, the Secretary General of the Council of Europe shall inform that Party that its reservation is considered to have been extended automatically for a period of six months. Failure by the Party concerned to notify its intention to uphold or modify its reservation before the expiry of that period shall cause the reservation to lapse.

7   Where a Party does not extradite a person in application of this reservation, after receiving an extradition request from another Party, it shall submit the case, without exception whatsoever and without undue delay, to its competent authorities for the purpose of prosecution, unless the requesting Party and the requested Party agree otherwise. The competent authorities, for the purpose of prosecution in the requested Party, shall take their decision in the same manner as in the case of any offence of a grave nature under the law of that Party. The requested Party shall communicate, without undue delay, the final outcome of the proceedings to the requesting Party and to the Secretary General of the Council of Europe, who shall forward it to the Consultation of the Parties provided for in Article 30.

8   The decision to refuse the extradition request on the basis of this reservation shall be forwarded promptly to the requesting Party. If within a reasonable time no judicial decision on the merits has been taken in the requested Party according to paragraph 7, the requesting Party may communicate this fact to the Secretary General of the Council of Europe, who shall submit the matter to the Consultation of the Parties provided for in Article 30. This Consultation shall consider the matter and issue an opinion on the conformity of the refusal with the Convention and shall submit it to the Committee of Ministers for the purpose of issuing a declaration thereon. When performing its functions under this paragraph, the Committee of Ministers shall meet in its composition restricted to the States Parties.

Article 21 – Discrimination clause

1   Nothing in this Convention shall be interpreted as imposing an obligation to extradite or to afford mutual legal assistance, if the requested Party has substantial grounds for believing that the request for extradition for offences set forth in Articles 5 to 7 and 9 or for mutual legal assistance with respect to such offences has been made for the purpose of prosecuting or punishing a person on account of that person's race, religion, nationality, ethnic origin or political opinion or that compliance

with the request would cause prejudice to that person's position for any of these reasons.

2   Nothing in this Convention shall be interpreted as imposing an obligation to extradite if the person who is the subject of the extradition request risks being exposed to torture or to inhuman or degrading treatment or punishment.

3   Nothing in this Convention shall be interpreted either as imposing an obligation to extradite if the person who is the subject of the extradition request risks being exposed to the death penalty or, where the law of the requested Party does not allow for life imprisonment, to life imprisonment without the possibility of parole, unless under applicable extradition treaties the requested Party is under the obligation to extradite if the requesting Party gives such assurance as the requested Party considers sufficient that the death penalty will not be imposed or, where imposed, will not be carried out, or that the person concerned will not be subject to life imprisonment without the possibility of parole.

Article 22 – Spontaneous information

1   Without prejudice to their own investigations or proceedings, the competent authorities of a Party may, without prior request, forward to the competent authorities of another Party information obtained within the framework of their own investigations, when they consider that the disclosure of such information might assist the Party receiving the information in initiating or carrying out investigations or proceedings, or might lead to a request by that Party under this Convention.

2   The Party providing the information may, pursuant to its national law, impose conditions on the use of such information by the Party receiving the information.

3   The Party receiving the information shall be bound by those conditions.

4   However, any Party may, at any time, by means of a declaration addressed to the Secretary General of the Council of Europe, declare that it reserves the right not to be bound by the conditions imposed by the Party providing the information under paragraph 2 above, unless it receives prior notice of the nature of the information to be provided and agrees to its transmission.

Article 23 – Signature and entry into force

1   This Convention shall be open for signature by the member States of the Council of Europe, the European Community and by non-member States which have participated in its elaboration.

2   This Convention is subject to ratification, acceptance or approval. Instruments of ratification, acceptance or approval shall be deposited with the Secretary General of the Council of Europe.

3   This Convention shall enter into force on the first day of the month following the expiration of a period of three months after the date on which six Signatories, including at least four member States of the Council of Europe, have expressed their consent to be bound by the Convention in accordance with the provisions of paragraph 2.

4   In respect of any Signatory which subsequently expresses its consent to be bound by it, the Convention shall enter into force on the first day of the month following the expiration of a period of three months after the date of the expression of its consent to be bound by the Convention in accordance with the provisions of paragraph 2.

Article 24 – Accession to the Convention

1   After the entry into force of this Convention, the Committee of Ministers of the Council of Europe, after consulting with and obtaining the unanimous consent of the Parties to the Convention, may invite any State which is not a member of the Council of Europe and which has not participated in its elaboration to accede to this convention. The decision shall be taken by the majority provided for in Article 20.d of the Statute of the Council of Europe and by the unanimous vote of the representatives of the Parties entitled to sit on the Committee of Ministers.

2   In respect of any State acceding to the convention under paragraph 1 above, the Convention shall enter into force on the first day of the month following the expiration of a period of three months after the date of deposit of the instrument of accession with the Secretary General of the Council of Europe.

Article 25 – Territorial application

1   Any State or the European Community may, at the time of signature or when depositing its instrument of ratification, acceptance, approval or accession, specify the territory or territories to which this Convention shall apply.

2   Any Party may, at any later date, by a declaration addressed to the Secretary General of the Council of Europe, extend the application of this Convention to any other territory specified in the declaration. In respect of such territory the Convention shall enter into force on the first day of the month following the expiration of a period of three months after the date of receipt of the declaration by the Secretary General.

3   Any declaration made under the two preceding paragraphs may, in respect of any territory specified in such declaration, be withdrawn by a

notification addressed to the Secretary General of the Council of Europe. The withdrawal shall become effective on the first day of the month following the expiration of a period of three months after the date of receipt of such notification by the Secretary General.

Article 26 – Effects of the Convention

1   The present Convention supplements applicable multilateral or bilateral treaties or agreements between the Parties, including the provisions of the following Council of Europe treaties:
 −   European Convention on Extradition, opened for signature, in Paris, on 13 December 1957 (ETS No. 24);
 −   European Convention on Mutual Assistance in Criminal Matters, opened for signature, in Strasbourg, on 20 April 1959 (ETS No. 30);
 −   European Convention on the Suppression of Terrorism, opened for signature, in Strasbourg, on 27 January 1977 (ETS No. 90);
 −   Additional Protocol to the European Convention on Mutual Assistance in Criminal Matters, opened for signature in Strasbourg on 17 March 1978 (ETS No. 99);
 −   Second Additional Protocol to the European Convention on Mutual Assistance in Criminal Matters, opened for signature in Strasbourg on 8 November 2001 (ETS No. 182);
 −   Protocol amending the European Convention on the Suppression of Terrorism, opened for signature in Strasbourg on 15 May 2003 (ETS No. 190).

2   If two or more Parties have already concluded an agreement or treaty on the matters dealt with in this Convention or have otherwise established their relations on such matters, or should they in future do so, they shall also be entitled to apply that agreement or treaty or to regulate those relations accordingly. However, where Parties establish their relations in respect of the matters dealt with in the present Convention other than as regulated therein, they shall do so in a manner that is not inconsistent with the Convention's objectives and principles.

3   Parties which are members of the European Union shall, in their mutual relations, apply Community and European Union rules in so far as there are Community or European Union rules governing the particular subject concerned and applicable to the specific case, without prejudice to the object and purpose of the present Convention and without prejudice to its full application with other Parties.

4   Nothing in this Convention shall affect other rights, obligations and responsibilities of a Party and individuals under international law, including international humanitarian law.

5   The activities of armed forces during an armed conflict, as those terms are understood under international humanitarian law, which are governed by that law, are not governed by this Convention, and the

activities undertaken by military forces of a Party in the exercise of their official duties, inasmuch as they are governed by other rules of international law, are not governed by this Convention.

Article 27 – Amendments to the Convention

1   Amendments to this Convention may be proposed by any Party, the Committee of Ministers of the Council of Europe or the Consultation of the Parties.

2   Any proposal for amendment shall be communicated by the Secretary General of the Council of Europe to the Parties.

3   Moreover, any amendment proposed by a Party or the Committee of Ministers shall be communicated to the Consultation of the Parties, which shall submit to the Committee of Ministers its opinion on the proposed amendment.

4   The Committee of Ministers shall consider the proposed amendment and any opinion submitted by the Consultation of the Parties and may approve the amendment.

5   The text of any amendment approved by the Committee of Ministers in accordance with paragraph 4 shall be forwarded to the Parties for acceptance.

6   Any amendment approved in accordance with paragraph 4 shall come into force on the thirtieth day after all Parties have informed the Secretary General of their acceptance thereof.

Article 28 – Revision of the Appendix

1   In order to update the list of treaties in the Appendix, amendments may be proposed by any Party or by the Committee of Ministers. These proposals for amendment shall only concern universal treaties concluded within the United Nations system dealing specifically with international terrorism and having entered into force. They shall be communicated by the Secretary General of the Council of Europe to the Parties.

2   After having consulted the non-member Parties, the Committee of Ministers may adopt a proposed amendment by the majority provided for in Article 20.d of the Statute of the Council of Europe. The amendment shall enter into force following the expiry of a period of one year after the date on which it has been forwarded to the Parties. During this period, any Party may notify the Secretary General of the Council of Europe of any objection to the entry into force of the amendment in respect of that Party.

3   If one third of the Parties notifies the Secretary General of the Council of Europe of an objection to the entry into force of the amendment, the amendment shall not enter into force.

4   If less than one third of the Parties notifies an objection, the amendment shall enter into force for those Parties which have not notified an objection.

5   Once an amendment has entered into force in accordance with paragraph 2 and a Party has notified an objection to it, this amendment shall come into force in respect of the Party concerned on the first day of the month following the date on which it notifies the Secretary General of the Council of Europe of its acceptance.

Article 29 – Settlement of disputes

In the event of a dispute between Parties as to the interpretation or application of this Convention, they shall seek a settlement of the dispute through negotiation or any other peaceful means of their choice, including submission of the dispute to an arbitral tribunal whose decisions shall be binding upon the Parties to the dispute, or to the International Court of Justice, as agreed upon by the Parties concerned.

Article 30 – Consultation of the Parties

1   The Parties shall consult periodically with a view to:
   a   making proposals to facilitate or improve the effective use and implementation of this Convention, including the identification of any problems and the effects of any declaration made under this Convention;
   b   formulating its opinion on the conformity of a refusal to extradite which is referred to them in accordance with Article 20, paragraph 8;
   c   making proposals for the amendment of this Convention in accordance with Article 27;
   d   formulating their opinion on any proposal for the amendment of this Convention which is referred to them in accordance with Article 27, paragraph 3;
   e   expressing an opinion on any question concerning the application of this Convention and facilitating the exchange of information on significant legal, policy or technological developments.

2   The Consultation of the Parties shall be convened by the Secretary General of the Council of Europe whenever he finds it necessary and in any case when a majority of the Parties or the Committee of Ministers request its convocation.

3   The Parties shall be assisted by the Secretariat of the Council of Europe in carrying out their functions pursuant to this Article.

Article 31 – Denunciation

1   Any Party may, at any time, denounce this Convention by means of a notification addressed to the Secretary General of the Council of Europe.

2   Such denunciation shall become effective on the first day of the month following the expiration of a period of three months after the date of receipt of the notification by the Secretary General.

Article 32 – Notification

The Secretary General of the Council of Europe shall notify the member States of the Council of Europe, the European Community, the non-member States which have participated in the elaboration of this Convention as well as any State which has acceded to, or has been invited to accede to, this Convention of:
a   any signature;
b   the deposit of any instrument of ratification, acceptance, approval or accession;
c   any date of entry into force of this Convention in accordance with Article 23;
d   any declaration made under Article 1, paragraph 2, 22, paragraph 4, and 25 ;
e   any other act, notification or communication relating to this Convention.

In witness whereof the undersigned, being duly authorised thereto, have signed this Convention.

Done at Warsaw, this 16th day of May 2005, in English and in French, both texts being equally authentic, in a single copy which shall be deposited in the archives of the Council of Europe. The Secretary General of the Council of Europe shall transmit certified copies to each member State of the Council of Europe, to the European Community, to the non-member States which have participated in the elaboration of this Convention, and to any State invited to accede to it.

Appendix

1   Convention for the Suppression of Unlawful Seizure of Aircraft, signed at The Hague on 16 December 1970;

2   Convention for the Suppression of Unlawful Acts Against the Safety of Civil Aviation, concluded at Montreal on 23 September 1971;

3   Convention on the Prevention and Punishment of Crimes Against Internationally Protected Persons, Including Diplomatic Agents, adopted in New York on 14 December 1973;

4   International Convention Against the Taking of Hostages, adopted in New York on 17 December 1979;

5   Convention on the Physical Protection of Nuclear Material, adopted in Vienna on 3 March 1980;

6   Protocol for the Suppression of Unlawful Acts of Violence at Airports Serving International Civil Aviation, done at Montreal on 24 February 1988;

7   Convention for the Suppression of Unlawful Acts Against the Safety of Maritime Navigation, done at Rome on 10 March 1988;

8   Protocol for the Suppression of Unlawful Acts Against the Safety of Fixed Platforms Located on the Continental Shelf, done at Rome on 10 March 1988;

9   International Convention for the Suppression of Terrorist Bombings, adopted in New York on 15 December 1997;

10 International Convention for the Suppression of the Financing of Terrorism, adopted in New York on 9 December 1999.

Council of Europe Convention on Action against Trafficking in Human Beings (CETS No. 197)

Preamble

The member States of the Council of Europe and the other Signatories hereto,

Considering that the aim of the Council of Europe is to achieve a greater unity between its members;

Considering that trafficking in human beings constitutes a violation of human rights and an offence to the dignity and the integrity of the human being;

Considering that trafficking in human beings may result in slavery for victims;

Considering that respect for victims' rights, protection of victims and action to combat trafficking in human beings must be the paramount objectives;

Considering that all actions or initiatives against trafficking in human beings must be non-discriminatory, take gender equality into account as well as a child-rights approach;

Recalling the declarations by the Ministers for Foreign Affairs of the member States at the 112th (14-15 May 2003) and the 114th (12-13 May 2004) Sessions of the Committee of Ministers calling for reinforced action by the Council of Europe on trafficking in human beings;

Bearing in mind the Convention for the Protection of Human Rights and Fundamental Freedoms (1950) and its protocols;

Bearing in mind the following recommendations of the Committee of Ministers to member States of the Council of Europe: Recommendation No. R (91) 11 on sexual exploitation, pornography and prostitution of, and trafficking in, children and young adults; Recommendation No. R (97) 13 concerning intimidation of witnesses and the rights of the defence; Recommendation No. R (2000) 11 on action against trafficking in human beings for the purpose of sexual exploitation and Recommendation Rec(2001)16 on the protection of children against sexual exploitation; Recommendation Rec(2002)5 on the protection of women against violence;

Bearing in mind the following recommendations of the Parliamentary Assembly of the Council of Europe: Recommendation 1325 (1997) on traffic in women and forced prostitution in Council of Europe member states; Recommendation 1450 (2000) on violence against women in Europe; Recommendation 1545 (2002) on a campaign against trafficking in women; Recommendation 1610 (2003) on migration connected with trafficking in women and prostitution; Recommendation 1611 (2003) on trafficking in organs in Europe; Recommendation 1663 (2004) Domestic slavery: servitude, au pairs and mail-order brides;

Bearing in mind the European Union Council Framework Decision of 19 July 2002 on combating trafficking in human beings the European Union Council Framework Decision of 15 March 2001 on the standing of victims in criminal proceedings and the European Union Council Directive of 29 April 2004 on the residence permit issued to third-country nationals who are victims of trafficking in human beings or who have been the subject of an action to facilitate illegal immigration, who co-operate with the competent authorities;

Taking due account of the United Nations Convention against Transnational Organized Crime and the Protocol thereto to Prevent, Suppress and Punish Trafficking in Persons, Especially Women and Children with a view to improving the protection which they afford and developing the standards established by them;

Taking due account of the other international legal instruments relevant in the field of action against trafficking in human beings;

Taking into account the need to prepare a comprehensive international legal instrument focusing on the human rights of victims of trafficking and setting up a specific monitoring mechanism,

Have agreed as follows:

Chapter I – Purposes, scope, non-discrimination principle and definitions

Article 1 – Purposes of the Convention

1 The purposes of this Convention are:
   a to prevent and combat trafficking in human beings, while guaranteeing gender equality
   b to protect the human rights of the victims of trafficking, design a comprehensive framework for the protection and assistance of victims and witnesses, while guaranteeing gender equality, as well as to ensure effective investigation and prosecution;
   c to promote international co-operation on action against trafficking in human beings.

2 In order to ensure effective implementation of its provisions by the Parties, this Convention sets up a specific monitoring mechanism.

Article 2 – Scope

This Convention shall apply to all forms of trafficking in human beings, whether national or transnational, whether or not connected with organised crime.

Article 3 – Non-discrimination principle

The implementation of the provisions of this Convention by Parties, in particular the enjoyment of measures to protect and promote the rights of victims, shall be secured without discrimination on any ground such as sex, race, colour, language, religion, political or other opinion, national or social origin, association with a national minority, property, birth or other status.

Article 4 – Definitions

For the purposes of this Convention :

a   "Trafficking in human beings" shall mean the recruitment, transportation, transfer, harbouring or receipt of persons, by means of the threat or use of force or other forms of coercion, of abduction, of fraud, of deception, of the abuse of power or of a position of vulnerability or of the giving or receiving of payments or benefits to achieve the consent of a person having control over another person, for the purpose of exploitation. Exploitation shall include, at a minimum, the exploitation of the prostitution of others or other forms of sexual exploitation, forced labour or services, slavery or practices similar to slavery, servitude or the removal of organs;

b   The consent of a victim of "trafficking in human beings" to the intended exploitation set forth in subparagraph (a) of this article shall be irrelevant where any of the means set forth in subparagraph (a) have been used;

c   The recruitment, transportation, transfer, harbouring or receipt of a child for the purpose of exploitation shall be considered "trafficking in human beings" even if this does not involve any of the means set forth in subparagraph (a) of this article;

d   "Child" shall mean any person under eighteen years of age;

e   "Victim" shall mean any natural person who is subject to trafficking in human beings as defined in this article.

Chapter II – Prevention, co-operation and other measures

Article 5 – Prevention of trafficking in human beings

1   Each Party shall take measures to establish or strengthen national co-ordination between the various bodies responsible for preventing and combating trafficking in human beings.

2   Each Party shall establish and/or strengthen effective policies and programmes to prevent trafficking in human beings, by such means as: research, information, awareness raising and education campaigns, social and economic initiatives and training programmes, in particular for persons vulnerable to trafficking and for professionals concerned with trafficking in human beings.

3   Each Party shall promote a Human Rights-based approach and shall use gender mainstreaming and a child-sensitive approach in the development, implementation and assessment of all the policies and programmes referred to in paragraph 2.

4   Each Party shall take appropriate measures, as may be necessary, to enable migration to take place legally, in particular through dissemination of accurate information by relevant offices, on the conditions enabling the legal entry in and stay on its territory.

5   Each Party shall take specific measures to reduce children's vulnerability to trafficking, notably by creating a protective environment for them.

6   Measures established in accordance with this article shall involve, where appropriate, non-governmental organisations, other relevant organisations and other elements of civil society committed to the prevention of trafficking in human beings and victim protection or assistance.

Article 6 – Measures to discourage the demand

To discourage the demand that fosters all forms of exploitation of persons, especially women and children, that leads to trafficking, each Party shall adopt or strengthen legislative, administrative, educational, social, cultural or other measures including:
a   research on best practices, methods and strategies;
b   raising awareness of the responsibility and important role of media and civil society in identifying the demand as one of the root causes of trafficking in human beings;
c   target information campaigns involving, as appropriate, inter alia, public authorities and policy makers;
d   preventive measures, including educational programmes for boys and girls during their schooling, which stress the unacceptable nature of discrimination based on sex, and its disastrous consequences, the

importance of gender equality and the dignity and integrity of every human being.

Article 7 – Border measures

1   Without prejudice to international commitments in relation to the free movement of persons, Parties shall strengthen, to the extent possible, such border controls as may be necessary to prevent and detect trafficking in human beings.

2   Each Party shall adopt legislative or other appropriate measures to prevent, to the extent possible, means of transport operated by commercial carriers from being used in the commission of offences established in accordance with this Convention.

3   Where appropriate, and without prejudice to applicable international conventions, such measures shall include establishing the obligation of commercial carriers, including any transportation company or the owner or operator of any means of transport, to ascertain that all passengers are in possession of the travel documents required for entry into the receiving State.

4   Each Party shall take the necessary measures, in accordance with its internal law, to provide for sanctions in cases of violation of the obligation set forth in paragraph 3 of this article.

5   Each Party shall adopt such legislative or other measures as may be necessary to permit, in accordance with its internal law, the denial of entry or revocation of visas of persons implicated in the commission of offences established in accordance with this Convention.

6   Parties shall strengthen co-operation among border control agencies by, *inter alia*, establishing and maintaining direct channels of communication.

Article 8 – Security and control of documents

Each Party shall adopt such measures as may be necessary:
a   To ensure that travel or identity documents issued by it are of such quality that they cannot easily be misused and cannot readily be falsified or unlawfully altered, replicated or issued; and
b   To ensure the integrity and security of travel or identity documents issued by or on behalf of the Party and to prevent their unlawful creation and issuance.

Article 9 – Legitimacy and validity of documents

At the request of another Party, a Party shall, in accordance with its internal law, verify within a reasonable time the legitimacy and validity of travel or identity documents issued or purported to have been issued in its name and suspected of being used for trafficking in human beings.

Chapter III – Measures to protect and promote the rights of victims, guaranteeing gender equality

Article 10 – Identification of the victims

1   Each Party shall provide its competent authorities with persons who are trained and qualified in preventing and combating trafficking in human beings, in identifying and helping victims, including children, and shall ensure that the different authorities collaborate with each other as well as with relevant support organisations, so that victims can be identified in a procedure duly taking into account the special situation of women and child victims and, in appropriate cases, issued with residence permits under the conditions provided for in Article 14 of the present Convention.

2   Each Party shall adopt such legislative or other measures as may be necessary to identify victims as appropriate in collaboration with other Parties and relevant support organisations. Each Party shall ensure that, if the competent authorities have reasonable grounds to believe that a person has been victim of trafficking in human beings, that person shall not be removed from its territory until the identification process as victim of an offence provided for in Article 18 of this Convention has been completed by the competent authorities and shall likewise ensure that that person receives the assistance provided for in Article 12, paragraphs 1 and 2.

3   When the age of the victim is uncertain and there are reasons to believe that the victim is a child, he or she shall be presumed to be a child and shall be accorded special protection measures pending verification of his/her age.

4   As soon as an unaccompanied child is identified as a victim, each Party shall:
  a   provide for representation of the child by a legal guardian, organisation or authority which shall act in the best interests of that child;
  b   take the necessary steps to establish his/her identity and nationality;
  c   make every effort to locate his/her family when this is in the best interests of the child.

Article 11 – Protection of private life

1   Each Party shall protect the private life and identity of victims. Personal data regarding them shall be stored and used in conformity with the conditions provided for by the Convention for the Protection of

Individuals with regard to Automatic Processing of Personal Data (ETS No. 108).

2   Each Party shall adopt measures to ensure, in particular, that the identity, or details allowing the identification, of a child victim of trafficking are not made publicly known, through the media or by any other means, except, in exceptional circumstances, in order to facilitate the tracing of family members or otherwise secure the well-being and protection of the child.

3   Each Party shall consider adopting, in accordance with Article 10 of the Convention for the Protection of Human Rights and Fundamental Freedoms as interpreted by the European Court of Human Rights, measures aimed at encouraging the media to protect the private life and identity of victims through self-regulation or through regulatory or co-regulatory measures.

Article 12 – Assistance to victims

1   Each Party shall adopt such legislative or other measures as may be necessary to assist victims in their physical, psychological and social recovery. Such assistance shall include at least:
a   standards of living capable of ensuring their subsistence, through such measures as: appropriate and secure accommodation, psychological and material assistance;
b   access to emergency medical treatment;
c   translation and interpretation services, when appropriate;
d   counselling and information, in particular as regards their legal rights and the services available to them, in a language that they can understand;
e   assistance to enable their rights and interests to be presented and considered at appropriate stages of criminal proceedings against offenders;
f   access to education for children.

2   Each Party shall take due account of the victim's safety and protection needs.

3   In addition, each Party shall provide necessary medical or other assistance to victims lawfully resident within its territory who do not have adequate resources and need such help.

4   Each Party shall adopt the rules under which victims lawfully resident within its territory shall be authorised to have access to the labour market, to vocational training and education.

5   Each Party shall take measures, where appropriate and under the conditions provided for by its internal law, to co-operate with non-

governmental organisations, other relevant organisations or other elements of civil society engaged in assistance to victims.

6   Each Party shall adopt such legislative or other measures as may be necessary to ensure that assistance to a victim is not made conditional on his or her willingness to act as a witness.

7   For the implementation of the provisions set out in this article, each Party shall ensure that services are provided on a consensual and informed basis, taking due account of the special needs of persons in a vulnerable position and the rights of children in terms of accommodation, education and appropriate health care.

Article 13 – Recovery and reflection period

1   Each Party shall provide in its internal law a recovery and reflection period of at least 30 days, when there are reasonable grounds to believe that the person concerned is a victim. Such a period shall be sufficient for the person concerned to recover and escape the influence of traffickers and/or to take an informed decision on co-operating with the competent authorities. During this period it shall not be possible to enforce any expulsion order against him or her. This provision is without prejudice to the activities carried out by the competent authorities in all phases of the relevant national proceedings, and in particular when investigating and prosecuting the offences concerned. During this period, the Parties shall authorise the persons concerned to stay in their territory.

2   During this period, the persons referred to in paragraph 1 of this Article shall be entitled to the measures contained in Article 12, paragraphs 1 and 2.

3   The Parties are not bound to observe this period if grounds of public order prevent it or if it is found that victim status is being claimed improperly.

Article 14 – Residence permit

1   Each Party shall issue a renewable residence permit to victims, in one or other of the two following situations or in both:
    a   the competent authority considers that their stay is necessary owing to their personal situation;
    b   the competent authority considers that their stay is necessary for the purpose of their co-operation with the competent authorities in investigation or criminal proceedings.

2   The residence permit for child victims, when legally necessary, shall be issued in accordance with the best interests of the child and, where appropriate, renewed under the same conditions.

3   The non-renewal or withdrawal of a residence permit is subject to the conditions provided for by the internal law of the Party.

4   If a victim submits an application for another kind of residence permit, the Party concerned shall take into account that he or she holds, or has held, a residence permit in conformity with paragraph 1.

5   Having regard to the obligations of Parties to which Article 40 of this Convention refers, each Party shall ensure that granting of a permit according to this provision shall be without prejudice to the right to seek and enjoy asylum.

Article 15 – Compensation and legal redress

1   Each Party shall ensure that victims have access, as from their first contact with the competent authorities, to information on relevant judicial and administrative proceedings in a language which they can understand.

2   Each Party shall provide, in its internal law, for the right to legal assistance and to free legal aid for victims under the conditions provided by its internal law.

3   Each Party shall provide, in its internal law, for the right of victims to compensation from the perpetrators.

4   Each Party shall adopt such legislative or other measures as may be necessary to guarantee compensation for victims in accordance with the conditions under its internal law, for instance through the establishment of a fund for victim compensation or measures or programmes aimed at social assistance and social integration of victims, which could be funded by the assets resulting from the application of measures provided in Article 23.

Article 16 – Repatriation and return of victims

1   The Party of which a victim is a national or in which that person had the right of permanent residence at the time of entry into the territory of the receiving Party shall, with due regard for his or her rights, safety and dignity, facilitate and accept, his or her return without undue or unreasonable delay.

2   When a Party returns a victim to another State, such return shall be with due regard for the rights, safety and dignity of that person and for the status of any legal proceedings related to the fact that the person is a victim, and shall preferably be voluntary.

3   At the request of a receiving Party, a requested Party shall verify whether a person is its national or had the right of permanent residence in its territory at the time of entry into the territory of the receiving Party.

4   In order to facilitate the return of a victim who is without proper documentation, the Party of which that person is a national or in which he or she had the right of permanent residence at the time of entry into the territory of the receiving Party shall agree to issue, at the request of the receiving Party, such travel documents or other authorisation as may be necessary to enable the person to travel to and re-enter its territory.

5   Each Party shall adopt such legislative or other measures as may be necessary to establish repatriation programmes, involving relevant national or international institutions and non governmental organisations. These programmes aim at avoiding re-victimisation. Each Party should make its best effort to favour the reintegration of victims into the society of the State of return, including reintegration into the education system and the labour market, in particular through the acquisition and improvement of their professional skills. With regard to children, these programmes should include enjoyment of the right to education and measures to secure adequate care or receipt by the family or appropriate care structures.

6   Each Party shall adopt such legislative or other measures as may be necessary to make available to victims, where appropriate in co-operation with any other Party concerned, contact information of structures that can assist them in the country where they are returned or repatriated, such as law enforcement offices, non-governmental organisations, legal professions able to provide counselling and social welfare agencies.

7   Child victims shall not be returned to a State, if there is indication, following a risk and security assessment, that such return would not be in the best interests of the child.

Article 17 – Gender equality

Each Party shall, in applying measures referred to in this chapter, aim to promote gender equality and use gender mainstreaming in the development, implementation and assessment of the measures.

Chapter IV – Substantive criminal law

Article 18 – Criminalisation of trafficking in human beings

Each Party shall adopt such legislative and other measures as may be necessary to establish as criminal offences the conduct contained in Article 4 of this Convention, when committed intentionally.

Article 19 – Criminalisation of the use of services of a victim

Each Party shall consider adopting such legislative and other measures as may be necessary to establish as criminal offences under its internal law, the use of services which are the object of exploitation as referred to in Article 4 paragraph a of this Convention, with the knowledge that the person is a victim of trafficking in human beings.

Article 20 – Criminalisation of acts relating to travel or identity documents

Each Party shall adopt such legislative and other measures as may be necessary to establish as criminal offences the following conducts, when committed intentionally and for the purpose of enabling the trafficking in human beings:

a   forging a travel or identity document;
b   procuring or providing such a document;
c   retaining, removing, concealing, damaging or destroying a travel or identity document of another person.

Article 21 – Attempt and aiding or abetting

1   Each Party shall adopt such legislative and other measures as may be necessary to establish as criminal offences when committed intentionally, aiding or abetting the commission of any of the offences established in accordance with Articles 18 and 20 of the present Convention.

2   Each Party shall adopt such legislative and other measures as may be necessary to establish as criminal offences when committed intentionally, an attempt to commit the offences established in accordance with Articles 18 and 20, paragraph a, of this Convention.

Article 22 – Corporate liability

1   Each Party shall adopt such legislative and other measures as may be necessary to ensure that a legal person can be held liable for a criminal offence established in accordance with this Convention, committed for its benefit by any natural person, acting either individually or as part of an organ of the legal person, who has a leading position within the legal person, based on:

a   a power of representation of the legal person;
b   an authority to take decisions on behalf of the legal person;
c   an authority to exercise control within the legal person.

2   Apart from the cases already provided for in paragraph 1, each Party shall take the measures necessary to ensure that a legal person can be held liable where the lack of supervision or control by a natural person referred to in paragraph 1 has made possible the commission of a criminal offence established in accordance with this Convention for the benefit of that legal person by a natural person acting under its authority.

3   Subject to the legal principles of the Party, the liability of a legal person may be criminal, civil or administrative.

4   Such liability shall be without prejudice to the criminal liability of the natural persons who have committed the offence.

Article 23 – Sanctions and measures

1   Each Party shall adopt such legislative and other measures as may be necessary to ensure that the criminal offences established in accordance with Articles 18 to 21 are punishable by effective, proportionate and dissuasive sanctions. These sanctions shall include, for criminal offences established in accordance with Article 18 when committed by natural persons, penalties involving deprivation of liberty which can give rise to extradition.

2   Each Party shall ensure that legal persons held liable in accordance with Article 22 shall be subject to effective, proportionate and dissuasive criminal or non-criminal sanctions or measures, including monetary sanctions.

3   Each Party shall adopt such legislative and other measures as may be necessary to enable it to confiscate or otherwise deprive the instrumentalities and proceeds of criminal offences established in accordance with Articles 18 and 20, paragraph a, of this Convention, or property the value of which corresponds to such proceeds.

4   Each Party shall adopt such legislative or other measures as may be necessary to enable the temporary or permanent closure of any establishment which was used to carry out trafficking in human beings, without prejudice to the rights of *bona fide* third parties or to deny the perpetrator, temporary or permanently, the exercise of the activity in the course of which this offence was committed.

Article 24 – Aggravating circumstances

Each Party shall ensure that the following circumstances are regarded as aggravating circumstances in the determination of the penalty for offences established in accordance with Article 18 of this Convention:
a   the offence deliberately or by gross negligence endangered the life of the victim;
b   the offence was committed against a child;
c   the offence was committed by a public official in the performance of her/his duties;
d   the offence was committed within the framework of a criminal organisation.

Article 25 – Previous convictions

Each Party shall adopt such legislative and other measures providing for the possibility to take into account final sentences passed by another Party in relation to offences established in accordance with this Convention when determining the penalty.

Article 26 – Non-punishment provision

Each Party shall, in accordance with the basic principles of its legal system, provide for the possibility of not imposing penalties on victims for their involvement in unlawful activities, to the extent that they have been compelled to do so.

Chapter V – Investigation, prosecution and procedural law

Article 27 – *Ex parte* and *ex officio* applications

1   Each Party shall ensure that investigations into or prosecution of offences established in accordance with this Convention shall not be dependent upon the report or accusation made by a victim, at least when the offence was committed in whole or in part on its territory.

2   Each Party shall ensure that victims of an offence in the territory of a Party other than the one where they reside may make a complaint before the competent authorities of their State of residence. The competent authority to which the complaint is made, insofar as it does not itself have competence in this respect, shall transmit it without delay to the competent authority of the Party in the territory in which the offence was committed. The complaint shall be dealt with in accordance with the internal law of the Party in which the offence was committed.

3   Each Party shall ensure, by means of legislative or other measures, in accordance with the conditions provided for by its internal law, to any group, foundation, association or non-governmental organisations which aims at fighting trafficking in human beings or protection of human rights, the possibility to assist and/or support the victim with his or her consent during criminal proceedings concerning the offence established in accordance with Article 18 of this Convention.

Article 28 – Protection of victims, witnesses and collaborators with the judicial authorities

1   Each Party shall adopt such legislative or other measures as may be necessary to provide effective and appropriate protection from potential retaliation or intimidation in particular during and after investigation and prosecution of perpetrators, for:
a   Victims;

b   As appropriate, those who report the criminal offences established in accordance with Article 18 of this Convention or otherwise co-operate with the investigating or prosecuting authorities;

c   witnesses who give testimony concerning criminal offences established in accordance with Article 18 of this Convention;

d   when necessary, members of the family of persons referred to in subparagraphs a and c.

2   Each Party shall adopt such legislative or other measures as may be necessary to ensure and to offer various kinds of protection. This may include physical protection, relocation, identity change and assistance in obtaining jobs.

3   A child victim shall be afforded special protection measures taking into account the best interests of the child.

4   Each Party shall adopt such legislative or other measures as may be necessary to provide, when necessary, appropriate protection from potential retaliation or intimidation in particular during and after investigation and prosecution of perpetrators, for members of groups, foundations, associations or non-governmental organisations which carry out the activities set out in Article 27, paragraph 3.

5   Each Party shall consider entering into agreements or arrangements with other States for the implementation of this article.

Article 29 – Specialised authorities and co-ordinating bodies

1   Each Party shall adopt such measures as may be necessary to ensure that persons or entities are specialised in the fight against trafficking and the protection of victims. Such persons or entities shall have the necessary independence in accordance with the fundamental principles of the legal system of the Party, in order for them to be able to carry out their functions effectively and free from any undue pressure. Such persons or the staffs of such entities shall have adequate training and financial resources for their tasks.

2   Each Party shall adopt such measures as may be necessary to ensure co-ordination of the policies and actions of their governments' departments and other public agencies against trafficking in human beings, where appropriate, through setting up co-ordinating bodies.

3   Each Party shall provide or strengthen training for relevant officials in the prevention of and fight against trafficking in human beings, including Human Rights training. The training may be agency-specific and shall, as appropriate, focus on: methods used in preventing such trafficking, prosecuting the traffickers and protecting the rights of the victims, including protecting the victims from the traffickers.

4   Each Party shall consider appointing National Rapporteurs or other mechanisms for monitoring the anti-trafficking activities of State institutions and the implementation of national legislation requirements.

Article 30 – Court proceedings

In accordance with the Convention for the Protection of Human Rights and Fundamental Freedoms, in particular Article 6, each Party shall adopt such legislative or other measures as may be necessary to ensure in the course of judicial proceedings:
a   the protection of victims' private life and, where appropriate, identity;
b   victims' safety and protection from intimidation,
in accordance with the conditions under its internal law and, in the case of child victims, by taking special care of children's needs and ensuring their right to special protection measures.

Article 31 – Jurisdiction

1   Each Party shall adopt such legislative and other measures as may be necessary to establish jurisdiction over any offence established in accordance with this Convention, when the offence is committed:
a   in its territory; or
b   on board a ship flying the flag of that Party; or
c   on board an aircraft registered under the laws of that Party; or
d   by one of its nationals or by a stateless person who has his or her habitual residence in its territory, if the offence is punishable under criminal law where it was committed or if the offence is committed outside the territorial jurisdiction of any State;
e   against one of its nationals.

2   Each Party may, at the time of signature or when depositing its instrument of ratification, acceptance, approval or accession, by a declaration addressed to the Secretary General of the Council of Europe, declare that it reserves the right not to apply or to apply only in specific cases or conditions the jurisdiction rules laid down in paragraphs 1 (d) and (e) of this article or any part thereof.

3   Each Party shall adopt such measures as may be necessary to establish jurisdiction over the offences referred to in this Convention, in cases where an alleged offender is present in its territory and it does not extradite him/her to another Party, solely on the basis of his/her nationality, after a request for extradition.

4   When more than one Party claims jurisdiction over an alleged offence established in accordance with this Convention, the Parties involved shall, where appropriate, consult with a view to determining the most appropriate jurisdiction for prosecution.

5   Without prejudice to the general norms of international law, this Convention does not exclude any criminal jurisdiction exercised by a Party in accordance with internal law.

Chapter VI – International co-operation and co-operation with civil society

Article 32 – General principles and measures for international co-operation

The Parties shall co-operate with each other, in accordance with the provisions of this Convention, and through application of relevant applicable international and regional instruments, arrangements agreed on the basis of uniform or reciprocal legislation and internal laws, to the widest extent possible, for the purpose of:
–   preventing and combating trafficking in human beings;
–   protecting and providing assistance to victims;
–   investigations or proceedings concerning criminal offences established in accordance with this Convention.

Article 33 – Measures relating to endangered or missing persons

1   When a Party, on the basis of the information at its disposal has reasonable grounds to believe that the life, the freedom or the physical integrity of a person referred to in Article 28, paragraph 1, is in immediate danger on the territory of another Party, the Party that has the information shall, in such a case of emergency, transmit it without delay to the latter so as to take the appropriate protection measures.

2   The Parties to this Convention may consider reinforcing their co-operation in the search for missing people, in particular for missing children, if the information available leads them to believe that she/he is a victim of trafficking in human beings. To this end, the Parties may conclude bilateral or multilateral treaties with each other.

Article 34 – Information

1   The requested Party shall promptly inform the requesting Party of the final result of the action taken under this chapter. The requested Party shall also promptly inform the requesting Party of any circumstances which render impossible the carrying out of the action sought or are likely to delay it significantly.

2   A Party may, within the limits of its internal law, without prior request, forward to another Party information obtained within the framework of its own investigations when it considers that the disclosure of such information might assist the receiving Party in initiating or carrying out investigations or proceedings concerning criminal offences established

in accordance with this Convention or might lead to a request for co-operation by that Party under this chapter.

3   Prior to providing such information, the providing Party may request that it be kept confidential or used subject to conditions. If the receiving Party cannot comply with such request, it shall notify the providing Party, which shall then determine whether the information should nevertheless be provided. If the receiving Party accepts the information subject to the conditions, it shall be bound by them.

4   All information requested concerning Articles 13, 14 and 16, necessary to provide the rights conferred by these articles, shall be transmitted at the request of the Party concerned without delay with due respect to Article 11 of the present Convention.

Article 35 – Co-operation with civil society

Each Party shall encourage state authorities and public officials, to co-operate with non-governmental organisations, other relevant organisations and members of civil society, in establishing strategic partnerships with the aim of achieving the purpose of this Convention.

Chapter VII – Monitoring mechanism

Article 36 – Group of experts on action against trafficking in human beings

1   The Group of experts on action against trafficking in human beings (hereinafter referred to as "GRETA"), shall monitor the implementation of this Convention by the Parties.

2   GRETA shall be composed of a minimum of 10 members and a maximum of 15 members, taking into account a gender and geographical balance, as well as a multidisciplinary expertise. They shall be elected by the Committee of the Parties for a term of office of 4 years, renewable once, chosen from amongst nationals of the States Parties to this Convention.

3   The election of the members of GRETA shall be based on the following principles:
a   they shall be chosen from among persons of high moral character, known for their recognised competence in the fields of Human Rights, assistance and protection of victims and of action against trafficking in human beings or having professional experience in the areas covered by this Convention;
b   they shall sit in their individual capacity and shall be independent and impartial in the exercise of their functions and shall be available to carry out their duties in an effective manner;

c   no two members of GRETA may be nationals of the same State;
d   they should represent the main legal systems.

4   The election procedure of the members of GRETA shall be determined by the Committee of Ministers, after consulting with and obtaining the unanimous consent of the Parties to the Convention, within a period of one year following the entry into force of this Convention. GRETA shall adopt its own rules of procedure.

Article 37 – Committee of the Parties

1   The Committee of the Parties shall be composed of the representatives on the Committee of Ministers of the Council of Europe of the member States Parties to the Convention and representatives of the Parties to the Convention, which are not members of the Council of Europe.

2   The Committee of the Parties shall be convened by the Secretary General of the Council of Europe. Its first meeting shall be held within a period of one year following the entry into force of this Convention in order to elect the members of GRETA. It shall subsequently meet whenever one-third of the Parties, the President of GRETA or the Secretary General so requests.

3   The Committee of the Parties shall adopt its own rules of procedure.

Article 38 – Procedure

1   The evaluation procedure shall concern the Parties to the Convention and be divided in rounds, the length of which is determined by GRETA. At the beginning of each round GRETA shall select the specific provisions on which the evaluation procedure shall be based.

2   GRETA shall define the most appropriate means to carry out this evaluation. GRETA may in particular adopt a questionnaire for each evaluation round, which may serve as a basis for the evaluation of the implementation by the Parties of the present Convention. Such a questionnaire shall be addressed to all Parties. Parties shall respond to this questionnaire, as well as to any other request of information from GRETA.

3   GRETA may request information from civil society.

4   GRETA may subsidiarily organise, in co-operation with the national authorities and the "contact person" appointed by the latter, and, if necessary, with the assistance of independent national experts, country visits. During these visits, GRETA may be assisted by specialists in specific fields.

5   GRETA shall prepare a draft report containing its analysis concerning the implementation of the provisions on which the evaluation is based, as well as its suggestions and proposals concerning the way in which the Party concerned may deal with the problems which have been identified. The draft report shall be transmitted for comments to the Party which undergoes the evaluation. Its comments are taken into account by GRETA when establishing its report.

6   On this basis, GRETA shall adopt its report and conclusions concerning the measures taken by the Party concerned to implement the provisions of the present Convention. This report and conclusions shall be sent to the Party concerned and to the Committee of the Parties. The report and conclusions of GRETA shall be made public as from their adoption, together with eventual comments by the Party concerned.

7   Without prejudice to the procedure of paragraphs 1 to 6 of this article, the Committee of the Parties may adopt, on the basis of the report and conclusions of GRETA, recommendations addressed to this Party (a) concerning the measures to be taken to implement the conclusions of GRETA, if necessary setting a date for submitting information on their implementation, and (b) aiming at promoting co-operation with that P>arty for the proper implementation of the present Convention.

Chapter VIII – Relationship with other international instruments

Article 39 – Relationship with the Protocol to prevent, suppress and punish trafficking in persons, especially women and children, supplementing the United Nations Convention against transnational organised crime

This Convention shall not affect the rights and obligations derived from the provisions of the Protocol to prevent, suppress and punish trafficking in persons, especially women and children, supplementing the United Nations Convention against transnational organised crime, and is intended to enhance the protection afforded by it and develop the standards contained therein.

Article 40 – Relationship with other international instruments

1   This Convention shall not affect the rights and obligations derived from other international instruments to which Parties to the present Convention are Parties or shall become Parties and which contain provisions on matters governed by this Convention and which ensure greater protection and assistance for victims of trafficking.

2   The Parties to the Convention may conclude bilateral or multilateral agreements with one another on the matters dealt with in this Convention, for purposes of supplementing or strengthening its provisions or facilitating the application of the principles embodied in it.

3   Parties which are members of the European Union shall, in their mutual relations, apply Community and European Union rules in so far as there are Community or European Union rules governing the particular subject concerned and applicable to the specific case, without prejudice to the object and purpose of the present Convention and without prejudice to its full application with other Parties. [1]

4   Nothing in this Convention shall affect the rights, obligations and responsibilities of States and individuals under international law, including international humanitarian law and international human rights law and, in particular, where applicable, the 1951 Convention and the 1967 Protocol relating to the Status of Refugees and the principle of *non-refoulement* as contained therein.

Chapter IX – Amendments to the Convention

Article 41 – Amendments

1   Any proposal for an amendment to this Convention presented by a Party shall be communicated to the Secretary General of the Council of Europe and forwarded by him or her to the member States of the Council of Europe, any signatory, any State Party, the European Community, to any State invited to sign this Convention in accordance with the provisions of Article 42 and to any State invited to accede to this Convention in accordance with the provisions of Article 43.

2   Any amendment proposed by a Party shall be communicated to GRETA, which shall submit to the Committee of Ministers its opinion on that proposed amendment.

3   The Committee of Ministers shall consider the proposed amendment and the opinion submitted by GRETA and, following consultation of the Parties to this Convention and after obtaining their unanimous consent, may adopt the amendment.

4   The text of any amendment adopted by the Committee of Ministers in accordance with paragraph 3 of this article shall be forwarded to the Parties for acceptance.

5   Any amendment adopted in accordance with paragraph 3 of this article shall enter into force on the first day of the month following the expiration of a period of one month after the date on which all Parties have informed the Secretary General that they have accepted it.

Chapter X – Final clauses

Article 42 – Signature and entry into force

1 This Convention shall be open for signature by the member States of the Council of Europe, the non member States which have participated in its elaboration and the European Community.

2 This Convention is subject to ratification, acceptance or approval. Instruments of ratification, acceptance or approval shall be deposited with the Secretary General of the Council of Europe.

3 This Convention shall enter into force on the first day of the month following the expiration of a period of three months after the date on which 10 Signatories, including at least 8 member States of the Council of Europe, have expressed their consent to be bound by the Convention in accordance with the provisions of the preceding paragraph.

4 In respect of any State mentioned in paragraph 1 or the European Community, which subsequently expresses its consent to be bound by it, the Convention shall enter into force on the first day of the month following the expiration of a period of three months after the date of the deposit of its instrument of ratification, acceptance or approval.

Article 43 – Accession to the Convention

1 After the entry into force of this Convention, the Committee of Ministers of the Council of Europe may, after consultation of the Parties to this Convention and obtaining their unanimous consent, invite any non-member State of the Council of Europe, which has not participated in the elaboration of the Convention, to accede to this Convention by a decision taken by the majority provided for in Article 20 d. of the Statute of the Council of Europe, and by unanimous vote of the representatives of the Contracting States entitled to sit on the Committee of Ministers.

2 In respect of any acceding State, the Convention shall enter into force on the first day of the month following the expiration of a period of three months after the date of deposit of the instrument of accession with the Secretary General of the Council of Europe.

Article 44 – Territorial application

1 Any State or the European Community may, at the time of signature or when depositing its instrument of ratification, acceptance, approval or accession, specify the territory or territories to which this Convention shall apply.

2 Any Party may, at any later date, by a declaration addressed to the Secretary General of the Council of Europe, extend the application of

this Convention to any other territory specified in the declaration and for whose international relations it is responsible or on whose behalf it is authorised to give undertakings. In respect of such territory, the Convention shall enter into force on the first day of the month following the expiration of a period of three months after the date of receipt of such declaration by the Secretary General.

3   Any declaration made under the two preceding paragraphs may, in respect of any territory specified in such declaration, be withdrawn by a notification addressed to the Secretary General of the Council of Europe. The withdrawal shall become effective on the first day of the month following the expiration of a period of three months after the date of receipt of such notification by the Secretary General.

Article 45 – Reservations

No reservation may be made in respect of any provision of this Convention, with the exception of the reservation of Article 31, paragraph 2.

Article 46 – Denunciation

1   Any Party may, at any time, denounce this Convention by means of a notification addressed to the Secretary General of the Council of Europe.

2   Such denunciation shall become effective on the first day of the month following the expiration of a period of three months after the date of receipt of the notification by the Secretary General.

Article 47 – Notification

The Secretary General of the Council of Europe shall notify the member States of the Council of Europe, any State signatory, any State Party, the European Community, to any State invited to sign this Convention in accordance with the provisions of Article 42 and to any State invited to accede to this Convention in accordance with the provisions of Article 43 of:
a   any signature;
b   the deposit of any instrument of ratification, acceptance, approval or accession;
c   any date of entry into force of this Convention in accordance with Articles 42 and 43;
d   any amendment adopted in accordance with Article 41 and the date on which such an amendment enters into force;
e   any denunciation made in pursuance of the provisions of Article 46;
f   any other act, notification or communication relating to this Convention,
g   any reservation made under Article 45.

In witness whereof the undersigned, being duly authorised thereto, have signed this Convention.

Done at Warsaw, this 16th day of May 2005, in English and in French, both texts being equally authentic, in a single copy which shall be deposited in the archives of the Council of Europe. The Secretary General of the Council of Europe shall transmit certified copies to each member State of the Council of Europe, to the non-member States which have participated in the elaboration of this Convention, to the European Community and to any State invited to accede to this Convention.

Committee of Ministers

Recommendation Rec(2006)8 of the Committee of Ministers to member states on assistance to crime victims
(Adopted by the Committee of Ministers on 14 June 2006 at the 967th meeting of the Ministers' Deputies)

The Committee of Ministers, under the terms of Article 15.*b* of the Statute of the Council of Europe,

Aware of the fact that criminal victimisation is a daily phenomenon affecting the lives of citizens throughout Europe;

Having regard to Recommendation No. R (87) 21 on the assistance to victims and the prevention of victimisation, intended to complement the European Convention on the Compensation of Victims of Violent Crime (ETS No. 116, 1983) and Recommendation No. R (85) 11 on the position of the victim in the framework of criminal law and procedure;

Noting that, since the adoption of Recommendation No. R (87) 21, several recommendations have been adopted by the Committee of Ministers and significant developments have occurred in the field of assistance to victims including developments in national legislation and practice, a better understanding of the victims' needs and new research;

Bearing in mind the Convention for the Protection of Human Rights and Fundamental Freedoms (ETS No. 5, 1950), the European Convention on the Compensation of Victims of Violent crimes (see above), the Council of Europe Convention on the Prevention of Terrorism (CETS No. 196, 2005) and the Council of Europe Convention on Action against trafficking in Human Beings (CETS No. 197, 2005);

Recalling the resolutions of the conferences of the European ministers of justice in 2003 and 2005, inviting the Committee of Ministers to adopt new rules concerning the support of victims of terrorist acts and their families;

Noting the work of the Committee of Experts on Terrorism (CODEXTER), with regard to victims of terrorism;

Having considered the Guidelines on human rights and the fight against terrorism adopted by the Committee of Ministers on 11 July 2002 and the Guidelines on the protection of victims of terrorist acts, adopted on 2 March 2005;

Taking account of the standards developed by the European Union and by the United Nations with regard to victims;

Noting with appreciation the achievements of non-governmental organisations in assisting victims;

Aware of the need for co-operation between States particularly to assist victims of terrorism and other forms of transnational crimes;

Aware of the need to prevent repeat victimisation, in particular for victims belonging to vulnerable groups;

Convinced that it is as much the responsibility of the State to ensure that victims are assisted as it is to deal with offenders,

Recommends that the governments of member States disseminate and be guided in their internal legislation and practice by the principles set out in the appendix to this recommendation which replaces Recommendation No. R (87) 21 on the assistance to victims and the prevention of victimisation.

Appendix to Recommendation Rec(2006)8

1.   Definitions

For the purpose of this recommendation,

1.1.   Victim means a natural person who has suffered harm, including physical or mental injury, emotional suffering or economic loss, caused by acts or omissions that are in violation of the criminal law of a member State. The term victim also includes, where appropriate, the immediate family or dependants of the direct victim.

1.2.   Repeat victimisation means a situation when the same person suffers from more than one criminal incident over a specific period of time.

1.3.   Secondary victimisation means the victimisation that occurs not as a direct result of the criminal act but through the response of institutions and individuals to the victim.

2.   Principles

2.1.   States should ensure the effective recognition of, and respect for, the rights of victims with regard to their human rights; they should, in particular, respect the security, dignity, private and family life of victims and recognise the negative effects of crime on victims.

2.2.   States should ensure that the measures set forth in this recommendation are made available to victims without discrimination.

2.3.   The granting of these services and measures should not depend on the identification, arrest, prosecution or conviction of the perpetrator of the criminal act.

3.   Assistance

3.1.   States should identify and support measures to alleviate the negative effects of crime and to undertake that victims are assisted in all aspects of their rehabilitation, in the community, at home and in the workplace.

3.2.   The assistance available should include the provision of medical care, material support and psychological health services as well as social care and counselling. These services should be provided free of charge at least in the immediate aftermath of the crime.

3.3.   Victims should be protected as far as possible from secondary victimisation.

3.4.　　States should ensure that victims who are particularly vulnerable, either through their personal characteristics or through the circumstances of the crime, can benefit from special measures best suited to their situation.

3.5.　　Wherever possible, the assistance should be provided in a language understood by the victim.

4.　　Role of the public services

4.1.　　States should identify and support measures to encourage respect and recognition of victims and understanding of the negative effects of crime amongst all personnel and organisations coming into contact with victims.

Criminal justice agencies

4.2.　　The police and other criminal justice agencies should identify the needs of victims to ensure that appropriate information, protection and support is made available.

4.3.　　In particular, States should facilitate the referral of victims by the police to assistance services so that the appropriate services may be offered.

4.4.　　Victims should be provided with explanations of decisions made with regard to their case and have the opportunity to provide relevant information to the criminal justice personnel responsible for making these decisions.

4.5.　　Legal advice should be made available where appropriate.

Agencies in the community

4.6.　　States should promote the provision of special measures for the support or protection of victims by organisations providing, for example, health services, social security, housing, education and employment.

Role of embassies and consulates

4.7.　　Embassies and consulates should provide their nationals who become victims of crime with appropriate information and assistance.

5.　　Victim support services

5.1.　　States should provide or promote dedicated services for the support of victims and encourage the work of non governmental organisations in assisting victims.

Minimum standards

5.2.   Such services should:
-    be easily accessible;
-    provide victims with free emotional, social and material support before, during and after the investigation and legal proceedings;
-    be fully competent to deal with the problems faced by the victims they serve;
-    provide victims with information on their rights and on the services available;
-    refer victims to other services when necessary;
-    respect confidentiality when providing services.

Specialised centres

5.3.   States are encouraged to support the setting up or the maintenance of specialised centres for victims of crimes such as sexual and domestic violence and to facilitate access to these centres.

5.4.   States may also consider it necessary to encourage the establishment or maintenance of specialised centres for victims of crimes of mass victimisation, including terrorism.

National help lines

5.5.   States are encouraged to set up or to support free national telephone help lines for victims.

Co-ordination of services for victims

5.6.   States should take steps to ensure that the work of services offering assistance to victims is co-ordinated and that:
-    a comprehensive range of services is available and accessible;
-    standards of good practice for services offering help to victims are prepared and maintained;
-    appropriate training is provided and co-ordinated;
-    services are accessible to government for consultation on proposed policies and legislation.

This co-ordination could be provided by a single national organisation or by some other means.

6.   Information

Provision of information

6.1.   States should ensure that victims have access to information of relevance to their case and necessary for the protection of their interests and the exercise of their rights.

6.2.   This information should be provided as soon as the victim comes into contact with law enforcement or criminal justice agencies or with social or health care services. It should be communicated orally as well as in writing, and as far as possible in a language understood by the victim.

Content of the information

6.3.   All victims should be informed of the services or organisations which can provide support and the type and, where relevant, the costs of the support.

6.4.   When an offence has been reported to law enforcement or criminal justice agencies, the information provided to the victim should also include as a minimum:
  i.   the procedures which will follow and the victims' role in these procedures;
  ii.   how and in what circumstances the victim can obtain protection;
  iii. how and in what circumstances the victim can obtain compensation from the offender;
  iv.   the availability and, where relevant, the cost of:
        - legal advice,
        - legal aid, or
        - any other sort of advice;
  v.   how to apply for state compensation, if eligible;
  vi.   if the victim is resident in another state, any existing arrangements which will help to protect his or her interests.

Information on legal proceedings

6.5.   States should ensure in an appropriate way that victims are kept informed and understand:
  -     the outcome of their complaint;
  -     relevant stages in the progress of criminal proceedings;
  -     the verdict of the competent court and, where relevant, the sentence.

Victims should be given the opportunity to indicate that they do not wish to receive such information.

7.   Right to effective access to other remedies

7.1.   Victims may need to seek civil remedies to protect their rights following a crime. States should therefore take the necessary steps to ensure that victims have effective access to all civil remedies, and within a reasonable time, through:
  -     the right of access to competent courts; and
  -     legal aid in appropriate cases.

7.2.   States should institute procedures for victims to claim compensation from the offender in the context of criminal proceedings. Advice and support should also be provided to victims in making these claims and in enforcing any payments awarded.

8.   State compensation

Beneficiaries

8.1.   Compensation should be provided by the state for:
-    victims of serious, intentional, violent crimes, including sexual violence;
-    the immediate family and dependants of victims who have died as a result of such crime.

Compensation scheme

8.2.   States should adopt a compensation scheme for the victims of crimes committed on their territory, irrespective of the victim's nationality.

8.3.   The compensation awarded to victims should be based on the principle of social solidarity.

8.4.   The compensation should be granted without undue delay, at a fair and appropriate level.

8.5.   Since many persons are victimised in European states other than their own, states are encouraged to co-operate to enable victims to claim compensation from the state in which the crime occurred by applying to a competent agency in their own country.

Damages requiring compensation

8.6.   Compensation should be provided for treatment and rehabilitation for physical and psychological injuries.

8.7.   States should consider compensation for loss of income, funeral expenses and loss of maintenance for dependants. States may also consider compensation for pain and suffering.

8.8.   States may consider means to compensate damage resulting from crimes against property.

Subsidiarity

8.9.   State compensation should be awarded to the extent that the damage is not covered by other sources such as the offender, insurance or state funded health and social provisions.

9.   Insurance

9.1.   States should evaluate the extent of cover available under public or private insurance schemes for the various categories of criminal victimisation. The aim should be to promote equal access to insurance for all residents.

9.2.   States should encourage the principle that insurance be made available to as many people as possible. Insurance should be available to cover the person's belongings, as well as their physical integrity.

9.3.   States are encouraged to promote the principle that insurance policies do not exclude damages caused by acts of terrorism unless other applicable provisions exist.

10.   Protection

Protection of physical and psychological integrity

10.1.   States should ensure, at all stages of the procedure, the protection of the victim's physical and psychological integrity. Particular protection may be necessary for victims who could be required to provide testimony.

10.2.   Specific protection measures should be taken for victims at risk of intimidation, reprisals or repeat victimisation.

10.3.   States should take the necessary measures to ensure that, at least in cases where there might be danger to the victims, when the person prosecuted or sentenced for an offence is released, a decision may be taken to notify the victims if necessary.

10.4.   In so far as a state forwards on its own initiative the information referred to in paragraph 10.3, it should ensure that victims have the right to choose not to receive it, unless communication thereof is compulsory under the terms of the relevant criminal proceedings.

Protection against repeat victimisation

10.5.   States should develop policies to identify and combat repeat victimisation. The prevention of repeat victimisation should be an essential element in all strategies for victim assistance and crime prevention.

10.6.   All personnel in contact with victims should receive adequate training on the risks of repeat victimisation and on ways to reduce such risks.

10.7.   Victims should be advised on the risk of repeat victimisation and of the means of reducing these risks as well as assistance in implementing the measures proposed.

Protection of privacy

10.8.   States should take appropriate steps to avoid as far as possible impinging on the private and family life of victims as well as to protect the personal data of victims, in particular during the investigation and prosecution of the crime.

10.9.   States should encourage the media to adopt and respect self regulation measures in order to protect victims' privacy and personal data.

11.   Confidentiality

11.1.   States should require all agencies, whether statutory or non-governmental, in contact with victims, to adopt clear standards by which they may only disclose to a third party information received from or relating to a victim under the condition that:
-    the victim has explicitly consented to such disclosure;
-    there is a legal requirement or authorisation to do so.

11.2.   In these two cases of exception, clear rules should govern the disclosure procedures. Complaints procedures should be published for dealing with alleged breaches to the rules.

12.   Selection and training of personnel

12.1.   States should assist and support victim support services to:
-    develop appropriate standards for the selection of all paid and voluntary staff providing direct assistance to victims;
-    organise training and support for all paid and voluntary staff to ensure that such assistance is delivered according to professional standards.

Training

12.2.   Training should as a minimum include:
-    awareness of the negative effects of crime on victims;
-    skills and knowledge required to assist victims;
-    awareness of the risk of causing secondary victimisation and the skills to prevent this.

Specialised training

12.3.   Specialised training should be provided to all personnel working with child victims and victims of special categories of crime, for example, domestic or sexual violence, terrorism, crimes motivated by racial, religious or other prejudice, as well as to families of murder victims.

12.4.   Member states should ensure that appropriate training is provided for:
- the police and personnel involved in the administration of justice;
- the emergency services and others attending the scene of a major incident;
- relevant staff in health, housing, social security, education and employment services.

12.5.   Such personnel should be trained to a level which is appropriate to their contact with victims. Training should include, as a minimum:
- general awareness of the effects of crime on a victim's attitudes and behaviour, including verbal behaviour;
- the risk of causing secondary victimisation and the skills required to minimise this risk;
- the availability of services providing information and support specific to the needs of victims and the means of accessing these services.

13.   Mediation

13.1.   Taking into account the potential benefits of mediation for victims, statutory agencies should, when dealing with victims, consider, where appropriate and available, the possibilities offered for mediation between the victim and the offender, in conformity with Committee of Ministers' Recommendation R (99) 19 on mediation in criminal matters.

13.2.   The interests of victims should be fully and carefully considered when deciding upon and during a mediation process. Due consideration should be given not only to the potential benefits but also to the potential risks for the victim.

13.3.   Where mediation is envisaged, states should support the adoption of clear standards to protect the interests of victims. These should include the ability of the parties to give free consent, issues of confidentiality, access to independent advice, the possibility to withdraw from the process at any stage and the competence of mediators.

14.   Co-ordination and co-operation

14.1.   Each state should develop and maintain co-ordinated strategies to promote and protect the rights and interests of victims.

14.2.   To this end, each state should ensure, both nationally and locally, that:
- all agencies involved in criminal justice, social provision and health care, in the statutory, private and voluntary sectors, work together to ensure a co-ordinated response to victims;

- additional procedures are elaborated to deal with large scale victimisation situations, together with comprehensive implementation plans including the identification of lead agencies.

15. International co-operation

Preparation of states' responses

15.1. States should co-operate in preparing an efficient and co-ordinated response for transnational crimes. They should ensure that a comprehensive response is available to victims and that services co-operate in providing assistance.

Co-operation with the state of residence

15.2. In cases where the victim does not normally reside in the state where the crime occurred, that state and the state of residence should co-operate to provide protection to the victim and to assist the victim in reporting the crime as well as in the judicial process.

16. Raising public awareness of the effects of crime

16.1. States should contribute to raising public awareness of the needs of victims, encouraging understanding and recognition of the effects of crime in order to prevent secondary victimisation and to facilitate the rehabilitation of victims.

16.2. This should be achieved through government funding and publicity campaigns, using all available media.

16.3. The role of the non-governmental sector in focusing public attention on the situation of victims should be recognised, promoted and supported.

17. Research

17.1. States should promote, support, and, to the extent possible, fund or facilitate fund-raising for victimological research, including comparative research by researchers from within or outside their own territory.

17.2 Research should include:
- criminal victimisation and its impact on victims;
- prevalence and risks of criminal victimisation including factors affecting risk;
- the effectiveness of legislative and other measures for the support and protection of victims of crime – both in criminal justice and in the community;
- the effectiveness of intervention by criminal justice agencies and victim services.

17.3   States should take into consideration the latest state of victimological research available in developing consistent and evidence-based policies towards victims.

17.4   States should encourage all governmental and non-governmental agencies dealing with victims of crime to share their expertise with other agencies and institutions nationally and internationally.

Explanatory memorandum

Introduction

Background to Recommendation R(87)21 on assistance to victims and the prevention of victimisation

1.   Statistics show that victimisation is a daily phenomenon in Europe. Threats of terrorism, as well as terrorist acts and other forms of transnational crimes, also call for improved forms of assistance to victims.

2.   In 2003, following a study[1] on the relevance of Recommendation No. R (87) 21, the Criminological Scientific Council (PC-CSC) concluded that a new recommendation should be developed on this topic that would update Recommendation No. R (87) 21.

3.   Recommendation No. R (87) 21 was designed to complement the 1983 European Convention on the Compensation of Victims of Violent Crime (ETS No. 116) and Recommendation No. R (85) 11 on the position of the victim within the framework of criminal law and procedure.

4.   Since the adoption of Recommendation No. R (87) 21 in 1987, there have been significant developments in the field of assistance to victims in Europe. Member states' legislation and practice have evolved, as documented in several related surveys.

5.   In 1996, the Council of Europe' Committee of Ministers adopted Recommendation No. R (96) 8 on "crime policy in Europe in a time of change", which calls member states to have a coherent and rational crime policy directed towards, *inter alia,* the provision of assistance to victims. In addition, the Committee of Ministers has adopted several other Recommendations[2] which provide for assistance to particular categories of victims.

6.   The United Nations[3] and the European Union[4] have elaborated several standards in the field of victims.

---

[1] Document PC-CSC (2003)1, "The relevance today of Recommendation R(87)21 on the assistance to victims", Helen Reeves, 16 January 2003.
[2] Notably: Recommendation nr R(85)4 on violence in the family, R(97)13 concerning intimidation of witnesses and the rights of the defence, R(99)19 concerning mediation in penal matters, R (2000)11 on action against trafficking in human beings for the purposes of sexual exploitation, R(2001)16 on the protection of children from sexual exploitation, R(2002)05 on protection of women against violence, R(2005)09 on the protection of witnesses and collaborators of justice.
[3] This includes the following UN Conventions: International Convention for the suppression of the financing of terrorism (1999), UN Convention against Transnational Organized Crime and its Protocol on the Trafficking in Human Beings (General Assembly Resolution 55/25, 8 January 2001); UN Convention against corruption (General Assembly, 21 November 2003, A/RES/58/4), as well as the

Victims of terrorism

7.   Assistance to victims of terrorism has been considered a priority after the terrorist acts in New York in 2001, in Beslan (Russian Federation), in Madrid in 2004, and in London in 2005.

8.   Within the Council of Europe, the work in the legal field has been involved to the Committee of Experts on Terrorism (CODEXTER), which has notably been involved in the elaboration of legal instruments to fight terrorism.

9.   At their Conferences in 2003 and in 2005, the European Ministers of Justice invited the Committee of Ministers, where necessary, to adopt new rules concerning the improvement of, *inter alia*, the types of support offered to victims of terrorist acts and their families[5].

10.   As a result of the CODEXTER's work, the Council of Europe's Convention on the Prevention of Terrorism (CETS No. 196) was opened for signature in May 2005. Article 13 of the Convention specifically deals with the protection of, compensation of, and assistance to victims of terrorism[6].

Terms of reference of the Group of Specialists on Assistance to Victims

11.   The Committee of Ministers approved, on 15 December 2004, the terms of reference for a Group of specialists on assistance to victims and prevention of victimisation (PC-S-AV).

Declaration of Basic Principles of Justice for Victims of Crime and Abuse of Power (General Assembly resolution 40/34 of 29 November 1985), Implementation of the Declaration of Basic Principles of Justice for Victims and of Crime and Abuse of Power (Economic and Social Council resolution 1989/57), Plan of Action for the Implementation of the Declaration of Basic Principles of Justice for Victims of Crime and Abuse of Power (Economic and Social Council resolution 1998/21), Vienna Declaration on Crime and Justice: Meeting the Challenges of the Twenty-first Century (General Assembly resolution 55/59 - 2000), Guidelines on Justice Matters involving Child Victims and Witnesses of Crime (adopted by Economic and Social Council resolution 2005/20 of 22 July 2005), Basic principles and guidelines on the right to a remedy and reparation for victims of gross violations on international human rights law and serious violations of international humanitarian law (adopted by UN General Assembly on 10 November 2005, document A/RES/60/147).

[4] In particular: the European Union Council Framework Decision of 15 March 2001 on the standing of victims in criminal proceedings, the European Union Council Directive 2004/80/EC of 29 April 2004 relating to compensation for victims of crime.

[5] Resolution No. 1 on Combating Terrorism of the 25th Conference of European Ministers of Justice, Sofia, 9-10 October 2003, Resolution no 3 on the Fight against Terrorism of the 26th Conference of European Ministers of Justice, Helsinki, 7-8 April 2005.

[6] Web site of the convention:
http://conventions.coe.int/Treaty/Commun/QueVoulezVous.asp?NT=196&CM=1&DF=24/02/2006&CL=ENG

12.   The Committee is called upon, under the authority of the CDPC, to elaborate a draft Recommendation (updating Recommendation No. R (87) 21) setting out, *inter alia*, appropriate standards and principles in this area, and notably taking into account the relevant Council of Europe Recommendations and Resolutions.

Work of the Group of Specialists on Assistance to Victims

13.   The PC-S-AV held five meetings between January 2005 and March 2006. In accordance with its terms of reference, the PC-S-AV followed a twin-track approach: initially it was requested to give priority, in terms of time and content, to assistance to the victims of terrorism, on which it reported to both the CDPC and to the CODEXTER in June 2005, while keeping the CDDH informed, and only subsequently did it concentrate on the wider aspects of assistance to victims, on which it reported to the CDPC.

14.   After having consulted the CODEXTER and kept the CDDH informed, the group adopted at its 5th meeting, 15-16 March 2006, the preliminary draft Recommendation and its explanatory memorandum, which were sent to the CDPC for approval.

15.   The draft recommendation was approved by the CDPC on 07 April 2006 and adopted by the Committee of Ministers of the Council of Europe on 14 June 2006.

General considerations: aims of the Recommendation

16.   The aims of the Recommendation are threefold.

17.   The first aim is to update Recommendation R(87)21 on the assistance to victims, taking into account developments in the legislation and practice of the member States since 1987.

18.   The second aim is to assist member States in the prevention of repeat victimisation, in particular for victims from vulnerable sections of society.

19.   The third aim is to provide member States with useful guidance in defining their legislation and practice on assistance to victims of terrorism.

Commentary on the provisions of the Recommendation and its Appendix

Preamble

Victims of crime and victims of terrorism – paras. iv, v and vi.

20.   From the outset, the Committee had to decide to what extent the new Recommendation should be devoted specifically to assistance to victims of terrorism as opposed to victims in general.

21.   Although the crime of terrorism has been prioritised in some countries, the Committee was of the opinion that the needs of victims of terrorism were essentially the same of those of victims of other crimes.

22.   It based its reflections on national legislation and practice of Member States. For this purpose, it requested the assistance of the Max Planck Institute for Foreign and International Criminal Law, which produced a study entitled "Victims of Terrorism – Policies and Legislation in Europe – an overview on victim related assistance and support". [7]

23.   The report shows that a few countries have specific assistance policies for victims of terrorism, such as France, Italy, Greece, Russian Federation, Spain, Turkey, United Kingdom (Northern Ireland). Most States have some assistance programmes which apply to victims in general and thus may apply also to victims of terrorism. Fewer States have implemented State compensation schemes for victims of crime in general or victims of terrorism in particular.

24.   The Group took also into particular account the relevant Resolutions of European Justice Ministers, the Guidelines on Human Rights and the Fight Against Terrorism adopted by the Committee of Ministers in July 2002, the Guidelines on the Protection of Victims of Terrorist Acts adopted by the Committee of Ministers on 2 March 2005[8] and the work of the CODEXTER, including their country profiles on relevant legal and institutional capacities in the fight against terrorism[9].

25.   On the basis of the materials provided to the Committee by the scientific expert from the Max Planck Institute, the Committee adopted a

---

[7] "Victims of Terrorism – policies and legislation in Europe. An overview on victim related assistance and support", by Hans-Joerg Albrecht and Michael Kilchling, Max Planck Institute for Foreign and International Criminal Law, May 2005 (PC-S-AV (2005) 04).
[8] The text of the guidelines are available on :
http://www.coe.int/T/CM/system/WCDdoc.asp?Ref=CM/Del/Dec%282005%29917/4. 2&Ver=0002&Sector=CM&Lang=en#
[9] The country profiles are available on the web site of the CODEXTER: www.coe.int/gmt

report on the assistance to victims of terrorism in June 2005, which was sent to the CODEXTER and to the CDPC,[10] which have given comments on it.

26.   In its discussions on the text of the new Recommendation on the assistance to victims in general, the Committee decided to discuss each Section successively and to   include, where appropriate, provisions applying specifically to victims of terrorism.

27.   Unless stated otherwise, the provisions included in the Recommendation should be understood as applying to all crime victims, including victims of terrorism.

28.   This Explanatory Memorandum contains some examples of national practice. In addition, the report "Victims of Terrorism – policies and legislation in Europe", as well as the country profiles gathered by the CODEXTER provide information about the main elements of national practices and legislation on the compensation of victims of terrorism. These elements may be considered by States when applying Art. 13 of the Council of Europe Convention on the Prevention of Terrorism (CETS No. 196).[11]

Scope of assistance to victims

29.   Assistance to victims has been understood, for the purposes of this Recommendation, as including various measures which States are encouraged to adopt with the overall aim of alleviating the negative effects of crime on victims and helping the victim's rehabilitation in the community.

30.   Accordingly, in addition to support services offered to victims, the recommendation also deals with such matters as the provision of information to victims, victim protection, social measures, selection and training of staff working with victims, aspects of criminal and civil justice systems, compensation and mediation. Such a holistic approach to victim assistance reflects the ways in which the different actors and institutions in society should interact with victims.

31.   The Recommendation provides detailed provisions on the various types of assistance to victims. The detailed character of the Recommendation is deliberate, and is intended to provide useful guidance for practitioners and public authorities in the development of practice and

---

[10] "Report on the assistance to victims of terrorism", 21 June 2005, sent to the European Committee of Crime Problems (CDPC) and to the CODEXTER (Committee of Experts on Terrorism) – document PC-S-AV (2005) 07.
[11] "Article 13 – Protection, compensation and support for victims of terrorism: Each Party shall adopt such measures as may be necessary to protect and support the victims of terrorism that has been committed within its own territory. These measures may include, through the appropriate national schemes and subject to domestic legislation, inter alia, financial assistance and compensation for victims of terrorism and their close family members."

legislation. The standards set forth in the Recommendation should contribute to defining new aspirations in the field of assistance to victims.

Role of Non-Governmental Organisations (NGO's) – para. viii

32.   The Committee paid tribute to the important role played by non-governmental organisations (NGO's) in assisting victims and in developing a dialogue with the relevant public authorities. NGOs have made a significant contribution to the promotion of victims' issues and to the strengthening of relevant institutional and legal frameworks.

33.   In particular, the Committee made reference to the work and experience gained by associations such as the "European Forum for Victim Services" (hereafter "the Forum"), a network of 21 non-governmental national organisations from nineteen European States. The Committee was assisted by policy statements adopted by the Forum on several issues[12].

Crime prevention and prevention of repeat victimisation - para. x

34.   The Recommendation covers assistance to victims and the prevention of repeat victimisation. Unlike the Recommendation R (87) 21, it does not deal with crime prevention in general, a matter now more commonly referred to as "crime reduction".

35.   Crime reduction is considered to be an issue that affects the whole community, not just those people who have become the victims of crime[13]. In view of the large volume of work carried out on this subject, it has been agreed that this topic should be made the subject of a separate document and excluded from the Committee's terms of reference.

36.   Far more is now known about the phenomenon known as "repeat victimisation"[14], which is the only aspect of crime reduction which does have immediate relevance for people who have already been the victims of crime. Research in various European countries has confirmed that once a crime has been committed, the possibility of a similar crime being committed against the same victim, or the same household, increases dramatically.

37.   The new Recommendation draws attention to this phenomenon and to the State's responsibility to include measures to prevent repeat victimisation within the general provision of services to victims.

---

[12] More information on the European forum of victim services on its web site: http://www.euvictimservices.org/.
[13] For more complete elements on the matter, see H. Reeves, "the relevance today of Recommendation R(87)21", doc PC-CSC (2003)01, 16 January 2003.
[14] This phenomenon is further elaborated under Chapter 10 B. of this document.

General considerations on assistance to victims – para. xi

38.   The Committee expressed its firm conviction that assistance to victims should be understood, developed and promoted for its own sake.

39.   In particular, assistance provided to victims needs to be conceived, organised and provided independently from the overall interests of the criminal justice system. Even when the interests and the position of victims are taken into consideration as part of the criminal justice procedure, the overall aim of assistance policies to victims should have the interests of victims as their primary focus.

Increased protection

40.   Nothing in the Recommendation prevents States from adopting more favourable measures and services than the ones described in the Recommendation.

1.   DEFINITIONS

41.   The definitions proposed in this Section aim to help the reader understand the scope for application of terms referred to in the Recommendation which are not defined in other Council of Europe instruments.

42.   Victim: the definition is consistent with the European Union Framework Decision on the standing of victims in criminal proceedings Art.1[15]. It covers natural persons who are victims of all types of crimes, including non-violent crimes and crimes committed through negligence.

43.   For the purposes of the Recommendation, the immediate family and dependents of the victim of crime have been included in the definition of victims. "Immediate family" includes partners, both married and unmarried.

44.   The definition of victims and the inclusion of family members and dependents is consistent with the UN standards, such as the Declaration of basic Principles of Justice for Victims of Crime and Abuse of Power (1985)[16].

45.   Repeat victimisation: the definition has been agreed by the PC-S-AV on the basis of the work of researchers and practitioners. It refers to situations when the same person suffers from more than one criminal

---

[15] Doc 2001/220/JHA adopted on 15 March 2001 Art1: "(a) "victim" shall mean a natural person who has suffered harm, including physical or mental injury, emotional suffering or economic loss, directly caused by acts or omissions that are in violation of the criminal law of a Member State;".

[16] Art 2: "The term "victim" also includes, where appropriate, the immediate family or dependants of the direct victim and persons who have suffered harm in intervening to assist victims in distress or to prevent victimisation."

incident over a specific period of time. It applies, for example, to victims of repeated burglaries, continuing domestic violence or any form of harassment.

46.   Secondary victimisation: Research and professional experience show that secondary victimisation, generated by institutions or individuals, is often experienced by victims in the aftermath of crime. Secondary victimisation involves a lack of understanding of the suffering of victims which can leave them feeling both isolated and insecure, loosing faith in the help available from their communities and the professional agencies. The experience of secondary victimisation intensifies the immediate consequences of crime by prolonging or aggravating the victim's trauma; attitudes, behaviour, acts or omissions can leave victims feeling alienated from society as a whole.[17]

2.   PRINCIPLES

47.   The State's responsibility to assist victims derives from the obligations set out in the European Convention on Human Rights (ECHR). States party to the Convention have a positive obligation to "secure to everyone within their jurisdiction the rights and freedoms defined in [the] Convention" (Art 1 ECHR), and in particular their rights to life (Art 2), security (Art 5), private and family life (Art 8).

48.   States should recognise the negative effects of crime on victims and take measures to alleviate these effects and help the victim's rehabilitation in the community.

49.   The personal characteristics of a victim, such as race, colour, sex, sexuality, age, language, religion, nationality, political or other opinion, cultural beliefs or practices, property, birth or family status, ethnic or social origin, and disability should not be grounds for refusing assistance.

50.   This does not however preclude States from making special provisions when specific characteristics or circumstances of the victims require.

51.   A number of States differentiate in the assistance given to a victim on the basis of the type of offence. It would nevertheless be desirable that States consider the victims' needs in priority.

52.   The conduct of the victim before, during and after the criminal event should not constitute grounds for refusing assistance to him or her. It could however be taken into account when considering the scope of compensation.

---

[17] Extract from the statement of the European Forum for Victim Services on the Social Rights of Victims of Crime (1998).

53.   Unrelated prior criminal conviction of the victim should not constitute grounds for refusing any provision of the Recommendation.

54.   The identification, arrest, prosecution or conviction of the perpetrator of the criminal act should not be the condition for granting these services. It is understood that some measures, such as mediation for instance, clearly depends on the identification of the offender.

3.   ASSISTANCE

General remarks

55.   The scope of assistance to victims has been elaborated in paras. 28-30 above.

56.   States should ensure that the services mentioned in the Recommendation are available for as long as needed by the victim.

57.   Where resources for assistance such as counselling are scarce, States may allocate those resources to victims of more serious crimes.

Types of assistance

58.   - Immediate assistance should consist of a preliminary medical assessment and first aid if needed, as well as general information on assistance available to victims. The personnel in contact with victims should be aware of the risk of secondary victimisation and should have adequate training to prevent it.
   - In the medium term, it has proved particularly useful to appoint a contact person or an "agent de liaison" between the victim, community services and investigation teams. The person should be well-trained in the available services and be able to understand and respond to the victim's emotional needs. In addition, the protection of the victim's privacy should be ensured.
   - In the longer term, the range of services that are proposed in the short and medium term should remain available as long as needed. The victim may wish to be referred to specialised services or to victims' self help groups where they can share their experiences with other victims. However, such initiatives should avoid unnecessarily prolonging the individual's perception of being a "victim".

Assistance to particularly vulnerable victims

59.   States should ensure the provision of assistance to particular groups of victims, who can be considered vulnerable either by virtue of their personal characteristics (as in the case of children or people with physical or learning disabilities) or of the type of crime they have been exposed to (e.g. domestic violence, sexual violence or organised crime). Such victims should benefit from special measures designed to suit their situation.

60.   Particular attention should be paid to victims who do not understand the local language. Wherever possible, assistance should be provided in a language understood by the victim.

Assistance to victims of multiple victimisation

61.   In cases of multiple victimisation, which may involve terrorism, some victims may benefit from group work or networking among victims of the same event.

62.   States should also foresee provisions for large scale assistance in the immediate aftermath of such incident, as described under Chapter 15 below.

4.   THE ROLE OF PUBLIC SERVICES

Criminal Justice Agencies

63.   Research has shown that victims benefit from referrals by law enforcement agencies to victims support services. Some States interpret data protection legislation in a way which precludes the transmission of the victim's personal data by referral. Research show however that victims are satisfied with the transmission of their personal data to victims support services. The practice in countries such as France, the Netherlands and in the United Kingdom has demonstrated the effectiveness of such referrals.

64.   Victims should be explicitly told that they can refuse referrals to victim services or offers of assistance from victim support services.

65.   Victim support services who receive referrals from the police should, in addition to offering their own services, provide victims with access to relevant specialist organisations dealing with victims of specific crimes (e.g. terrorism) or with specific victim groups (e.g. women, children).

66.   Although many States provide information on the main decisions taken during criminal proceedings, fewer States take measures to give explanations for these decisions. Explanations should be provided in particular regarding decisions described in Art 6.5 of the Recommendation.

67.   Whenever the victim is well aware of the decisions taken, he or she would more likely provide with additional information which could be relevant to the case.

68.   In addition to the training of criminal justice agencies to recognise victims' needs, as provided for in Chapter 12 of the Recommendation, it has been demonstrated that systems to monitor performance are more likely to encourage good practice.

69.   Victims should receive legal advice on any aspect of their involvement in the criminal justice process, including on the possibility to becoming "*partie civile*" or to claim compensation.

Agencies in the community

70.   The measures proposed in this Section relate to the wider aspects of the victim's life in the community, which are not covered by the criminal justice system or by State compensation. The Recommendation recognises that many victims require, for example, medical services for both physical and psychological injuries, whether or not the crime has been reported to the police.   Similarly, some victims of repeated burglaries or racist or other harassment will need help with home security or re-housing.

71.   Although these provisions are available in most countries, for instance the relocation of a victim who is a witness of organised crime, the rights of other victims have rarely been recognised and would deserve higher consideration.

72.   The policy statement adopted by the European Forum for Victim Services on "the social rights of victims of crime" (1998)[18] provides examples of social measures which could be considered by States in fields such as access to health care services, income, home security, employment, education.[19]

Role of Embassies and Consulates

73.   States should take the necessary steps to ensure that their embassies and consulates provide national victims with information on assistance available to them both in their host country and in their own countries. They should also, to the extent possible, provide national victims with immediate assistance by helping them to obtain such things as new identity documents, flight tickets and accommodation.

5.   VICTIM SUPPORT SERVICES

74.   In addition to assistance provided by criminal justice agencies and public services, States should provide or promote dedicated services for the support of victims. Such services can be of many different natures, although research[20] has indicated the positive value of the establishment and

---

[18] Available on http://www.euvictimservices.org/EFVSDocs/social_rights.pdf.
[19] See also the publication made by the United Kingdom Home Office, "a new deal for   victims   and   witnesses",   2003,   available   at: http://old.homeoffice.gov.uk/docs2/vicwitstrat.pdf.
[20] Brienen, M.E.I., Hoegen, E.H. Victims of Crime in 22 European Criminal Justice Systems: The Implementation of Recommendation (85) 11 of the Council of Europe on the Position of the Victim in the Framework of Criminal Law and Procedure, Niemegen, Netherlands: WLP, 2000.

promotion of independent non-governmental national victim support agencies.

75. While the majority of victim service organisations are formed within the voluntary sector, their success depends greatly upon the support of government. The 2001 EU Framework Decision on the standing of victims in criminal proceedings, requests Member States to "promote the involvement of victim support systems responsible for organising the initial reception of victims and for victim support and assistance, thereafter". [21]

76. Of the recommendations in the Phare Rule of Law Project, Module IV, one crucially asks that in every state, "named senior officials in the relevant ministries and criminal justice agencies be charged with express responsibility for the identification and promotion of policies and programmes for victims and witnesses". [22]

Minimum standards

77. Victim support services should adopt and abide by defined standards of services. As a minimum, the victims support services should respect the standards set forth in this Section of the Recommendation.

78. Nothing should prevent such services from going further in their definitions of standards of services. To this end, reference could be made to the Statement of victims' rights to standards of services adopted by the European Forum for Victim Services in 1999[23].

79. The services should be available to the victims regardless of when the victim makes contact with victim support services. Particularly in cases of violence against minors, a long period of time can elapse before the victim takes the initiative to contact a victim support service.

80. Training, as described under Chapter 12, should enable the relevant personnel to be fully competent to deal with the problems of the victims they serve.

81. Specialised services, dealing for example with children, victims of rape or victims of terrorism are of great value. General services are encouraged to provide these services or to refer victims to other specialists. Such services should be easily accessible. The co-ordination of victim

---

[21] Council Framework Decision of 15 March 2001 on the standing of victims of crime in criminal proceedings (2001/220/JHA) OJ, L82, 22 March 2001, Article 13.
[22] Phare Horizontal Programme on Justice and Home Affairs, Reinforcement of the Rule of Law: Final report on the first part of the project. European Commission: August 2002. p. 57.
[23] Available on:
http://www.euvictimservices.org/EFVSDocs/service_standard_rights.pdf.

support services, as mentioned under §§ 86 – 90 and 149 below is important in this perspective.

Specialised centres

82.   The existence of these centres has proved to be of particular value to victims of sexual violence, trafficking and domestic violence. Such victims may be fearful of reporting to the police and might prefer to turn to such centres first. They should be able to obtain support and information whether or not they decide to report the crime to the authorities. These centres should be aware of the importance of securing evidence for possible criminal proceedings at a later date.

83.   Some States consider that other forms of trauma, such as trauma resulting from terrorist acts or other forms of multiple victimisation, could also be addressed by such specialised centres.

National help lines

84.   It is recommended that national help lines should be available in addition to other services listed in the Recommendation. Help lines should as a minimum provide general support and information and referrals to victim support agencies.

85.   All personnel should be trained to provide basic support according to the needs expressed.

Co-ordination of victim services

86.   It is important that States ensure the effective provision of support to victims. They should ensure that adequate services are available and that they work in a co-ordinated manner. In several countries, the setting up of national generalist organisations contributes to achieving such objective.

87.   The co-ordination of dedicated victims services contributes to:
- voicing the needs and concerns of member associations and allowing for better access to and more influence on government policies and institutions;
- having an overview of the existing services available to victims, being in a position to assess them and identify their strengths and weaknesses;
- preparing and maintaining standards of good practice for victim services;
- co-ordinating assistance to victims
- co-ordinating the provision of training.

88.   The recommendations issued by the Phare Working Group, propose that in all states "strenuous efforts should be made either to aid the

development of an existing generalist organisation for victims or to create and aid the development of such an organisation where none exists".[24]

89.	The European Forum for Victim Services has also long advocated the establishment of effective national victim services. The forum is composed of 21 national organisations from 19 member States.

90.	National victim assistance services have emerged in many European states[25] and they have proved to be effective in lobbying for victim policy decisions on the part of governments. These organisations are consulted before important decisions are taken by government, and in some instances, the organisations themselves initiate the discussion.

## 6.	INFORMATION

91.	This Section of the Recommendation corresponds closely to the Art 4 of the EU Council Framework Decision of 15 March 2001 on the standing of victims in criminal proceedings[26].

Provision of information

92.	Victims should be informed as soon as possible of the services available when they report a crime to the police. They should also be informed of the possibility that victim support services will approach them.

93.	If the victim contacts victim support services before reporting the crime, he or she should be informed how to report the offence to the police.

94.	Procedures should be put in place to ensure that victims have easy access to information relevant to their case and necessary for the protection of their interests.

95.	In particular for cases where the information is to be given to a victim by a statutory agency (e.g. police), a review mechanism should be set up to ensure that the procedures are well-implemented and adhered to.

96.	In order to provide victims with additional information, many States have provided internet sites or leaflets and handbooks. The information

---

[24] Phare Horizontal Programme on Justice and Home Affairs, Reinforcement of the Rule of Law: Final report on the first part of the project. European Commission: August 2002. p. 57.

[25] Brienen, M.E.I., Hoegen, E.H. Victims of Crime in 22 European Criminal Justice Systems: The Implementation of Recommendation (85) 11 of the Council of Europe on the Position of the Victim in the Framework of Criminal Law and Procedure, Niemegen, Netherlands: WLP, 2000, p. 45.

[26] Available on:
http://europa.eu.int/smartapi/cgi/sga_doc?smartapi!celexapi!prod!CELEXnumdoc&lg=en&numdoc=32001F0220&model=guichett.

provided may be adapted to fit the needs of various types of victims (children, victims of domestic violence, murder, or sexual assault etc.).

Content of the information

97.   In case where the victim reports a crime, he or she should be informed of the procedures which will follow and of his or her role in these procedures. This should include, where appropriate, the possibility of exercising his or her rights in criminal proceedings, the possibility of obtaining protection, of being called as a witness, etc.

Information on criminal proceedings

98.   Victims should be informed of the progress of the case. It may include information on a decision to charge, not to charge, to discontinue the prosecution, the dates of court hearings and decisions relating to the release of the offender from pre-trial detention In particular, information on decisions to release offenders should be provided to the victim in cases of violent crimes against the person or harassment and when the offender has been given a lengthy sentence (e.g. 12 months or more).

99.   Sometimes victims do not want to receive information regarding the offender or the progress of criminal proceedings. Victims should therefore have the possibility to express their wish not to receive such information.

7.   RIGHT TO EFFECTIVE ACCESS TO OTHER REMEDIES

100.   Victims who suffer damages as a result of a crime should be entitled to effective access to justice in order to protect their rights. They should have access to justice to deal with such problems as child custody, property ownership, home security and claims for damages against the offender. Where relevant, exclusion orders or other injunctions should be made available.

101.   Victims should also be entitled to claim compensation from the offender in the context of criminal proceedings except where, in certain cases, national law provides for compensation to be awarded in another manner. This is in line with the Council framework decision of 15 March 2001 on the standing of victims in criminal proceedings (Art 9).

102.   Assistance should also be provided to victims to enforce any payment awarded. In some States, assistance is given by the State, to enforce a payment awarded by a criminal court. Research has demonstrated that this is the most effective way to ensure that payment is made. States should therefore consider what steps are needed to ensure payment.

8.   STATE COMPENSATION

Compensation scheme

103.   Each State should adopt a compensation scheme for victims.

104.   It is asserted that the obligation of the State to pay compensation is based on the principle of social solidarity by which the society, as a whole, accepts to share the burden produced by the crime.

105.   The practice, in terms of victim compensation, varies widely among States. They are therefore encouraged to compare systems of compensation, including the provision of funding. Sources of funding for State compensation schemes can be public funds, confiscation of perpetrators' assets, fines, a tax imposed on insurance contracts (as in the French practice) or other sources.

106.   National compensation schemes should compensate all eligible victims of crimes committed within their national borders. The access to compensation should be granted irrespective of the victim's nationality. Nationality could however be considered to some extent in the calculation of the amount to be compensated to victims.

Damages to be compensated

107.   As an expression of social solidarity, the treatment and rehabilitation for physical and psychological injuries should be compensated.

108.   The Recommendation invites States to consider, in addition to compensation for physical injuries, the compensation for pain and suffering. This is particularly relevant for numerous victims of sexual violence.

109.   Physical injuries and loss of income can often be covered by private insurances and/or social security. The immaterial damage is often the main damage to be compensated. The inclusion of pain and suffering as a damage to be compensated is therefore crucial in cases where there is no material injury but considerable moral harm caused by the crime.

110.   Compensation for special damages, such as loss of income, funeral expenses, loss of maintenance for dependants should be considered by States. Compensation for damages resulting from crimes against property may also be envisaged.

111.   As to the level of compensation to be awarded, it is suggested that it should be the same for all victims, regardless of the situation and needs of the individual victim.

Victims of terrorism

112.   As far as victims of terrorism are concerned, the Committee had an extensive discussion on the types of losses to be compensated as well as on the types of compensation to be awarded.

113.   The report on "Victims of Terrorism – policies and legislation in Europe. An overview on victim related assistance and support", elaborated by the Max Planck Institute for Foreign and International Criminal Law[27] as well as the "Report on the assistance to victims of terrorism", adopted by the Committee in June 2005[28] provide useful suggestions and national examples.

114.   As to the forms that compensation may take, due consideration should be given, in this regard, to Guideline VII of the Council of Europe Guidelines on the Protection of Victims of Terrorist Acts: "apart from the payment of pecuniary compensation, states are encouraged to consider, depending on the circumstances, taking other measures to mitigate the negative effects of the terrorist act suffered by the victims." Such other forms of acknowledgment for victims could be considered in all cases of multiple victimisation[29].

115.   In some countries, compensation is offered to the community which is associated with the victim of a terrorist act. This community could use this compensation to build a hospital, school or memorial, or to set up an association or foundation.

116.   A system of voluntary contributions to a trust fund for the benefit of an affected community can be considered.

117.   The level of evidence required from victims of terrorism during any judicial procedure for compensation should be limited. The evidence that a terrorist act has been committed and that the claimant is a victim should be sufficient. Evidence of intention should not be necessary.

---

[27] "Victims of Terrorism – policies and legislation in Europe. An overview on victim related assistance and support", by Hans-Joerg Albrecht and Michael Kilchling, Max Planck Institute for Foreign and International Criminal Law, May 2005 (PC-S-AV (2005) 04).
[28] "Report on the assistance to victims of terrorism", adopted by the PC-S-AV, 21 June 2005, transmitted to the European Committee of Crime Problems (CDPC) and to the CODEXTER (Committee of Experts on Terrorism); document PC-S-AV (2005) 07.
[29] See the UN Declaration of Basic Principles of Justice for Victims and Abuse of Power, 1985.

Subsidiarity

118.   State compensation should be awarded to the extent that the damage is not covered by other sources such as the offender, insurance company or State-funded health and social provisions.

119.   The application of this principle varies among States. In many States, for example, the compensation obtained from private insurance companies is taken into account when fixing the amount of compensation to be paid by the State. In some States, however, it is not and State compensation is received in addition to any indemnity received from the insurance company.

9.   INSURANCE

120.   States should evaluate the extent of insurance cover provided by public or private insurance schemes for the various relevant categories of criminal victimisation. Where necessary, states should also seek ways to make insurance more accessible for families at greatest risk of victimisation and for those with limited means.

121.   Research in the United Kingdom (1998 British Crime Survey) has shown that almost one in five United Kingdom households does not have home contents insurance. Low income households were the least likely to have insurance; about half of those living in accommodation rented from a public or social landlord were not insured. The survey also showed that those least likely to have insurance are most at risk of burglary.[30] Further research has shown that the most common reason for not being insured is cost – it is relatively more expensive to insure on a low income. Those families with the lowest incomes living in neighbourhoods with high crime levels are three to four times less likely to have insurance than households with high incomes.

122.   A valuable alternative for those who cannot afford conventional insurance cover is a "tenant's contents insurance scheme". These schemes, which can be operated by public or social landlords, generally involve the collection of insurance premiums with rent. The landlord is able to negotiate preferential rates with insurance companies and these savings can be passed on to tenants. Tenants receive cover that is affordable, flexible and meets their needs. Landlords are able to demonstrate that they have fulfilled their obligations to promote social inclusion. Research commissioned shows that schemes like this do operate successfully but much more needs to be done to set up and promote tenants contents insurance.[31]

---

[30] Budd, T. (1999) Burglary of domestic dwellings: findings from the British Crime Survey. (Home Office statistical bulletin; 4/99) London Home Office.
[31] Housing Corporation (2001) Insurance for all: a good practice guide. London: the Housing Corporation, 2001.

10. PROTECTION

A. Protection of physical and psychological integrity

123.   Special protective measures should be available to particularly vulnerable categories of victims, such as children, persons with learning disabilities, victims of domestic violence and other types of victims subject to repeat victimisation, including victims of trafficking in human beings, sexual violence, and victims of all forms of harassment. In such cases, police forces could inform the victims of the potential or actual risks of repeated crimes or reprisals and on ways to protect themselves. Adequate training and adequate resources should be provided to police forces for this purpose.

124.   Particular protection should be available for victims who might be called as witnesses and are at risk of harassment, intimidation or reprisals. The Council of Europe Recommendations R (1997) 13 concerning intimidation of witnesses and the rights of the defence[32] and R (2005) 09[33] on the protection of witnesses and collaborators of justice provides useful guidance on this matter.

125.   Protection can include legal and procedural measures. It could also include practical measures, such as alarm systems, closed circuit TV, video cameras and involving neighbours, the community, etc.

126.   Re-location should be made available as an option for particularly vulnerable victims or victims under threat. Where applicable, States are encouraged to enter into bi-lateral agreements to define the procedures for such re-location and the associated rights of the victim (residence, social rights, health care, education, etc).

B. Protection against repeat victimisation

127.   Wherever the possibility of repeat victimisation exists, measures to help victims to avoid further victimisation should be regarded as an essential element of the assistance to victims.

128.   Research in various countries in Europe has confirmed that once a crime has been committed, the possibility of a similar crime occurring against the same victim, or the same household, increases dramatically. For example, a household which has been burgled is four times more likely to be burgled again within six weeks of the first crime[34]. Statistics show, for

---

[32] Available on :
http://wcd.coe.int/com.instranet.InstraServlet?Command=com.instranet.CmdBlobGet&DocId=574854&SecMode=1&Admin=0&Usage=4&InstranetImage=43025.

[33] Available on :
http://wcd.coe.int/ViewDoc.jsp?id=849237&BackColorInternet=9999CC&BackColorIntranet=FFBB55&BackColorLogged=FFAC75.

[34] Graham Farrell, Multiple victimisation: Its Extent and Significance in: International Review of Victimology 2 (1992).

instance in Germany, that 70% of all self-reported crimes have been committed against only 14% of the adult population[35]. In the case of violent crimes, 45% are committed against 17% of the population.

129.   As an example of national practice, in some areas in England and Wales, Victim Support offers special projects to prevent burglary victims being targeted repeatedly. Repeat victims are identified using specialised referral software and assistance is given through the provision of appropriate crime prevention hardware and other advice.

130.   Other groups with specific victimisation risks such as victims of racist and hate crimes have been offered special services by Victim Support in conjunction with local government agencies and the police. Special reporting centres have been set up based at doctor's surgeries, council offices and Citizen Advice Bureaus, which enable repeat victims of racist and hate crime to report harassment or intimidation without having to increase their vulnerability by reporting directly to a police station.

C. Protection of privacy

131.   The protection of the victim's privacy should be ensured in particular when the crime receives a high level of media coverage.

132.   There is a tendency in some countries for journalists to harass victims, their families, friends and neighbours for personal information. Pressure is also placed on agencies in contact with the victim to provide access to victims which would not otherwise be available. This behaviour should not be tolerated.

133.   It is the responsibility of the State to protect the individual's right to respect of private and family life, as set forth in Art 8[36] of the European Convention on the protection of human rights and fundamental guarantees (ECHR).[37] Due consideration should be given to the legal requirements to protect personal data of victims, as well as, in some cases, the image of victims.

---

[35] Schneider, Hans Joachim, Victimological Developments in the World during the Last Three Decades: Proceedings of the Montreal Symposium 2000, World Society of Victimology.

[36] Article 8 – Right to respect for private and family life: (1) Everyone has the right to respect for his private and family life, his home and his correspondence. (2) There shall be no interference by a public authority with the exercise of this right except such as is in accordance with the law and is necessary in a democratic society in the interests of national security, public safety or the economic well-being of the country, for the prevention of disorder or crime, for the protection of health or morals, or for the protection of the rights and freedoms of others.

[37] The forum's Statement on Social Rights of Victims contains useful elements on this matter: http://www.euvictimservices.org/EFVSDocs/service_standard_rights.pdf.

11. CONFIDENTIALITY

134.   When dealing with the issue of confidentiality and without prejudice to the situations covered under 71-72, the interests of the victim should always be the priority, including the protection of his or her personal data. The disclosure of the victim's details can be granted only if the victim consents to it, or if there is a legal requirement or authorisation or an overriding ethical consideration to do so. In these circumstances three exceptions, clear rules should govern the disclosure procedures. Any disclosure should be respectful of the principle of proportionality. Within some limits, police forces can, for instance, disclose information on victims to other persons (e.g. a witness) for investigation purposes.

135.   Complaints procedures should be published for dealing with alleged breaches to the adopted rules.[38]

136.   Practitioners recognise in general that in situations where the health or security of anyone, including the victim, is at risk, this would constitute an overriding ethical consideration which would allow overruling the confidentiality principle.

12. SELECTION AND TRAINING OF PERSONNEL

137.   Rules for selection of staff and training should apply to all personnel whose work involves contact with victims. It applies to professional and voluntary staff.

138.   In many European States, victim services are supported by dedicated teams of volunteers.[39] The employment of trained volunteers is a preferred option with many non-governmental organisations and is crucial to the success of victim services, as volunteers are representative of the community which they serve. In these organisations, trained professional staff offer training and supervision, as well as administrative, financial, and personal support to the volunteer workforce.

139.   The development of a professional framework for the training, support and supervision of volunteers is crucial to the effectiveness of these organisations. Under Article 14 of the 2001 EU Framework decision, each member state must enable personnel involved with victims, "to receive suitable training with particular reference to the needs of the most vulnerable groups".

---

[38]   Ibidem.
[39]   Brienen, M.E.I., Hoegen, E.H. (2000) Victims of Crime in 22 European Criminal Justice Systems: The Implementation of Recommendation (85) 11 of the Council of Europe on the Position of the Victim in the Framework of Criminal Law and Procedure, Niemegen, Netherlands: WLP, 2000.

Training

140. Training of personnel should include, as a minimum, awareness of the negative effects of crimes, the range of victims' reactions, the risks of causing secondary victimisation and the skills and competences to assist victims.

141. The competences to be taught vary according to the type of service provided by the personnel concerned. To the extent necessary, the training will cover psychological aspects of victimisation, the types of assistance available and the ways to access them, information on legal and judicial provisions etc.

142. Training can be facilitated by national victim assistance services, which can co-ordinate the organisation of training both to public services (medical and social services, magistrates, police forces) and to associations and organisations providing assistance to victims.

Training of personnel in other services

143. Section underlines the necessity of providing training for personnel in police forces, the judiciary, Embassies and Consulates, as well as in health, housing, social security, education and employment services. Relevant personnel, i.e. persons in direct contact with victims, should be trained to recognise the effects of crime on victims, the risk of causing secondary victimisation and on the availability of services providing support or information.

13. MEDIATION

144. There is a shared consensus that victim-offender mediation, where available, offers benefits as well as presenting potential risks for the victim. Such benefits and risks need to be carefully balanced when involving a victim in a mediation process. This balance is especially important in situations linked to intimate relationships, such as domestic violence, where the victim may not be in a position to express free consent to the mediation process.

145. Cases which are unsuitable for mediation, as a diversion from the criminal justice system, may still benefit from mediation at any stage following the sentence.

146. In designing national legislation and practice on victim-offender mediation, member states should give particular attention to issues such as the risk of secondary victimisation, the ability of parties to give free consent, issues of confidentiality, competence of mediators and the possibility to withdraw from the process at any stage.

147.   Advice from an independent person on the possibilities offered by mediation is particularly important in order to provide the victim with objective information on the matters raised in the preceding paragraph. This could enable the victim to have a clearer idea on the benefits and potential risks offered by mediation.

148.   States should take into account the relevant international and national norms and practices, notably:
-    the Council of Europe Recommendation Rec(99)19 on mediation in criminal matters[40],
-    United Nations Basic principles on the use of restorative justice programmes in criminal matters, ECOSOC Resolution 2002/12, 24 July 2002[41]
-    European Forum of Victim Services' statement on the position of the victim within the process of mediation.[42]

14.   CO-ORDINATION AND CO-OPERATION

149.   The need for co-ordination is particularly important in countries where several victim services co-exist. If organisations with overlapping or similar services approach an individual victim without co-ordination, there is a higher risk of confusion and of secondary victimisation. The role of a national organisation in ensuring co-ordination and co-operation between services and institutions can be beneficial in this context.

15.   INTERNATIONAL CO-OPERATION

Preparation of States' responses

150.   Particularly in situations of mass victimisation such as terrorist acts, States should ensure a well-prepared and co-ordinated response. The emergency response should be part of the general civil and public disaster response schemes which are in place in most European countries.
These emergency plans should:
-    designate an agency to take the lead in co-ordinating the response,
-    identify the key actors who will deal with the victims, both statutory and voluntary, such as the police, medical staff, support services,
-    ensure a co-ordinated and immediate response.
The efficiency of such emergency plans presupposes:
-    well-trained specialised services, such as public services, police, victim services and NGO's.
-    realistic drill exercises with the participation of key actors to be involved at the disaster scene, in particular in trans-frontier situations.

---

[40] Available on : http://cm.coe.int/ta/rec/1999/99r19.htm.
[41] Available on:
http://www.un.org/docs/ecosoc/documents/2002/resolutions/eres2002-12.pdf.
[42] See on http://www.euvictimservices.org/.

151.   Measures taken by States in this area should meet the requirements of the Art 3 of the Council of Europe Convention on the Prevention of Terrorism (CETS No. 196), dealing with national prevention policies.

16. RAISING PUBLIC AWARENESS OF THE EFFECTS OF CRIME

152.   Although it is recommended that States have a primary role in public education, media also have an important role to pay in this context.

153.   The media should be encouraged to play a positive role in raising public awareness on the negative effects of crimes on victims. The media should avoid transmitting to the public mere sensationalist or emotive images or facts. They should be aware of the risks of provoking an increase in fear as well as secondary victimisation.

154.   The media are also encouraged to show examples of ways in which members of the public can contribute to the rehabilitation of victims.

17. RESEARCH

155.   States should contribute to or support the funding of victimological research. States could either provide direct funding, or give assistance to the raising of external research funds.

156.   States can also provide practical support for example by giving the necessary permissions to conduct particular research projects or by allowing access to data, etc.

157.   Comparative research should be promoted. Researchers from other countries should have equal access to research, research resources and research data.

158.   Such comparative research could be conducted for example on:
  - the effectiveness of the existing protection (procedural and practical) measures;
  - training programmes for public services and for associations and organisations providing assistance to victims;
  - compensation schemes for victims in general and victims of terrorism in particular;
  - the organisation of immediate assistance to victims and notably: the planning, training and co-ordination of these personnel, the specific role of the police at the crime scene, appropriate methods of taking victims' witness statements by investigators.

Recommendation Rec(2005)9 of the Committee of Ministers to member states on the protection of witnesses and collaborators of justice
(Adopted by the Committee of Ministers on 20 April 2005
at the 924th meeting of the Ministers' Deputies)

The Committee of Ministers, under the terms of Article 15.*b* of the Statute of the Council of Europe,

Recalling that the aim of the Council of Europe is to achieve greater unity among its members;

Aware of the need for member states to develop a common crime policy in relation to witness protection;

Noting that there is growing recognition of the special role of witnesses in criminal proceedings and that their evidence is often crucial to securing the conviction of offenders, especially in respect of serious crime;

Considering that in some areas of criminality, such as organised crime and terrorism, there is an increasing risk that witnesses will be subjected to intimidation;

Considering that the final report of the Multidisciplinary Group on International Action against Terrorism (GMT) and the subsequent decisions of the Committee of Ministers recognise the protection of witnesses and collaborators of justice as a priority area of the Council of Europe's legal action against terrorism;

Recalling that in Resolution No. 1 on Combating International Terrorism approved at the 24th Conference of European Ministers of Justice (Moscow, 4-5 October 2001), the Committee of Ministers was invited to adopt urgently all normative measures considered necessary for assisting states to prevent, detect, prosecute and punish acts of terrorism, such as the improvement of the protection of witnesses and other persons participating in proceedings involving persons accused of terrorist crimes;

Recalling that in Resolution No. 1 on Combating Terrorism approved at the 25th Conference of European Ministers of Justice (Sofia, 9-10 October 2003), the Committee of Ministers was invited to, *inter alia*, pursue without delay the work with a view to adopting relevant international instruments on the protection of witnesses and collaborators of justice;

Convinced that, while all persons have a civic duty to give sincere testimony as witnesses if so required by the criminal justice system, there should also be greater recognition given to their rights and needs, including the right not to be subject to any undue interference or be placed at personal risk;

Considering that member states have a duty to protect witnesses against such interference by providing them with specific protection measures aimed at effectively ensuring their safety;

Considering that it is unacceptable for the criminal justice system to fail to bring defendants to trial and obtain a judgment because witnesses have been effectively discouraged from testifying freely and truthfully;

Aware that the protection of witnesses and collaborators of justice requires confidentiality and that efforts should be made to ensure that effective measures are taken to thwart attempts to trace witnesses and collaborators of justice, in particular by criminal organisations, including terrorist organisations;

Bearing in mind the provisions of the European Convention on Human Rights (ETS No. 5) and the case-law of its organs, which recognise the rights of the defence to examine the witness and to challenge his/her testimony;

Taking into account Recommendation No. R (97) 13 concerning intimidation of witnesses and the rights of the defence, in particular with respect to the measures to be taken in relation to vulnerable witnesses, especially in cases of crime within the family; Recommendation No. R (85) 4 on violence in the family, Recommendation No. R (85) 11 on the position of the victim in the framework of criminal law and procedure, Recommendation No. R (87) 21 on assistance to victims and the prevention of victimisation, Recommendation No. R (91) 11 concerning sexual exploitation, pornography and prostitution of, and trafficking in, children and young adults and Recommendation No. R (96) 8 on crime policy in Europe in a time of change,

Recommends that governments of member states:

i.   be guided, when formulating their internal legislation and reviewing their criminal policy and practice, by the principles and measures appended to this Recommendation;

ii.   ensure that all the necessary publicity for these principles and measures is distributed to all interested bodies, such as judicial organs, investigating and prosecuting authorities, bar associations, and relevant social institutions.

Appendix to Recommendation Rec(2005)9

I. Definitions

For the purposes of this Recommendation, the term:

- "witness" means any person who possesses information relevant to criminal proceedings about which he/she has given and/or is able to give testimony (irrespective of his/her status and of the direct or indirect, oral or written form of the testimony, in accordance with national law), who is not included in the definition of "collaborator of justice";

- "collaborator of justice" means any person who faces criminal charges, or has been convicted of taking part in a criminal association or other criminal organisation of any kind, or in offences of organised crime, but who agrees to co-operate with criminal justice authorities, particularly by giving testimony about a criminal association or organisation, or about any offence connected with organised crime or other serious crimes;

- "intimidation" means any direct or indirect threat carried out or likely to be carried out to a witness or collaborator of justice, which may lead to interference with his/her willingness to give testimony free from undue interference, or which is a consequence of his/her testimony;

- "anonymity" means that the identifying particulars of the witness are not generally divulged to the opposing party or to the public in general;

- "people close to witnesses and collaborators of justice" includes the relatives and other persons in a close relationship to the witnesses and the collaborators of justice, such as the partner, (grand)children, parents and siblings;

- "protection measures" are all individual procedural or non-procedural measures aimed at protecting the witness or collaborator of justice from any intimidation and/or any dangerous consequences of the decision itself to co-operate with justice;

- "protection programme" means a standard or tailor-made set of individual protection measures which are, for example, described in a memorandum of understanding, signed by the responsible authorities and the protected witness or collaborator of justice.

II. General Principles

1. Appropriate legislative and practical measures should be taken to ensure that witnesses and collaborators of justice may testify freely and without being subjected to any act of intimidation.

2.   While respecting the rights of the defence, the protection of witnesses, collaborators of justice and people close to them should be organised, where necessary, before, during and after the trial.

3.   Acts of intimidation of witnesses, collaborators of justice and people close to them should, where necessary, be made punishable either as separate criminal offences or as part of the offence of using illegal threats.

4.   Subject to legal privileges providing the right of some persons to refuse to give testimony, witnesses and collaborators of justice should be encouraged to report any relevant information regarding criminal offences to the competent authorities and thereafter agree to give testimony in court.

5.   While taking into account the principle of free assessment of evidence by courts and the respect of the rights of the defence, procedural law should enable the impact of intimidation on testimonies to be taken into consideration and statements made during the preliminary phase of the procedure to be allowed (and/or used) in court.

6.   While respecting the rights of the defence, alternative methods of giving evidence which protect witnesses and collaborators of justice from intimidation resulting from face-to-face confrontation with the accused should be considered.

7.   Criminal justice personnel should have adequate training and guidelines to deal with cases where witnesses might require protection measures or programmes.

8.   All the stages of the procedure related to the adoption, implementation, modification and revocation of protection measures or programmes should be kept confidential; the unauthorised disclosure of this information should be made punishable as a criminal offence where appropriate, especially to ensure the security of a protected person.

9.   The adoption of protection measures or programmes should also take into account the need to strike an adequate balance with the principle of safeguarding the rights and expectations of victims.

III. Protection measures and programmes

10. When designing a framework of measures to combat serious offences, including those related to organised crime and terrorism, and violations of international humanitarian law, appropriate measures should be adopted to protect witnesses and collaborators of justice against intimidation.

11. No terrorism-related crimes should be excluded from the offences for which specific witness protection measures/programmes are envisaged.

12. The following criteria should, *inter alia*, be taken into consideration when deciding upon the entitlement of a witness/collaborator of justice to protection measures or programmes:
-   involvement of the person to be protected (as a victim, witness, co-perpetrator, accomplice or aider and abetter) in the investigation and/or in the case;
-   relevance of the contribution;
-   seriousness of the intimidation;
-   willingness and suitability to being subject to protection measures or programmes

13. When deciding upon the adoption of protection measures it should also be considered, in addition to the criteria mentioned in paragraph 12, whether there is no other evidence available that could be deemed sufficient to establish a case related to serious offences.

14. Proportionality between the nature of the protection measures and the seriousness of the intimidation of the witness/collaborator of justice should be ensured.

15. Witnesses/collaborators of justice being subjected to the same kind of intimidation should be entitled to similar protection. However, any protection measures/programmes adopted will need to take into account the particular characteristics of the matter and the individual needs of the person(s) to be protected.

16. Procedural rules aimed at the protection of witnesses and collaborators of justice should ensure that the balance necessary in a democratic society is maintained between the prevention of crime, the needs of the victims and witnesses and the safeguarding of the right to a fair trial.

17. While ensuring that the parties have adequate opportunity to challenge the evidence given by a witness/collaborator of justice, the following measures aimed at preventing identification of the witness may, *inter alia*, be considered:
-   audiovisual recording of statements made by witnesses/collaborators of justice during the preliminary phase of the procedure;
-   using statements given during the preliminary phase of the procedure as evidence in court when it is not possible for witnesses to appear before the court or when appearing in court might result in great and actual danger to the witnesses/collaborators of justice or to people close to them; pre-trial statements should be regarded as valid evidence if the parties have, or have had, the chance to participate in the examination and interrogate and/or cross-examine the witness and to discuss the contents of the statement during the procedure;

- disclosing information which enables the witness to be identified at the latest possible stage of the proceedings and/or releasing only selected details;
- excluding or restricting the media and/or the public from all or part of the trial;
- using devices preventing the physical identification of witnesses and collaborators of justice, such as using screens or curtains, disguising the face of the witness or distorting his/her voice;
- using video-conferencing.

18. Any decision to grant anonymity to a witness in criminal proceedings will be made in accordance with domestic law and European human rights law.

19. Where available, and in accordance with domestic law, anonymity of persons who might give evidence should be an exceptional measure. Where the guarantee of anonymity has been requested by such persons and/or temporarily granted by the competent authorities, criminal procedural law should provide for a verification procedure to maintain a fair balance between the needs of criminal justice and the rights of the parties. The parties should, through this procedure, have the opportunity to challenge the alleged need for anonymity of the witness, his/her credibility and the origin of his/her knowledge.

20. Any decision to grant anonymity should only be taken when the competent judicial authority finds that the life or freedom of the person involved, or of the persons close to him or her, is seriously threatened, the evidence appears to be significant and the person appears to be credible.

21. When anonymity has been granted, the conviction should not be based solely, or to a decisive extent, on the evidence provided by anonymous witnesses.

22. Where appropriate, witness protection programmes should be set up and made available to witnesses and collaborators of justice who need protection. The main objective of these programmes should be to safeguard the life and personal security of witnesses/collaborators of justice, and people close to them, aiming in particular at providing the appropriate physical, psychological, social and financial protection and support.

23. Protection programmes implying dramatic changes in the life/privacy of the protected person (such as relocation and change of identity) should be applied to witnesses and collaborators of justice who need protection beyond the duration of the criminal trials where they give testimony. Such programmes, which may last for a limited period or for life, should be adopted only if no other measures are deemed sufficient to protect the witness/collaborator of justice and persons close to them.

24. The adoption of such programmes requires the informed consent of the person(s) to be protected and an adequate legal framework, including

appropriate safeguards for the rights of the witnesses or collaborators of justice according to national law.

25. Where appropriate, protection measures could be adopted on an urgent and provisional basis before a protection programme is formally adopted.

26. Given the essential role that collaborators of justice may play in the fight against serious offences, they should be given adequate consideration. Where necessary, protection programmes applicable to collaborators of justice serving a prison sentence may also include specific arrangements such as special penitentiary regimes.

27. Protection of collaborators of justice should also be aimed at preserving their credibility and public security. Adequate measures should be undertaken to protect against the risk of the collaborators of justice committing further crimes while under protection and therefore, even involuntarily, jeopardising the case in court. The intentional perpetration of an offence by a collaborator of justice under protection should, according to the relevant circumstances, imply the revocation of protection measures.

28. While respecting the fundamental principles of administrative organisation of each state, staff dealing with the implementation of protection measures should be afforded operational autonomy and should not be involved either in the investigation or in the preparation of the case where the witness/collaborator of justice is to give evidence. Therefore, an organisational separation between these functions should be provided for. However, an adequate level of co-operation/contact with or between law-enforcement agencies should be ensured in order to successfully adopt and implement protection measures and programmes.

IV. International co-operation

29. While respecting the different legal systems and the fundamental principles of administrative organisation of each state, a common approach in international issues related to the protection of witnesses and collaborators of justice should be followed. Such a common approach should aim at ensuring proper professional standards, at least in the crucial aspects of confidentiality, integrity and training. Member states should ensure sufficient exchange of information and co-operation between the authorities responsible for protection programmes.

30. Measures aimed at fostering international co-operation should be adopted and implemented in order to facilitate the examination of protected witnesses and collaborators of justice and to allow protection programmes to be implemented across borders.

31. The scope and the effective and rapid implementation of international co-operation in matters related to the protection of witnesses and

collaborators of justice, including with relevant international jurisdictions, should be improved.

32. The following objectives should, for example, be considered:
- to provide assistance in relocating abroad protected witnesses, collaborators of justice and persons close to them and ensuring their protection, in particular in those cases where no other solution can be found for their protection;
- to facilitate and improve the use of modern means of telecommunication such as video-links, and the security thereof, while safeguarding the rights of the parties;
- to co-operate and exchange best practices through the use of already existing networks of national experts;
- to contribute to the protection of witnesses and collaborators of justice within the context of co-operation with international criminal courts.

Guidelines on the Protection of Victims of Terrorist Acts

(Adopted by the Committee of Ministers on 2 March 2005
at the 917th meeting of the Ministers' Deputies)

Preamble

The Committee of Ministers,

a.   Considering that terrorism seriously jeopardises human rights, threatens democracy, aims notably to destabilise legitimately constituted governments and to undermine pluralistic civil society and challenges the ideals of everyone to live free from fear;

b.   Unequivocally condemning all acts of terrorism as criminal and unjustifiable, wherever and by whomever committed;

c.   Recognising the suffering endured by the victims of terrorist acts and their close family and considering that these persons must be shown national and international solidarity and support;

d.   Recognising in that respect the important role of associations for the protection of victims of terrorist acts;

e.   Reaffirming the Guidelines on Human Rights and the Fight against Terrorism, adopted on 11 July 2002 at the 804th meeting of the Ministers' Deputies, as a permanent and universal reference;

f.   Underlining in particular the states' obligation to take the measures needed to protect the fundamental rights of everyone within their jurisdiction against terrorist acts, especially the right to life;

g.   Recalling also that all measures taken by states to fight terrorism must respect human rights and the principle of the rule of law, while excluding any form of arbitrariness, as well as any discriminatory or racist treatment, and must be subject to appropriate supervision;

h.   Considering that the present Guidelines aim at addressing the needs and concerns of the victims of terrorist acts in identifying the means to be implemented to help them and to protect their fundamental rights while excluding any form of arbitrariness, as well as any discriminatory or racist treatment;

i.   Considering that the present Guidelines should not, under any circumstances, be construed as restricting in any way the Guidelines of 11 July 2002.

Adopts the following Guidelines and invites member states to implement them and ensure that they are widely disseminated among all authorities responsible for the fight against terrorism and for the protection of the victims of terrorist acts, as well as among representatives of civil society.

I. Principles

1. States should ensure that any person who has suffered direct physical or psychological harm as a result of a terrorist act as well as, in appropriate circumstances, their close family can benefit from the services and measures prescribed by these Guidelines. These persons are considered victims for the purposes of these Guidelines.

2. The granting of these services and measures should not depend on the identification, arrest, prosecution or conviction of the perpetrator of the terrorist act.

3. States must respect the dignity, private and family life of victims of terrorist acts in their treatment.

II. Emergency assistance

In order to cover the immediate needs of the victims, states should ensure that appropriate (medical, psychological, social and material) emergency assistance is available free of charge to victims of terrorist acts; they should also facilitate access to spiritual assistance for victims at their request.

III. Continuing assistance

1. States should provide for appropriate continuing medical, psychological, social and material assistance for victims of terrorist acts.

2. If the victim does not normally reside on the territory of the state where the terrorist act occurred, that state should co-operate with the state of residence in ensuring that the victim receives such assistance.

IV. Investigation and prosecution

1. Where there have been victims of terrorist acts, states must launch an effective official investigation into those acts.

2. In this framework, special attention must be paid to victims without it being necessary for them to have made a formal complaint.

3. In cases where, as a result of an investigation, it is decided not to take action to prosecute a suspected perpetrator of a terrorist act, states should allow victims to ask for this decision to be re-examined by a competent authority.

V. Effective access to the law and to justice

States should provide effective access to the law and to justice for victims of terrorist acts by providing:

(i) the right of access to competent courts in order to bring a civil action in support of their rights, and

(ii) legal aid in appropriate cases.

VI. Administration of justice

1. States should, in accordance with their national legislation, strive to bring individuals suspected of terrorist acts to justice and obtain a decision from a competent tribunal within a reasonable time.

2. States should ensure that the position of victims of terrorist acts is adequately recognised in criminal proceedings.

VII. Compensation

1. Victims of terrorist acts should receive fair, appropriate and timely compensation for the damages which they suffered. When compensation is not available from other sources, in particular through the confiscation of the property of the perpetrators, organisers and sponsors of terrorist acts, the state on the territory of which the terrorist act happened must contribute to the compensation of victims for direct physical or psychological harm, irrespective of their nationality.

2. Compensation should be easily accessible to victims, irrespective of nationality. To this end, the state on the territory of which the terrorist act happened should introduce a mechanism allowing for a fair and appropriate compensation, after a simple procedure and within a reasonable time.

3. States whose nationals were victims of a terrorist act on the territory of another state should also encourage administrative co-operation with the competent authorities of that state to facilitate access to compensation for their nationals.

4. Apart from the payment of pecuniary compensation, states are encouraged to consider, depending on the circumstances, taking other measures to mitigate the negative effects of the terrorist act suffered by the victims.

VIII.Protection of the private and family life of victims of terrorist acts

1. States should take appropriate steps to avoid as far as possible undermining respect for the private and family life of victims of terrorist acts, in particular when carrying out investigations or providing assistance after the

terrorist act as well as within the framework of proceedings initiated by victims.

2.   States should, where appropriate, in full compliance with the principle of freedom of expression, encourage the media and journalists to adopt self-regulatory measures in order to ensure the protection of the private and family life of victims of terrorist acts in the framework of their information activities.

3.   States must ensure that victims of terrorist acts have an effective remedy where they raise an arguable claim that their right to respect for their private and family life has been violated.

IX. Protection of the dignity and security of victims of terrorist acts

1.   At all stages of the proceedings, victims of terrorist acts should be treated in a manner which gives due consideration to their personal situation, their rights and their dignity.

2.   States must ensure the protection and security of victims of terrorist acts and should take measures, where appropriate, to protect their identity, in particular where they intervene as witnesses.

X.   Information for victims of terrorist acts

States should give information, in an appropriate way, to victims of terrorist acts about the act of which they suffered, except where victims indicate that they do not wish to receive such information. For this purpose, states should:

(i)   set up appropriate information contact points for the victims, concerning in particular their rights, the existence of victim support bodies, and the possibility of obtaining assistance, practical and legal advice as well as redress or compensation;

(ii) ensure the provision to the victims of appropriate information in particular about the investigations, the final decision concerning prosecution, the date and place of the hearings and the conditions under which they may acquaint themselves with the decisions handed down.

XI. Specific training for persons responsible for assisting victims of terrorist acts

States should encourage specific training for persons responsible for assisting victims of terrorist acts, as well as granting the necessary resources to that effect.

XII. Increased protection

Nothing in these Guidelines restrains states from adopting more favorable services and measures than described in these Guidelines.

Recommendation Rec(2002)5 of the Committee of Ministers to member states on the protection of women against violence[43]
(Adopted by the Committee of Ministers on 30 April 2002
at the 794th meeting of the Ministers' Deputies)

The Committee of Ministers, under the terms of Article 15.*b* of the Statute of the Council of Europe,

Reaffirming that violence towards women is the result of an imbalance of power between men and women and is leading to serious discrimination against the female sex, both within society and within the family;

Affirming that violence against women both violates and impairs or nullifies the enjoyment of their human rights and fundamental freedoms;

Noting that violence against women constitutes a violation of their physical, psychological and/or sexual integrity;

Noting with concern that women are often subjected to multiple discrimination on ground of their gender as well as their origin, including as victims of traditional or customary practices inconsistent with their human rights and fundamental freedoms;

Considering that violence against women runs counter to the establishment of equality and peace and constitutes a major obstacle to citizens' security and democracy in Europe;

Noting with concern the extent of violence against women in the family, whatever form the family takes, and at all levels of society;

Considering it urgent to combat this phenomenon which affects all European societies and concerns all their members;

Recalling the Final Declaration adopted at the Second Council of Europe Summit (Strasbourg, 1997), in which the heads of state and government of the member states affirmed their determination to combat violence against women and all forms of sexual exploitation of women;

Bearing in mind the provisions of the European Convention on Human Rights (1950) and the case-law of its organs, which safeguard, *inter alia*, the right to life and the right not to be subjected to torture or to inhuman or degrading treatment or punishment, the right to liberty and security and the right to a fair trial;

---

[43] In conformity with Article 10.2c of the Rules of Procedure of the Ministers' Deputies, Sweden reserved its right to comply or not with paragraph 54 of this recommendation.

Considering the European Social Charter (1961) and the revised European Social Charter (1996), in particular the provisions therein concerning equality between women and men with regard to employment, as well as the Additional Protocol to the European Social Charter providing for a system of collective complaints;

Recalling the following recommendations of the Committee of Ministers to member states of the Council of Europe: Recommendation No. R (79) 17 concerning the protection of children against ill-treatment; Recommendation No. R (85) 4 on violence in the family; Recommendation No. R (85) 11 on the position of the victim within the framework of criminal law and procedure; Recommendation No. R (87) 21 on assistance to victims and the prevention of victimisation; Recommendation No. R (90) 2 on social measures concerning violence within the family; Recommendation No. R (91) 11 concerning sexual exploitation, pornography and prostitution of, and trafficking in, children and young adults; Recommendation No. R (93) 2 on the medico-social aspects of child abuse, Recommendation No. R (2000) 11 on action against trafficking in human beings for the purpose of sexual exploitation and Recommendation Rec(2001)16 on the protection of children against sexual exploitation;

Recalling also the Declarations and Resolutions adopted by the 3rd European Ministerial Conference on Equality between Women and Men held by the Council of Europe (Rome, 1993);

Bearing in mind the United Nations Declaration on the Elimination of Violence against Women (1993), the United Nations Convention on the Elimination of All Forms of Discrimination against Women (1979), the United Nations Convention against Transnational Organised Crime and its Protocol to Prevent, Suppress and Punish Trafficking in Persons, especially Women and Children (2000), the Platform for Action adopted at the Fourth World Conference on Women (Beijing, 1995) and the Resolution on Further actions and initiatives to implement the Beijing Declaration and Platform for Action adopted by the United Nations General Assembly (23rd extraordinary session, New York, 5-9 June 2000);

Bearing in mind the United Nations Convention on the Rights of the Child (1989), as well as its Optional Protocol on the sale of children, child prostitution and child pornography (2000);

Also bearing in mind the International Labour Organisation Convention No. 182 concerning the Prohibition and Immediate Action for the Elimination of the Worst Forms of Child Labour (1999) and Recommendation (R 190) on the Worst Forms of Child Labour (1999);

Recalling the basic principles of international humanitarian law, and especially the 4th Geneva Convention relative to the protection of civilian persons in time of war (1949) and the 1st and 2nd additional Protocols thereto;

Recalling also the inclusion of gender-related crimes and sexual violence in the Statute of the International Criminal Court (Rome, 17 July 1998),

Recommends that the governments of member states:

I.   Review their legislation and policies with a view to:

1.   guaranteeing women the recognition, enjoyment, exercise and protection of their human rights and fundamental freedoms;

2.   taking necessary measures, where appropriate, to ensure that women are able to exercise freely and effectively their economic and social rights;

3.   ensuring that all measures are co-ordinated nation-wide and focused on the needs of the victims and that relevant state institutions as well as non-governmental organisations (NGOs) be associated with the elaboration and the implementation of the necessary measures, in particular those mentioned in this recommendation;

4.   encouraging at all levels the work of NGOs involved in combating violence against women and establishing active co-operation with these NGOs, including appropriate logistic and financial support;

II.   Recognise that states have an obligation to exercise due diligence to prevent, investigate and punish acts of violence, whether those acts are perpetrated by the state or private persons, and provide protection to victims;

III.   Recognise that male violence against women is a major structural and societal problem, based on the unequal power relations between women and men and therefore encourage the active participation of men in actions aiming at combating violence against women;

IV.   Encourage all relevant institutions dealing with violence against women (police, medical and social professions) to draw up medium- and long-term co-ordinated action plans, which provide activities for the prevention of violence and the protection of victims;

V.   Promote research, data collection and networking at national and international level;

VI.   Promote the establishment of higher education programmes and research centres including at university level, dealing with equality issues, in particular with violence against women;

VII.   Improve interactions between the scientific community, the NGOs in the field, political decision-makers and legislative, health, educational, social and police bodies in order to design co-ordinated actions against violence;

VIII. Adopt and implement the measures described in the appendix to this recommendation in the manner they consider the most appropriate in the light of national circumstances and preferences, and, for this purpose, consider establishing a national plan of action for combating violence against women;

IX. Inform the Council of Europe on the follow-up given at national level to the provisions of this recommendation.

Appendix to Recommendation Rec(2002)5

Definition

1. For the purposes of this recommendation, the term "violence against women" is to be understood as any act of gender-based violence, which results in, or is likely to result in, physical, sexual or psychological harm or suffering to women, including threats of such acts, coercion, or arbitrary deprivation of liberty, whether occurring in public or private life. This includes, but is not limited to, the following:

  a. violence occurring in the family or domestic unit, including, *inter alia*, physical and mental aggression, emotional and psychological abuse, rape and sexual abuse, incest, rape between spouses, regular or occasional partners and cohabitants, crimes committed in the name of honour, female genital and sexual mutilation and other traditional practices harmful to women, such as forced marriages;

  b. violence occurring within the general community, including, inter alia, rape, sexual abuse, sexual harassment and intimidation at work, in institutions or elsewhere trafficking in women for the purposes of sexual exploitation and economic exploitation and sex tourism;

  c. violence perpetrated or condoned by the state or its officials;

  d. violation of the human rights of women in situations of armed conflict, in particular the taking of hostages, forced displacement, systematic rape, sexual slavery, forced pregnancy, and trafficking for the purposes of sexual exploitation and economic exploitation.

General measures concerning violence against women

2. It is the responsibility and in the interest of states as well as a priority of national policies to safeguard the right of women not to be subjected to violence of any kind or by any person. To this end, states may not invoke custom, religion or tradition as a means of evading this obligation.

3. Member states should introduce, develop and/or improve where necessary, national policies against violence based on:

  a. maximum safety and protection of victims;

  b. empowerment of victimised women by optimal support and assistance structures which avoid secondary victimisation;

  c. adjustment of the criminal and civil law including the judicial procedure;

  d. raising of public awareness and education of children and young persons;

  e. ensuring special training for professionals confronted with violence against women;

  f. prevention in all respective fields.

4. In this framework, it will be necessary to set up, wherever possible, at national level, and in co-operation with, where necessary, regional and/or local authorities, a governmental co-ordination institution or body in charge

of the implementation of measures to combat violence against women as well as of regular monitoring and evaluation of any legal reform or new form of intervention in the field of action against violence, in consultation with NGOs and academic and other institutions.

5.   Research, data collection and networking at national and international level should be developed, in particular in the following fields:
   a.   the preparation of statistics sorted by gender, integrated statistics and common indicators in order to better evaluate the scale of violence against women;
   b.   the medium- and long-term consequences of assaults on victims;
   c.   the consequence of violence on those who are witness to it, *inter alia*, within the family;
   d.   the health, social and economic costs of violence against women;
   e.   the assessment of the efficiency of the judiciary and legal systems in combating violence against women;
   f.   the causes of violence against women, i.e. the reasons which cause men to be violent and the reasons why society condones such violence;
   g.   the elaboration of criteria for benchmarking in the field of violence.

Information, public awareness, education and training

Member states should:

6.   compile and make available to the general public appropriate information concerning the different types of violence and their consequences for victims, including integrated statistical data, using all the available media (press, radio and television, etc.);

7.   mobilise public opinion by organising or supporting conferences and information campaigns so that society is aware of the problem and its devastating effects on victims and society in general and can therefore discuss the subject of violence towards women openly, without prejudice or preconceived ideas;

8.   include in the basic training programmes of members of the police force, judicial personnel and the medical and social fields, elements concerning the treatment of domestic violence, as well as all other forms of violence affecting women;

9.   include in the vocational training programmes of these personnel, information and training so as to give them the means to detect and manage crisis situations and improve the manner in which victims are received, listened to and counselled;

10. encourage the participation of these personnel in specialised training programmes, by integrating the latter in a merit-awarding scheme;

11. encourage the inclusion of questions concerning violence against women in the training of judges;

12. encourage self-regulating professions, such as therapists, to develop strategies against sexual abuse which could be committed by persons in positions of authority;

13. organise awareness-raising campaigns on male violence towards women, stressing that men should be responsible for their acts and encouraging them to analyse and dismantle mechanisms of violence and to adopt different behaviour;

14. introduce or reinforce a gender perspective in human rights education programmes, and reinforce sex education programmes that give special importance to gender equality and mutual respect;

15. ensure that both boys and girls receive a basic education that avoids social and cultural patterns, prejudices and stereotyped roles for the sexes and includes training in assertiveness skills, with special attention to young people in difficulty at school; train all members of the teaching profession to integrate the concept of gender equality in their teaching;

16. include specific information in school curricula on the rights of children, help-lines, institutions where they can seek help and persons they can turn to in confidence.

Media

Member states should:

17. encourage the media to promote a non-stereotyped image of women and men based on respect for the human person and human dignity and to avoid programmes associating violence and sex; as far as possible, these criteria should also be taken into account in the field of the new information technologies;

18. encourage the media to participate in information campaigns to alert the general public to violence against women;

19. encourage the organisation of training to inform media professionals and alert them to the possible consequences of programmes that associate violence and sex;

20. encourage the elaboration of codes of conduct for media professionals, which would take into account the issue of violence against women and, in the terms of reference of media watch organisations, existing or to be established, encourage the inclusion of tasks dealing with issues concerning violence against women and sexism.

Local, regional and urban planning

Member states should:

21. encourage decision-makers in the field of local, regional and urban planning to take into account the need to reinforce women's safety and to prevent the occurrence of violent acts in public places;

22. as far as possible, take all necessary measures in this respect, concerning in particular public lighting, organisation of public transport and taxi services, design and planning of car parks and residential buildings.

Assistance for and protection of victims (reception, treatment and counselling)

Member states should:

23. ensure that victims, without any discrimination, receive immediate and comprehensive assistance provided by a co-ordinated, multidisciplinary and professional effort, whether or not they lodge a complaint, including medical and forensic medical examination and treatment, together with post-traumatic psychological and social support as well as legal assistance; this should be provided on a confidential basis, free of charge and be available around the clock;

24. in particular, ensure that all services and legal remedies available for victims of domestic violence are provided to immigrant women upon their request;

25. take all the necessary measures in order to ensure that collection of forensic evidence and information is carried out according to standardised protocol and forms;

26. provide documentation particularly geared to victims, informing them in a clear and comprehensible manner of their rights, the service they have received and the actions they could envisage or take, regardless of whether they are lodging a complaint or not, as well as of their possibilities to continue to receive psychological, medical and social support and legal assistance;

27. promote co-operation between the police, health and social services and the judiciary system in order to ensure such co-ordinated actions, and encourage and support the establishment of a collaborative network of non-governmental organisations;

28. encourage the establishment of emergency services such as anonymous, free of charge telephone help-lines for victims of violence and/or persons confronted or threatened by situations of violence; regularly

monitor calls and evaluate the data obtained from the assistance provided with due respect for data protection standards;

29. ensure that the police and other law-enforcement bodies receive, treat and counsel victims in an appropriate manner, based on respect for human beings and dignity, and handle complaints confidentially; victims should be heard without delay by specially-trained staff in premises that are designed to establish a relationship of confidence between the victim and the police officer and ensure, as far as possible, that the victims of violence have the possibility to be heard by a female officer should they so wish;

30. to this end, take steps to increase the number of female police officers at all levels of responsibility;

31. ensure that children are suitably cared for in a comprehensive manner by specialised staff at all the relevant stages (initial reception, police, public prosecutor's department and courts) and that the assistance provided is adapted to the needs of the child;

32. take steps to ensure the necessary psychological and moral support for children who are victims of violence by setting up appropriate facilities and providing trained staff to treat the child from initial contact to recovery; these services should be provided free of charge;

33. take all necessary measures to ensure that none of the victims suffer secondary (re)victimisation or any gender-insensitive treatment by the police, health and social personnel responsible for assistance, as well as by judiciary personnel.

Criminal law, civil law and judicial proceedings

Criminal law

Member states should:

34. ensure that criminal law provides that any act of violence against a person, in particular physical or sexual violence, constitutes a violation of that person's physical, psychological and/or sexual freedom and integrity, and not solely a violation of morality, honour or decency;

35. provide for appropriate measures and sanctions in national legislation, making it possible to take swift and effective action against perpetrators of violence and redress the wrong done to women who are victims of violence. In particular, national law should:
-   penalise sexual violence and rape between spouses, regular or occasional partners and cohabitants;
-   penalise any sexual act committed against non-consenting persons, even if they do not show signs of resistance;

- penalise sexual penetration of any nature whatsoever or by any means whatsoever of a non-consenting person;
- penalise any abuse of the vulnerability of a pregnant, defenceless, ill, physically or mentally handicapped or dependent victim;
- penalise any abuse of the position of a perpetrator, and in particular of an adult *vis-à-vis* a child.

Civil law

Member states should:

36. ensure that, in cases where the facts of violence have been established, victims receive appropriate compensation for any pecuniary, physical, psychological, moral and social damage suffered, corresponding to the degree of gravity, including legal costs incurred;

37. envisage the establishment of financing systems in order to compensate victims.

Judicial proceedings

Member states should:

38. ensure that all victims of violence are able to institute proceedings as well as, where appropriate, public or private organisations with legal personality acting in their defence, either together with the victims or on their behalf;

39. make provisions to ensure that criminal proceedings can be initiated by the public prosecutor;

40. encourage prosecutors to regard violence against women and children as an aggravating or decisive factor in deciding whether or not to prosecute in the public interest;

41. take all necessary steps to ensure that at all stages in the proceedings, the victims' physical and psychological state is taken into account and that they may receive medical and psychological care;

42. envisage the institution of special conditions for hearing victims or witnesses of violence in order to avoid the repetition of testimony and to lessen the traumatising effects of proceedings;

43. ensure that rules of procedure prevent unwarranted and/or humiliating questioning for the victims or witnesses of violence, taking into due consideration the trauma that they have suffered in order to avoid further trauma;

44. where necessary, ensure that measures are taken to protect victims effectively against threats and possible acts of revenge;

45. take specific measures to ensure that children's rights are protected during proceedings;

46. ensure that children are accompanied, at all hearings, by their legal representative or an adult of their choice, as appropriate, unless the court gives a reasoned decision to the contrary in respect of that person;

47. ensure that children are able to institute proceedings through the intermediary of their legal representative, a public or private organisation or any adult of their choice approved by the legal authorities and, if necessary, to have access to legal aid free of charge;

48. provide that, for sexual offences and crimes, any limitation period does not commence until the day on which the victim reaches the age of majority;

49. provide for the requirement of professional confidentiality to be waived on an exceptional basis in the case of persons who may learn of cases of children subject to sexual violence in the course of their work, as a result of examinations carried out or of information given in confidence.

Intervention programmes for the perpetrators of violence

Member states should:

50. organise intervention programmes designed to encourage perpetrators of violence to adopt a violence-free pattern of behaviour by helping them to become aware of their acts and recognise their responsibility;

51. provide the perpetrator with the possibility to follow intervention programmes, not as an alternative to sentence, but as an additional measure aiming at preventing violence; participation in such programmes should be offered on a voluntary basis;

52. consider establishing specialised state-approved intervention centres for violent men and support centres initiated by NGOs and associations within the resources available;

53. ensure co-operation and co-ordination between intervention programmes directed towards men and those dealing with the protection of women.

Additional measures with regard to sexual violence

A genetic data bank

Member states should:

54. consider setting up national and European data banks comprising the genetic profile of all identified and non-identified perpetrators of sexual violence in order to put in place an effective policy to catch offenders, prevent re-offending, and taking into account the standards laid down by domestic legislation and the Council of Europe in this field.

Additional measures with regard to violence within the family

Member states should:

55. classify all forms of violence within the family as criminal offence;

56. revise and/or increase the penalties, where necessary, for deliberate assault and battery committed within the family, whichever member of the family is concerned;

57. preclude adultery as an excuse for violence within the family;

58. envisage the possibility of taking measures in order to:
    a. enable police forces to enter the residence of an endangered person, arrest the perpetrator and ensure that he or she appears before the judge;
    b. enable the judiciary to adopt, as interim measures aimed at protecting the victims, the banning of a perpetrator from contacting, communicating with or approaching the victim, residing in or entering certain defined areas;
    c. establish a compulsory protocol for operation so that the police and medical and social services follow the same procedure;
    d. promote pro-active victim protection services which take the initiative to contact the victim as soon as a report is made to the police;
    e. ensure smooth co-operation of all relevant institutions, such as police authorities, courts and victim protection services, in order to enable the victim to take all relevant legal and practical measures for receiving assistance and taking actions against the perpetrator within due time limits and without unwanted contact with the perpetrator;
    f. penalise all breaches of the measures imposed on the perpetrators by the authorities.

59. consider, where needed, granting immigrant women who have been/are victims of domestic violence an independent right to residence in order to enable them to leave their violent husbands without having to leave the host country.

Additional measures with regard to sexual harassment

Member states should:

60. take steps to prohibit all conducts of a sexual nature, or other conduct based on sex affecting the dignity of women at work, including the behaviour of superiors and colleagues: all conduct of a sexual nature for which the perpetrator makes use of a position of authority, wherever it occurs (including situations such as neighbourhood relations, relations between students and teachers, telephone harassment, etc.), is concerned. These situations constitute a violation of the dignity of persons;

61. promote awareness, information and prevention of sexual harassment in the workplace or in relation to work or wherever it may occur and take the appropriate measures to protect women and men from such conduct.

Additional measures with regard to genital mutilation

Member states should:

62. penalise any mutilation of a woman's or girl's genital organs either with or without her consent; genital mutilation is understood to mean sewing up of the clitoris, excision, clitoridectomy and infibulation;

63. penalise any person who has deliberately participated in, facilitated or encouraged any form of female genital mutilation, with or without the person's consent; such acts shall be punishable even if only partly performed;

64. organise information and prevention campaigns aimed at the population groups concerned, in particular immigrants and refugees, on the health risks to victims and the criminal penalties for perpetrators;

65. alert the medical professions, in particular doctors responsible for pre- and post-natal medical visits and for monitoring the health of children;

66. arrange for the conclusion or reinforcement of bilateral agreements concerning prevention, and prohibition of female genital mutilation and the prosecution of perpetrators;

67. consider the possibility of granting special protection to these women as a threatened group for gender-based reasons.

Additional measures concerning violence in conflict and post-conflict situations

Member states should:

68. penalise all forms of violence against women and children in situations of conflict, in accordance with the provisions of international humanitarian law, whether they occur in the form of humiliation, torture, sexual slavery or death resulting from these actions;

69. penalise rape, sexual slavery, forced pregnancy, enforced sterilisation or any other form of sexual violence of comparable gravity as an intolerable violation of human rights, as crimes against humanity and, when committed in the context of an armed conflict, as war crimes;

70. ensure protection of witnesses before the national courts and international criminal tribunals trying genocide, crimes against humanity and war crimes, and provide them with legal residence at least during the proceedings;

71. ensure social and legal assistance to all persons called to testify before the national courts and international criminal tribunals trying genocide, crimes against humanity and war crimes;

72. consider providing refugee status or subsidiary protection for reasons of gender-based persecution and/or providing residence status on humanitarian grounds to women victims of violence during conflicts;

73. support and fund NGOs providing counselling and assistance to victims of violence during conflicts and in post-conflict situations;

74. in post-conflict situations, promote the inclusion of issues specific to women into the reconstruction and the political renewal process in affected areas;

75. at national and international levels, ensure that all interventions in areas which have been affected by conflicts are performed by personnel who have been offered gender-sensitive training;

76. support and fund programmes which follow a gender-sensitive approach in providing assistance to victims of conflicts and contributing to the reconstruction and repatriation efforts following a conflict.

Additional measures concerning violence in institutional environments

Member states should:

77. penalise all forms of physical, sexual and psychological violence perpetrated or condoned by the state or its officials, wherever it occurs and in particular in prisons or detention centres, psychiatric institutions, etc;

78. penalise all forms of physical, sexual and psychological violence perpetrated or condoned in situations in which the responsibility of the state or of a third party may be invoked, for example in boarding schools, retirement homes and other establishments.

Additional measures concerning failure to respect freedom of choice with regard to reproduction

Member states should:

79. prohibit enforced sterilisation or abortion, contraception imposed by coercion or force, and pre-natal selection by sex, and take all necessary measures to this end.

Additional measures concerning killings in the name of honour

Member states should:

80. penalise all forms of violence against women and children committed in accordance with the custom of "killings in the name of honour";

81. take all necessary measures to prevent "killings in the name of honour", including information campaigns aimed at the population groups and the professionals concerned, in particular judges and legal personnel;

82. penalise anyone having deliberately participated in, facilitated or encouraged a "killing in the name of honour";

83. support NGOs and other groups which combat these practices.

Additional measures concerning early marriages

Member states should:

84. prohibit forced marriages, concluded without the consent of the persons concerned;

85. take the necessary measures to prevent and stop practices related to the sale of children.

Recommendation No. R (2000) 11 of the Committee of Ministers to member states on action against trafficking in human beings for the purpose of sexual exploitation[44]
(Adopted by the Committee of Ministers on 19 May 2000 at the 710th meeting of the Ministers' Deputies)

The Committee of Ministers, under the terms of Article 15.*b* of the Statute of the Council of Europe,

Bearing in mind that Europe has recently experienced a considerable growth of activities connected with trafficking in human beings for the purpose of sexual exploitation, which is often linked to organised crime in as much as such lucrative practices are used by organised criminal groups as a basis for financing and expanding their other activities, such as drugs and arms trafficking and money laundering;

Considering that trafficking in human beings for the purpose of sexual exploitation extends well beyond national borders, and that it is therefore necessary to establish a pan-European strategy to combat this phenomenon and protect its victims, while ensuring that the relevant legislation of the Council of Europe member states is harmonised and uniformly and effectively applied;

Recalling the Declaration adopted at the Second Summit of the Council of Europe (October 1997), in which the heads of state and government of the member states of the Council of Europe decided "to seek common responses to the challenges posed by the growth (...) in organised crime (...) throughout Europe" and affirmed their determination "to combat violence against women and all forms of sexual exploitation of women";

Bearing in mind the Convention for the Protection of Human Rights and Fundamental Freedoms (1950) and its protocols;

Bearing in mind the European Social Charter (1961), the Revised European Social Charter (1996) and the Additional Protocol to the European Social Charter providing for a System of Collective Complaints;

Bearing in mind the following recommendations of the Committee of Ministers to member states of the Council of Europe: Recommendation No. R (91) 11 on sexual exploitation, pornography and prostitution of, and trafficking in, children and young adults; Recommendation No. R (96) 8 on crime policy in Europe in a time of change, and Recommendation

---

[44] When adopting this Recommendation, the Representatives of Germany and the Netherlands indicated that, in accordance with Article 10.2.c of the Rules of Procedure for the meetings of the Ministers' Deputies, they reserved the right, for their respective governments, to comply or not with paragraph I.1 of the Appendix to the Recommendation.

No. R (97) 13 concerning intimidation of witnesses and the rights of the defence;

Bearing in mind the following texts of the Parliamentary Assembly of the Council of Europe: Recommendation 1065 (1987) on the traffic in children and other forms of child exploitation, Recommendation 1211 (1993) on clandestine migration: traffickers and employers of clandestine migrants, Resolution 1099 (1996) on the sexual exploitation of children and Recommendation 1325 (1997) of the Council of Europe on trafficking in women and forced prostitution in Council of Europe member states;

Recalling also the Convention on the Elimination of all forms of Discrimination against Women (1979) and other international conventions such as the United Nations Convention for the Suppression of the Traffic in Persons and of the Exploitation of the Prostitution of Others (1949);

Considering that trafficking in human beings for the purpose of sexual exploitation, which mainly concerns women and young persons, may result in slavery for the victims;

Condemns trafficking in human beings for the purpose of sexual exploitation, which constitutes a violation of human rights and an offence to the dignity and the integrity of the human being,

Recommends that the governments of member states:

1. review their legislation and practice with a view to introducing, where necessary, and applying the measures described in the appendix to this recommendation;

2. ensure that this recommendation is brought to the attention of all relevant public and private bodies, in particular police and judicial authorities, diplomatic missions, migration authorities, professionals in the social, medical and education fields and non-governmental organisations.

Appendix to Recommendation No. R(2000)11

I.   Basic principles and notions

1.   The basic notions should be as follows: trafficking in human beings for the purpose of sexual exploitation includes the procurement by one or more natural or legal persons and/or the organisation of the exploitation and/or transport or migration – legal or illegal – of persons, even with their consent, for the purpose of their sexual exploitation, *inter alia* by means of coercion, in particular violence or threats, deceit, abuse of authority or of a position of vulnerability.

On this basis, the governments of member States are invited to consider the following measures:

II.   General measures

2.   Take appropriate legislative and practical measures to ensure the protection of the rights and the interests of the victims of trafficking, in particular the most vulnerable and most affected groups: women, adolescents and children.

3.   Give absolute priority to assisting the victims of trafficking through rehabilitation programmes, where applicable, and to protecting them from traffickers.

4.   Take action to apprehend, prosecute and punish all those responsible for trafficking, and to prevent sex tourism and all activities which might lead to forms of trafficking.

5.   Consider trafficking in human beings for the purposes of sexual exploitation as falling within the scope of international organised crime, and therefore calls for co-ordinated action adapted to realities both at national and international levels.

III. Basis for action and methods

6.   Take co-ordinated action using a multidisciplinary approach involving the relevant social, judicial, administrative, customs, law enforcement and immigration authorities and non-governmental organisations (NGOs).

7.   Encourage co-operation, involving both national authorities and NGOs, between countries of origin, transit and destination of the victims of trafficking, by means of bilateral and multilateral agreements.

8.   In order to ensure that these actions have a firm and reliable basis, encourage national and international research concerning, in particular:

- the influence of the media, and above all new information and communication techniques on trafficking in human beings for the purpose of sexual exploitation;
- the clients of the sex trade: trends in demand and their consequences for trafficking in human beings for the purpose of sexual exploitation;
- the origin of the phenomenon of trafficking and the methods used by traffickers.

9. Consider the establishment of research units specialising in trafficking in human beings for the purpose of sexual exploitation.

10. Take steps to develop, both at national and international level, data and statistics that will help to shed more light on the phenomenon of trafficking in human beings for the purpose of sexual exploitation and, if possible, compare the way the phenomenon is developing in the Council of Europe's different member States.

IV. Prevention

i. *Awareness-raising and information*

11. Organise information campaigns with a gender perspective in order to increase public awareness of the hazardous situations that may lead to trafficking and the negative effects of such trafficking and, in particular, discredit the notion that there are easy gains to be made from prostitution; these campaigns should be directed at all parties concerned, particularly female immigration applicants and women refugees.

12. Organise information campaigns intended to discredit sex tourism and discourage potential participants from joining in such activities.

13. Provide appropriate information, such as documentation, videos and leaflets on trafficking in and the sexual exploitation of women, children and young persons to diplomatic representatives, public authorities, the media, humanitarian NGOs and other public and private bodies working in the countries of origin of potential victims.

14. Disseminate widely, in every country, information on the health risks associated with sexual exploitation.

15. Encourage and organise activities to make media professionals more aware of issues relating to trafficking in human beings for the purpose of sexual exploitation and the influence the media can have in this field.

ii. *Education*

16. Introduce or step up sex education programmes in schools, with particular emphasis on equality between women and men and on respect for

human rights and individual dignity, taking into account the rights of the child as well as the rights of his or her parents, legal guardians and other individuals legally responsible for him or her.

17. Ensure that school curricula include information on the risks of exploitation, sexual abuse and trafficking that children and young people could face and ways of protecting themselves; this information should also be circulated to young people outside the education system and to parents.

18. Provide both boys and girls with an education that avoids gender stereotypes and ensures that all teachers and others involved in education are trained in such a way as to incorporate a gender dimension into their teaching.

iii. Training

19. Organise special training for social workers, as well as for medical, teaching, diplomatic, consular, judicial, customs and police personnel to enable them to identify cases of trafficking for the purpose of sexual exploitation and respond appropriately.

20. Introduce and/or develop training programmes to enable police personnel to acquire specialised skills in this field.

21. In particular, set up specific training programmes and exchanges of experiences in order to improve co-operation between the police and the NGOs specialising in victim protection.

22. Also introduce training programmes for immigration officials and frontier police so that they can contribute to prevention by making sure that persons travelling abroad, particularly young persons not accompanied by a parent or guardian, are not involved in trafficking.

iv. Long-term action

23. Combat the long-term causes of trafficking, which are often linked to the inequalities between economically developed countries and those that are less developed, particularly by improving the social status as well as the economic condition of women in the latter.

24. Take into account in economic, social, migration or other policies, the need to improve women's condition and prevent trafficking in human beings and sex tourism.

25. Disseminate information on the possibilities of legal migration in order to make women aware of the conditions and procedures for obtaining visas and residence permits.

V. Assistance to and protection of victims

i. Victim support

26. Encourage the establishment or development of reception centres or other facilities where the victims of human trafficking can benefit from information on their rights, as well as psychological, medical, social and administrative support with a view to their reintegration into their country of origin or the host country.

27. In particular, ensure that the victims have the opportunity, for example through the reception centres or other facilities, to benefit from legal assistance in their own language.

ii. Legal action

28. Provide, where possible, victims of trafficking, particularly children and witnesses, with special (audio or video) facilities to report and file complaints, and which are designed to protect their private lives and their dignity and reduce the number of official procedures and their traumatising effects.

29. If necessary, and particularly in the case of criminal networks, take steps to protect victims, witnesses and their families to avoid acts of intimidation and reprisals.

30. Establish victim protection systems which offer effective means to combat intimidation as well as real threats to the physical security of the victims and their families both in countries of destination and countries of origin.

31. Provide protection when needed in the country of origin for the families of victims of trafficking when the latter bring legal proceedings in the country of destination.

32. Extend, where appropriate, this protection to members of associations or organisations assisting the victims during civil and penal proceedings.

33. Enable the relevant courts to order offenders to pay compensation to victims.

34. Grant victims, if necessary, and in accordance with national legislation, a temporary residence status in the country of destination, in order to enable them to act as witnesses during judicial proceedings against offenders; during this time, it is essential to ensure that victims have access to social and medical assistance.

35. Consider providing, if necessary, a temporary residence status on humanitarian grounds.

iii.   Social measures for victims of trafficking in countries of origin

36. Encourage and support the establishment of a network of NGOs involved in assistance to victims of trafficking.

37. Promote co-operation between reception facilities and NGOs in countries of origin to assist the return and reintegration of victims.

iv.   Right of return and rehabilitation

38. Grant victims the right to return to their countries of origin, by taking all necessary steps, including through co-operation agreements between the countries of origin and countries of destination of the victims.

39. Establish, through bilateral agreements, a system of financing the return of victims and a contribution towards their reintegration.

40. Organise a system of social support for returnees to ensure that victims are assisted by the medical and social services and/or by their families.

41. Introduce special measures concerned with victims' occupational reintegration.

VI.   Penal legislation and judicial co-operation

42. Enact or strengthen legislation on trafficking in human beings for the purpose of sexual exploitation and introduce, where necessary, a specific offence.

43. Introduce or increase penal sanctions that are in proportion to the gravity of the offences, including dissuasive custodial sentences, and allow for effective judicial co-operation and the extradition of the persons charged or convicted.

44. Take such steps as are necessary to order, without prejudice to the rights of third parties in good faith, the seizure and confiscation of the instruments of, and proceeds from, trafficking.

45. Facilitate police investigation and monitoring of establishments in which victims of trafficking are exploited and organise their closure if necessary.

46. Provide for rules governing the liability of legal persons, with specific penalties.

47. Provide for traffickers to be extradited in accordance with applicable international standards, if possible, to the country where evidence of offences can be uncovered.

48. Establish rules governing extra-territorial jurisdiction to permit and facilitate the prosecution and conviction of persons who have committed offences relating to trafficking in human beings for the purpose of sexual exploitation, irrespective of the country where the offences were committed, and including cases where the offences took place in more than one country.

49. In accordance with national laws concerning the protection of personal data, as well as with the provisions of the Council of Europe Convention for the Protection of Individuals with regard to Automatic Processing of Personal Data, set up and maintain information systems which could be useful for the investigation and prosecution of trafficking offences.

VII. Measures for co-ordination and co-operation

i.   *At national level*

50. Set up a co-ordinating mechanism responsible for drawing up the national policy on combating trafficking and organising a multidisciplinary approach to the issue.

51. Use this mechanism to encourage the exchange of information, the compilation of statistics and the assessment of practical findings obtained in the field, trends in trafficking and the results of national policy.

52. Use this mechanism to liaise with mechanisms of other countries and international organisations in order to co-ordinate activities, and to monitor, review and implement national and international strategies aimed at combating trafficking;

ii.   *At international level*

53. As far as possible, make use of all the available international instruments and mechanisms applicable to trafficking, particularly regarding the seizure and confiscation of profits earned from trafficking.

54. Set up an international body to co-ordinate the fight against trafficking, with particular responsibility for establishing a European file of missing persons, in accordance with national laws concerning the protection of personal data.

55. Increase and improve exchanges of information and co-operation between countries at bilateral level as well as through international organisations involved in combating trafficking.

56. Governments are invited to consider signing and ratifying, if they have not already done so, the Council of Europe's Convention on Laundering, Search, Seizure and Confiscation of the Proceeds from Crime (1990), the Revised European Social Charter (1996) and the Additional Protocol to the European Social Charter providing for a System of Collective Complaints

(1995), the European Convention on the Exercise of Children's Rights (1996), the Convention on the Elimination of all forms of discrimination against Women (1979) and its Optional Protocol (1999), as well as the United Nations Convention on the Rights of the Child (1989) and/or to consider withdrawing existing reservations to these instruments.

57. Governments are invited to incorporate into their national systems all the measures necessary to apply the principles and standards laid down in the Action Programme adopted at the 4th World Conference on Women (Beijing, 4-15 September 1995), and in particular Part IV.D, and the agreed conclusions adopted at the 42nd session of the United Nations Commission on the Status of Women, the resolution adopted regularly by the General Assembly of the United Nations on the Traffic in Women and Girls, the declaration adopted at the Ministerial Conference containing European Guidelines for Measures to Prevent and Combat Trafficking in Women for the Purpose of Sexual Exploitation (The Hague, 24-26 April 1997), as well as in the following recommendations of the Committee of Ministers to the member states of the Council of Europe: Recommendation No. R (80) 10 on measures against the transfer and the safekeeping of funds of criminal origin, Recommendation No. R (85) 11 on the position of the victim in the framework of criminal law and procedure and Recommendation No. R (87) 21 on assistance to victims and the prevention of victimisation.

**Recommendation No. R (99) 19 of the Committee of Ministers
to member states concerning Mediation in Penal Matters**
*(Adopted by the Committee of Ministers on 15 September 1999
at the 679th meeting of the Ministers' Deputies)*

The Committee of Ministers, under the terms of Article 15.*b* of the Statute of the Council of Europe,

Noting the developments in member States in the use of mediation in penal matters as a flexible, comprehensive, problem-solving, participatory option complementary or alternative to traditional criminal proceedings;

Considering the need to enhance active personal participation in criminal proceedings of the victim and the offender and others who may be affected as parties as well as the involvement of the community;

Recognising the legitimate interest of victims to have a stronger voice in dealing with the consequences of their victimisation, to communicate with the offender and to obtain apology and reparation;

Considering the importance of encouraging the offenders' sense of responsibility and offering them practical opportunities to make amends, which may further their reintegration and rehabilitation;

Recognising that mediation may increase awareness of the important role of the individual and the community in preventing and handling crime and resolving its associated conflicts, thus encouraging more constructive and less repressive criminal justice outcomes;

Recognising that mediation requires specific skills and calls for codes of practice and accredited training;

Considering the potentially substantial contribution to be made by non-governmental organisations and local communities in the field of mediation in penal matters and the need to combine and to co-ordinate the efforts of public and private initiatives;

Having regard to the requirements of the Convention for the Protection of Human Rights and Fundamental Freedoms;

Bearing in mind the European Convention on the Exercise of Children's Rights as well as Recommendations No. R (85) 11 on the position of the victim in the framework of criminal law and procedure, No. R (87) 18 concerning the simplification of criminal justice, No. R (87) 21 on assistance to victims and the prevention of victimisation, No. R (87) 20 on social reactions to juvenile delinquency, No. R (88) 6 on social reactions to juvenile delinquency among young people coming from migrant families, No. R (92) 16 on the European Rules on community sanctions and measures, No. R (95) 12 on the management of criminal justice and No. R (98) 1 on family mediation;

Recommends that the governments of member States consider the principles set out in the appendix to this Recommendation when developing mediation in penal matters, and give the widest possible circulation to this text.

Appendix to Recommendation No. R(99)19

I. Definition

These guidelines apply to any process whereby the victim and the offender are enabled, if they freely consent, to participate actively in the resolution of matters arising from the crime through the help of an impartial third party (mediator).

II. General principles

1. Mediation in penal matters should only take place if the parties freely consent. The parties should be able to withdraw such consent at any time during the mediation.

2. Discussions in mediation are confidential and may not be used subsequently, except with the agreement of the parties.

3. Mediation in penal matters should be a generally available service.

4. Mediation in penal matters should be available at all stages of the criminal justice process.

5. Mediation services should be given sufficient autonomy within the criminal justice system.

III. Legal basis

6. Legislation should facilitate mediation in penal matters.

7. There should be guidelines defining the use of mediation in penal matters. Such guidelines should in particular address the conditions for the referral of cases to the mediation service and the handling of cases following mediation.

8. Fundamental procedural safeguards should be applied to mediation; in particular, the parties should have the right to legal assistance and, where necessary, to translation/interpretation. Minors should, in addition, have the right to parental assistance.

IV. The operation of criminal justice in relation to mediation

9. A decision to refer a criminal case to mediation, as well as the assessment of the outcome of a mediation procedure, should be reserved to the criminal justice authorities.

10. Before agreeing to mediation, the parties should be fully informed of their rights, the nature of the mediation process and the possible consequences of their decision.

11. Neither the victim nor the offender should be induced by unfair means to accept mediation.

12. Special regulations and legal safeguards governing minors' participation in legal proceedings should also be applied to their participation in mediation in penal matters.

13. Mediation should not proceed if any of the main parties involved is not capable of understanding the meaning of the process.

14. The basic facts of a case should normally be acknowledged by both parties as a basis for mediation. Participation in mediation should not be used as evidence of admission of guilt in subsequent legal proceedings.

15. Obvious disparities with respect to factors such as the parties' age, maturity or intellectual capacity should be taken into consideration before a case is referred to mediation.

16. A decision to refer a criminal case to mediation should be accompanied by a reasonable time-limit within which the competent criminal justice authorities should be informed of the state of the mediation procedure.

17. Discharges based on mediated agreements should have the same status as judicial decisions or judgments and should preclude prosecution in respect of the same facts (*ne bis in idem*).

18. When a case is referred back to the criminal justice authorities without an agreement between the parties or after failure to implement such an agreement, the decision as to how to proceed should be taken without delay.

V. The operation of mediation services

V.1.Standards

19. Mediation services should be governed by recognised standards.

20. Mediation services should have sufficient autonomy in performing their duties. Standards of competence and ethical rules, as well as procedures for the selection, training and assessment of mediators should be developed.

21. Mediation services should be monitored by a competent body.

V.2. Qualifications and training of mediators

22. Mediators should be recruited from all sections of society and should generally possess good understanding of local cultures and communities.

23. Mediators should be able to demonstrate sound judgment and interpersonal skills necessary to mediation.

24. Mediators should receive initial training before taking up mediation duties as well as in-service training. Their training should aim at providing for a high level of competence, taking into account conflict resolution skills, the specific requirements of working with victims and offenders and basic knowledge of the criminal justice system.

V.3. Handling of individual cases

25. Before mediation starts, the mediator should be informed of all relevant facts of the case and be provided with the necessary documents by the competent criminal justice authorities.

26. Mediation should be performed in an impartial manner, based on the facts of the case and on the needs and wishes of the parties. The mediator should always respect the dignity of the parties and ensure that the parties act with respect towards each other.

27. The mediator should be responsible for providing a safe and comfortable environment for the mediation. The mediator should be sensitive to the vulnerability of the parties.

28. Mediation should be carried out efficiently, but at a pace that is manageable for the parties.

29. Mediation should be performed *in camera*.

30. Notwithstanding the principle of confidentiality, the mediator should convey any information about imminent serious crimes, which may come to light in the course of mediation, to the appropriate authorities or to the persons concerned.

V.4. Outcome of mediation

31. Agreements should be arrived at voluntarily by the parties. They should contain only reasonable and proportionate obligations.

32. The mediator should report to the criminal justice authorities on the steps taken and on the outcome of the mediation. The mediator's report should not reveal the contents of mediation sessions, nor express any judgment on the parties' behaviour during mediation.

VI. Continuing development of mediation

33. There should be regular consultation between criminal justice authorities and mediation services to develop common understanding.

34. Member States should promote research on, and evaluation of, mediation in penal matters.

Recommendation No. R (97) 13 of the Committee of Ministers to member states concerning Intimidation of Witnesses and the Rights of the Defence

(Adopted by the Committee of Ministers on 10 September 1997 at the 600th Meeting of the Ministers' Deputies)

The Committee of Ministers, under the terms of Article 15.*b* of the Statute of the Council of Europe,

Recalling that the aim of the Council of Europe is to achieve a greater unity among its Members;

Aware of the need for member States to develop a common crime policy in relation to witness protection;

Considering that in some areas of criminality, such as organised crime and crime within the family, there is an increasing risk that witnesses will be subjected to intimidation;

Considering that it is unacceptable that the criminal justice system might fail to bring defendants to trial and obtain a judgment because witnesses are effectively discouraged from testifying freely and truthfully;

Noting that there is growing recognition of the special role of witnesses in criminal proceedings and that their evidence is often crucial to securing the conviction of offenders, especially in respect of organised crime and crime in the family;

Convinced that while all persons have a civic duty to give sincere testimony as witnesses, if so required by the criminal justice system, there should also be greater recognition given to their rights and needs, including the right not to be subject to any interference or be placed at personal risk;

Considering that member States have a duty to protect witnesses against such interference by providing them with specific measures of protection that effectively ensure their safety;

Bearing in mind the provisions of the European Convention of Human Rights and the case-law of its organs, which recognize the rights of the defence to examine the witness and to challenge his testimony but do not provide for a face to face confrontation between the witness and the alleged offender;

Taking into account Recommendation No. R (85) 4 on violence in the family, Recommendation No. R (85) 11 on the position of the victim in the framework of criminal law and procedure, Recommendation No. R (87) 21 on assistance to victims and prevention of victimisation, Recommendation No. (91) 11 on sexual exploitation, pornography and prostitution of, and trafficking in, children and young adults and Recommendation No. (96) 8 on crime policy in Europe in a time of change;

Recommends that Governments of member States:

i.   be guided, when formulating their internal legislation and reviewing their criminal policy and practice, by the principles appended to this recommendation;

ii.   ensure that all the necessary publicity for these principles is distributed to all interested bodies, such as bar associations, judicial organs, law enforcement agencies and social institutions involved in family care.

Appendix

I.   Definitions

For the purposes of this Recommendation:
-   "witness" means any person, irrespective of his status under national criminal procedural law, who possesses information relevant to criminal proceedings. This definition includes experts as well as interpreters;
-   "intimidation" means any direct, indirect or potential threat to a witness, which may lead to interference with his duty to give testimony free from influence of any kind whatsoever. This includes intimidation resulting either (i) from the mere existence of a criminal organisation having a strong reputation of violence and reprisal, or (ii) from the mere fact that the witness belongs to a closed social group and is in a position of weakness therein;
-   "anonymity" means that the identifying particulars of the witness remain totally unknown to the defendant;
-   "collaborator of justice" means any person who faces criminal charges, or was convicted, of having taken part in an association of criminals or other criminal organisation of any kind, or in organised crime offences but agrees to co-operate with criminal justice authorities, particularly by giving information about the criminal association or organisation or any criminal offence connected with organised crime.

II.   General Principles

1.   Appropriate legislative and practical measures should be taken to ensure that witnesses may testify freely and without intimidation.

2.   While respecting the rights of the defence, the protection of witnesses, their relatives and other persons close to them should be organised, where necessary, including the protection of their life and personal security before, during and after trial.

3.   Acts of intimidation of witnesses should be made punishable either as separate criminal offences or as part of the offence of using illegal threats.

4.   While taking into account the principle of free assessment of evidence by courts, procedural law should allow for consideration of the impact of intimidation on testimonies.

5.   Subject to legal privileges, witnesses should be encouraged to report any relevant information regarding criminal offences to the competent authorities and thereafter agree to give testimony in court.

6.   While respecting the rights of the defence, witnesses should be provided with alternative methods of giving evidence which protect them from

intimidation resulting from face to face confrontation with the accused, e.g. by allowing witnesses to give evidence in a separate room.

7. Criminal justice personnel should have adequate training to deal with cases where witnesses might be at risk of intimidation.

III. Measures to be taken in relation to organised crime

8. When designing a framework of measures to combat organised crime, specific rules of procedure should be adopted to cope with intimidation. These measures may also be applicable to other serious offences. Such rules shall ensure the necessary balance in a democratic society between the prevention of disorder or crime and the safeguarding of the right of the accused to a fair trial.

9. While ensuring that the defence has adequate opportunity to challenge the evidence given by a witness, the following measures should, inter alia, be considered :
- recording by audio-visual means of statements made by witnesses during pre-trial examination;
- using pre-trial statements given before a judicial authority as evidence in court when it is not possible for witnesses to appear before the court or when appearing in court might result in great and actual danger to the life and security of witnesses, their relatives or other persons close to them;
- revealing the identity of witnesses at the latest possible stage of the proceedings and/or releasing only selected details;
- excluding the media and/or the public from all or part of the trial.

10. Where available and in accordance with domestic law, anonymity of persons who might give evidence should be an exceptional measure. Where the guarantee of anonymity has been requested by such persons and/or temporarily granted by the competent authorities, criminal procedural law should provide for a verification procedure to maintain a fair balance between the needs of criminal proceedings and the rights of the defence. The defence should, through this procedure, have the opportunity to challenge the alleged need for anonymity of the witness, his credibility and the origin of his knowledge.

11. Anonymity should only be granted when the competent judicial authority, after hearing the parties, finds that:
- i. the life or freedom of the person involved is seriously threatened or, in the case of an undercover agent, his potential to work in the future is seriously threatened;
  and
- ii. the evidence is likely to be significant and the person appears to be credible.

12. Where appropriate, further measures should be available to protect witnesses giving evidence, including preventing identification of the witness by the defence e.g. by using screens, disguising his face or distorting his voice.

13. When anonymity has been granted, the conviction shall not be based solely or to a decisive extent on the evidence of such persons.

14. Where appropriate, special programmes, such as witness protection programmes, should be set up and made available to witnesses who need protection. The main objective of these programmes should be to safeguard the life and personal security of witnesses, their relatives and other persons close to them.

15. Witness protection programmes should offer various methods of protection; this may include giving witnesses and their relatives and other persons close to them an identity change, relocation, assistance in obtaining new jobs, providing them with body-guards and other physical protection.

16. Given the prominent role that collaborators of justice play in the fight against organised crime, they should be given adequate consideration, including the possibility of benefitting from measures provided by witness protection programmes. Where necessary, such programmes may also include specific arrangements such as special penitentiary regimes for collaborators of justice serving a prison sentence.

IV. Measures to be taken in relation to vulnerable witnesses, especially in cases of crime within the family

17. Adequate legislative and practical measures should be taken to ensure protection against intimidation, and to relieve pressure on witnesses giving evidence against family members in criminal cases.

18. Such measures should be designed for different categories of vulnerable witnesses. They should take into account that in the family environment intimidation is often latent and usually affects the witness' psychological and/or emotional well-being. In the absence of overt acts of intimidation, preference should therefore be given to non-criminal law measures.

19. Special protection should be made available to children together with support against any abuse of authority in the family. Children should be made aware of their rights, in particular, the right to report crime.

20. The specific interests of the child should be protected throughout proceedings by a social agency and, if appropriate, through specially trained lawyers.

21. Women who suffer domestic violence and elderly persons subjected to ill-treatment by their family should receive adequate protection from

intimidation aimed at preventing them from reporting crimes and giving evidence.

22. Programmes should be set up to assist witnesses in giving evidence against other members of the family. Such programmes could provide a framework for:
- legal, psychological and social assistance, and, if appropriate, care and financial assistance;
- measures to remove the accused from the vicinity of the witness in order to avoid further intimidation; alternatively measures to remove the witness;
- psycho-social measures (such as psychiatric training) for the accused to prevent further offending.

23. The different institutions within the criminal justice system should be made aware that they can have a traumatic effect on witnesses; they should strive to counter that effect.

24. When a vulnerable witness first reports allegations to the police, there should be immediate access to professional help. Furthermore, the examination of the witness should be conducted by suitably trained staff.

25. Vulnerable witnesses should, whenever possible, be examined at the earliest stage of the criminal proceedings, as soon as possible after the facts have been reported. Such examination should be carried out in a particularly careful, respectful and thorough manner.

26. Such examination should not be repeated. The examination should be conducted by or in the presence of a judicial authority, and the defence should have sufficient opportunity to challenge this testimony.

27. If appropriate, statements made at the pre-trial stage should be recorded by video to avoid face to face confrontation and unnecessary repetitive examinations that may cause trauma. During the trial, audio-visual techniques may be used in order to enable the competent authority to hear the persons concerned out of each other's physical presence.

28. At the court hearing, examination of the witness should be closely supervised by the judge. Where cross-examination, especially in cases concerning allegations of sexual offences, might have an unduly traumatic effect on the witness, the judge should consider taking appropriate measures to control the manner of questioning.

29. The mere fact that evidence by children is not given under oath should not be, in itself, a reason for its exclusion.

V.   International co-operation

30. Instruments aiming to foster international co-operation as well as national laws should be supplemented in order to facilitate the examination of witnesses at risk of intimidation and to allow witness protection programmes to be implemented across borders. The following measures should, for example, be considered:

- use of modern means of telecommunication, such as video-links, to facilitate simultaneous examination of protected witnesses or witnesses whose appearance in court in the requesting state is otherwise impossible, difficult or costly, while safeguarding the rights of the defence;
- assistance in relocating protected witnesses abroad and ensuring their protection;
- exchange of information between authorities responsible for witness protection programmes

Recommendation No. R (96) 8 of the Committee of Ministers to member states on Crime Policy in Europe in a Time of Change
(Adopted by the Committee of Ministers on 5 September 1996
at the 572nd meeting of the Ministers' Deputies)

The Committee of Ministers, under the terms of Article 15.*b* of the Statute of the Council of Europe,

Recalling that the aim of the Council of Europe is to achieve a greater unity between its members;

Bearing in mind the political, economic and social as well as the legal and institutional changes which have taken place in Europe over the past few years, in particular since 1989, the fall of the totalitarian regimes in central and eastern Europe, as well as the creation of the single market in western Europe;

Realising that such changes, albeit for different reasons, concern as much central and eastern as western Europe;

Considering that such changes have had, and will continue to have, major consequences at international, national and individual level;

Considering moreover that, in particular, such changes have a bearing in particular on crime and consequently call for appropriate responses, both at domestic and international level;

Being aware that the effectiveness of such responses depends greatly on their being harmonised within a coherent and concerted European crime policy;

Conscious of the indissoluble connections between criminality in western, central and eastern Europe;

Having regard to the work already achieved by the Council of Europe aimed at bringing closer the crime policies of its member states, which is reflected in a comprehensive set of principles and standards that emerges, *inter alia*, from the texts that it has adopted during the past forty years;

Conscious of the growing need for the Council of Europe to further contribute to that end;

Taking into consideration the recommendations adopted by the Committee of Ministers of the Council of Europe in the field of crime problems,

Recommends the governments of member states to be guided in their policies, legislations and practices concerning responses to present-day crime problems, by the following principles and recommendations:

I. Domestic responses to crime

a. *In general*

1. Every response to crime must conform to the basic principles of democratic states governed by the rule of law and subject to the paramount aim of guaranteeing respect for human rights.

2. Therefore, however serious the situation of a society might be with respect to crime, any measures aimed at dealing with that situation that do not take account of the values of democracy, human rights and the rule of law are inadmissible.

3. It must be one of the fundamental functions of criminal justice to safeguard the interests of the victims of crime. To this end it is necessary both to enhance the confidence of victims in criminal justice and to have adequate regard, within the criminal justice system, to the physical, psychological, material and social harm suffered by victims.

4. No society is crime-free, and thus the main objective of crime policy cannot be to eliminate crime but rather to contain crime at the lowest possible limits.

5. Subject to the above principles, each member state should have a coherent and rational crime policy directed towards the prevention of crime, including social prevention (for example social and economic policy, education, information, and so on) and situational prevention (for example measures to reduce the opportunities and means of committing offences, and so on), the individualisation of criminal reactions, the promotion of alternatives to custodial sentences, the social reintegration of offenders and the provision of assistance to victims.

6. On drawing up crime policy, governments should take advice from and actively co-operate with professionals directly concerned with the implementation of the policy; they should at the same time take advice from scientists in different fields having a bearing on crime policy.

7. Both because social, economic and other measures often have a direct impact on crime and because effective crime prevention requires a stable environment, crime policy must be co-ordinated with other policies.

8. To this end it is advisable in particular that states create either a crime policy co-ordination unit within central government or a horizontal structure for co-operation between the relevant bodies; it is further advisable that states encourage the development of crime prevention strategies at local or regional level.

9. Governments should participate regularly and actively in international schemes for the collection of relevant statistical information on crime.

10. Material and non-material costs to society of crime in general should be weighed against the costs of crime control.

11. The public must be kept informed of crime problems. Neither crime policy nor, indeed, the criminal justice system can be effective without a favourable public attitude and even active participation by the public.

b. *With respect to economic crime*

12. Measures should be taken in order to make the criminal justice system better fitted to deal effectively with the sophisticated business transactions that conceal economic crime or themselves constitute economic crimes.

13. Administrative law, commercial law, tax law, competition law and civil law should be called upon more often to play an active part in countering economic crime.

14. Prosecutors, investigating magistrates and judges dealing with economic crime should be given special training.

15. Where appropriate, economic crime should be dealt with in specialised chambers.

16. Provisions relating to time limitations should be reviewed in order to allow the competent authorities sufficient time to gather evidence in economic crime cases.

17. Rules governing evidence should be designed in such a manner as to pay due attention to the requirements of fighting against economic and organised crime.

18. Rules governing bank secrecy should not impede effective action against economic and organised crime.

19. The range of sanctions available in respect of persons convicted of economic offences should include disqualification from engaging in certain economic activities for a given period of time.

20. Provision should be made either for the liability of corporate bodies for criminal offences or for other measures with similar effect.

c. *With respect to organised crime*

21. Governments should consider the possibility of making it an offence to belong to or support an organised crime association.

22. Governments should endeavour to develop a good knowledge of the features of criminal organisations and to share that knowledge with the governments of other member states.

23. Governments should act on the basis of a strategy, in particular by using intelligence and crime analysis to achieve identified aims.

24. Specialised police, investigation and prosecutorial structures should be created and vested with means to carry out financial investigation and computerised analysis systems.

25. Adequate protection for witnesses and other participants in proceedings relating to the fight against organised crime should be provided for.

26. Interception of communications - both telecommunications and direct communications - should be envisaged in order to cope better with the requirements of fighting against criminal organisations.

27. Money laundering should be made an offence and provisions made for the search, seizure and confiscation of the proceeds of crime.

28. Governments should envisage the possibility of providing for an investigation/prosecution magistrate with jurisdiction over the entire national territory, or providing for the establishment of a central co-ordination body.

II. International responses to crime

a. *In general*

29. Governments should:
   - improve as far as possible their ratification position with regard to the European Conventions on Extradition (ETS No. 24) and Mutual Assistance in Criminal Matters (ETS No. 30), their additional Protocols (ETS Nos. 86, 98 and 99) the additional Protocol to the European Convention on Information on Foreign Law (ETS No. 97), as well as the Convention on the Transfer of Sentenced Persons (ETS No. 112) and the Convention on Laundering, Search, Seizure and Confiscation of the Proceeds from Crime (ETS No. 141);
   - review their need to uphold reservations and declarations made when ratifying the above-mentioned European Conventions on extradition and mutual assistance;
   - exchange between competent authorities of the member states information on those parts of domestic legislation which appear to be relevant for handling requests for co-operation in criminal matters based on the different conventions;
   - provide, when requested by another government, information and other forms of assistance for drafting domestic legislation on criminal matters, in particular those which have international features (for example computer crime, environmental crime, fraud, organised

crime) with a view to member states adopting domestic legislation which is compatible and harmonised with legislation in other member states, in such a manner as to make international co-operation both possible and uncomplicated;

- exchange, where appropriate, liaison magistrates with other governments, especially those with whom co-operation is more intensive, with a view to assisting the competent authorities when drafting or executing requests for legal co-operation and, moreover, to contributing to harmonising procedures and reducing delays;
- organise seminars for the competent authorities on particular subjects related to international co-operation;
- set up exchange programmes for judicial authorities, in particular judges and prosecutors specialised in organised and economic crime, with a view to enabling them to visit their counterparts in other member states for short periods and acquaint themselves with the working methods and legal systems in other member states;
- examine the advisability of developing amongst member states a computerised information network including all components of criminal justice systems in member states, as well as a database containing, *inter alia*, legislation and case-law.

30. Governments should bear in mind existing structures for police and judicial co-operation, such as ICPO-Interpol, and make optimal use of them.

31. Training of judges, prosecutors and police officers should take into account international aspects of crime as well as international co-operation instruments and practices.

32. In the long term, existing structures of mutual assistance based on the traditional concept of separate states might be complemented by adequate measures of co-operation and be improved by the creation of new supra-national structures for the judiciary.

b. *With respect to economic and organised crime*

33. European standards should be adopted on mutual legal assistance involving the use of sensitive data.

34. European standards should be adopted on mutual assistance for the purpose of the use of telecommunications in the giving of evidence.

35. Procedures should be developed on simultaneous and co-ordinated multilateral mutual legal assistance between three or more countries.

36. Bearing in mind existing structures for police co-operation, methods should be provided for better co-ordination of police teams working together across borders in the investigation of given cases.

37. Controlled delivery techniques and the use of undercover agents should be studied at international level.

38. Provision should be made for setting up international multi-disciplinary expert teams working together in given cases.

39. International administrative assistance should be provided for and made available to national control authorities with jurisdiction over areas that are prone to economic crime.

40. Efforts should be undertaken in order to find the right balance and the necessary co-ordination between international administrative assistance and mutual legal assistance in criminal matters.

41. Differences between national rules governing bank secrecy should not hamper effective international co-operation in the fight against economic crime and organised crime.

42. The possibility should be studied of giving international effect to the disqualifications mentioned in item 19 above.

Recommendation No. R (91) 11 of the Committee of Ministers to member states concerning Sexual Exploitation, Pornography and Prostitution of, and Trafficking in, Children and Young Adults

(adopted by the Committee of Ministers on 9 September 1991 at the 461st meeting of the Ministers' Deputies)

The Committee of Ministers, under the terms of Article 15.*b* of the Statute of the Council of Europe,

Considering that the well-being and interests of children and young adults are fundamental issues for any society;

Considering that sexual exploitation of children and young adults for profit-making purposes in the form of pornography, prostitution and traffic of human beings has assumed new and alarming dimensions at national and international level;

Considering that sexual experience linked to this social phenomenon, often associated with early sexual abuse within the family or outside of it, may be detrimental to a child's and young adult's psychosocial development;

Considering that it is in the interests of member States of the Council of Europe to harmonise their national legislation on sexual exploitation of children and young adults in order to improve the co-ordination and effectiveness of action taken at national and international level with a view to tackling this problem;

Having regard to Recommendation 1065 (1987) of the Parliamentary Assembly of the Council of Europe on the traffic in children and other forms of child exploitation;

Recalling Resolution No. 3 on sexual exploitation, pornography and prostitution of, and trafficking in, children and young adults of the 16th Conference of European Ministers of Justice (Lisbon, 1988);

Recalling Recommendation No. R (85) 4 on violence in the family, Recommendation No. R (85) 11 on the position of the victim in the framework of criminal law and procedure, Recommendation No. R (87) 20 on social reactions to juvenile delinquency and Recommendation No. R (89) 7 concerning principles on the distribution of videograms having a violent, brutal or pornographic content;

Bearing in mind the Convention for the Protection of Human Rights and Fundamental Freedoms (1950) and the European Social Charter (1961);

Bearing also in mind the United Nations Convention on the Rights of the Child (1989),

I. Recommends that the governments of member States review their legislation and practice with a view to introducing, if necessary, and implementing the following measures:

A. General measures

a. Public awareness, education and information

1. Make appropriate documentation on sexual exploitation of children and young adults available to parents, persons having minors in their care and other concerned groups and associations;

2. Include in the programmes of primary and secondary school education information about the dangers of sexual exploitation and abuse to which children and young adults might be exposed, and about how they may defend themselves;

3. Promote and encourage programmes aimed at furthering awareness and training for those who have functions involving support and protection of children and young adults in the fields of education, health, social welfare, justice and the police force in order to enable them to identify cases of sexual exploitation and to take the necessary measures;

4. Make the public aware of the devastating effects of sexual exploitation which transforms children and young adults into consumer objects and urge the general public to take part in the efforts of associations and organisations intervening in the field;

5. Invite the media to contribute to a general awareness of the subject and to adopt appropriate rules of conduct;

6. Discourage and prevent any abuse of the picture and the voice of the child in an erotic context;

b. Collection and exchange of information

7. Urge public and private institutions and agencies dealing with children and young adults who have been victims of all forms of sexual exploitation, to keep appropriate statistical information for scientific purposes and crime policy, while respecting anonymity and confidentiality;

8. Encourage co-operation between the police and all public and private organisations handling cases of sexual abuse within the family or outside of it and of various forms of sexual exploitation;

c. Prevention, detection, assistance

9.   Urge police services to give special attention to prevention, detection, and investigation of offences involving sexual exploitation of children and young adults, and allocate to them sufficient means towards that end;

10. Promote and further the creation and operation of specialised public and private services for the protection of children and young adults at risk in order to prevent and detect all forms of sexual exploitation;

11. Support public and private initiatives at local level to set up helplines and centres with a view to providing medical, psychological, social or legal assistance to children and young adults who are at risk or who have been victims of sexual exploitation;

d. Criminal law and criminal procedure

12. Ensure that the rights and interests of children and young adults are safeguarded throughout proceedings while respecting the rights of the alleged offenders;

13. Ensure throughout judicial and administrative proceedings confidentiality of record and the respect for privacy rights of children and young adults who have been victims of sexual exploitation by avoiding, in particular, the disclosure of any information that could lead to their identification;

14. Provide for special conditions at hearings involving children who are victims or witnesses of sexual exploitation, in order to diminish the traumatising effects of such hearings and to increase the credibility of their statements while respecting their dignity;

15. Provide under an appropriate scheme for compensation of children and young adults who have been victims of sexual exploitation;

16. Provide for the possibility of seizing and confiscating the proceeds from offences relating to sexual exploitation of children and young adults.

B.   Measures relating to pornography involving children

1.   Provide for appropriate sanctions taking into account the gravity of the offence committed by those involved in the production and distribution of any pornographic material involving children;

2.   Examine the advisability of introducing penal sanctions for mere possession of pornographic material involving children;

3.   Ensure, particularly through international co-operation, the detection of firms, associations or individuals often linked with two or more countries, using children for the production of pornographic material;

4.   Envisage informing the public, in order to raise awareness, of the implementation of penal policy, the number of prosecutions and convictions in cases involving child pornography, while ensuring the anonymity of the children concerned and of the alleged offenders.

C. Measures relating to the prostitution of children and young adults

1.   Increase the material and human resources of welfare and police services and improve their working methods so that places where child prostitution may occur are regularly inspected;

2.   Encourage and support the setting up of mobile welfare units for the surveillance of, or establishment of contact with, children at risk, particularly street children, in order to assist them to return to their families, if possible, and, if necessary, direct them to the appropriate agencies for health care, training or education;

3.   Intensify efforts with a view to identifying and sanctioning those who foster or encourage the prostitution of children or young adults, or who profit from it, on the one hand, and of the customers of child prostitution, on the other;

4.   Create or develop special units within the police and, if necessary, improve their working methods, in order to combat procuring of children and young adults;

5.   Dissuade travel agencies from promoting sex tourism in any form, especially through publicity, in particular by instituting consultations between them and the public services;

6.   Give priority to vocational training and reintegration programmes involving children and young adults who are occasionally or habitually prostituting themselves.

D. Measures relating to the trafficking in children and young adults

1.   Supervise the activities of artistic, marriage and adoption agencies in order to control the movement within, or between countries, of children and young adults to prevent the possibility that they will be led into prostitution or other forms of sexual exploitation;

2.   Increase surveillance by immigration authorities and frontier police in order to ensure that travel abroad by children, especially those not accompanied by their parents or their guardian, is not related to trafficking in human beings;

3.   Set up facilities and support those existing, in order to protect and assist the victims of traffic in children and young adults.

II. International aspects

Recommends that the Governments of member States:

1. Examine the advisability of signing and ratifying, if they have not done so:
- the United Nations Convention for the Suppression of the Traffic in Persons and the Exploitation of the Prostitution of Others (1950);
- the Hague Convention on Jurisdiction, Applicable Law and Recognition of Decrees relating to Adoptions (1965);
- the European Convention on the Adoption of Children (1967);
- Convention No. 138 concerning Minimum Age for Admission to Employment of the International Labour Organisation (1973);
- the United Nations Convention on the Rights of the Child (1989).

2. Introduce rules on extraterritorial jurisdiction in order to allow the prosecution and punishment of nationals who have committed offences concerning sexual exploitation of children outside the national territory, or, if applicable, review existing rules to that effect, and improve international co-operation to that end;

3. Increase and improve exchanges of information between countries through Interpol, in order to identify and prosecute offenders involved in sexual exploitation, and particularly in trafficking in children and young adults, or those who organise it;

4. Establish links with international associations and organisations working for the welfare of children and young adults in order to benefit from data available to them and secure, if necessary, their collaboration in combating sexual exploitation;

5. Take steps towards the creation of a European register of missing children.

III. Research priorities

Recommends that the Governments of member States promote research at national and international level, in particular, in the following fields:
1. Nature and extent of various forms of sexual exploitation of children and young adults, especially with a cross-cultural view;
2. Nature of paedophilia and factors contributing to it;
3. Links between adoption and sexual exploitation;
4. Links between sexual abuse within the family and prostitution;
5. Characteristics, role and needs of the consumers of child prostitution and child pornography;
6. Evaluation studies of vocational training and reintegration programmes concerning youth involved in prostitution;

7. Structure, international networks, interconnections and earnings of the sex industry;
8. Links between the sex industry and organised crime;
9. Possibilities and limitations of the criminal justice system as an instrument of prevention and repression of various forms of sexual exploitation of children and young adults;
10. Epidemiology, causes and consequences of sexually transmitted diseases in children and young persons, and analysis of their links with sexual abuse and exploitation.

Recommendation No. R (85) 11 of the Committee of Ministers to member states on the Position of the Victim in the Framework of Criminal Law and Procedure

(Adopted by the Committee of Ministers on 28 June 1985 at the 387th meeting of the Ministers' Deputies)

The Committee of Ministers, under the terms of Article 15.*b* of the Statute of the Council of Europe,

Considering that the objectives of the criminal justice system have traditionally been expressed in terms which primarily concern the relationship between the state and the offender;

Considering that consequently the operation of this system has sometimes tended to add to rather than to diminish the problems of the victim;

Considering that it must be a fundamental function of criminal justice to meet the needs and to safeguard the interests of the victim;

Considering that it is also important to enhance the confidence of the victim in criminal justice and to encourage his co-operation, especially in his capacity as a witness;

Considering that, to these ends, it is necessary to have more regard in the criminal justice system to the physical, psychological, material and social harm suffered by the victim, and to consider what steps are desirable to satisfy his needs in these respects;

Considering that measures to this end need not necessarily conflict with other objectives of criminal law and procedure, such as the reinforcement of social norms and the rehabilitation of offenders, but may in fact assist in their achievement and in an eventual reconciliation between the victim and the offender;

Considering that the needs of the victim should be taken into account to a greater degree, throughout all stages of the criminal justice process;

Having regard to the European Convention on the Compensation of Victims of Violent Crimes,

I.   Recommends the governments of member states to review their legislation and practice in accordance with the following guidelines :

A. *At police level*

1.   Police officers should be trained to deal with victims in a sympathetic, constructive and reassuring manner;

2.   The police should inform the victim about the possibilities of obtaining assistance, practical and legal advice, compensation from the offender and state compensation;

3.   The victim should be able to obtain information on the outcome of the police investigation;

4.   In any report to the prosecuting authorities, the police should give as clear and complete a statement as possible of the injuries and losses suffered by the victim;

B. *In respect of prosecution*

5.   A discretionary decision whether to prosecute the offender should not be taken without due consideration of the question of compensation of the victim, including any serious effort made to that end by the offender;

6.   The victim should be informed of the final decision concerning prosecution, unless he indicates that he does not want this information;

7.   The victim should have the right to ask for a review by a competent authority of a decision not to prosecute, or the right to institute private proceedings;

C. *Questioning of the victim*

8.   At all stages of the procedure, the victim should be questioned in a manner which gives due consideration to his personal situation, his rights and his dignity. Whenever possible and appropriate, children and the mentally ill or handicapped should be questioned in the presence of their parents or guardians or other persons qualified to assist them;

D. *Court proceedings*

9.   The victim should be informed of
   - the date and place of a hearing concerning an offence which caused him suffering;
   - his opportunities of obtaining restitution and compensation within the criminal justice process, legal assistance and advice;
   - how he can find out the outcome of the case;

10. It should be possible for a criminal court to order compensation by the offender to the victim. To that end, existing limitations, restrictions or technical impediments which prevent such a possibility from being generally realised should be abolished;

11. Legislation should provide that compensation may either be a penal sanction, or a substitute for a penal sanction or be awarded in addition to a penal sanction;

12. All relevant information concerning the injuries and losses suffered by the victim should be made available to the court in order that it may, when deciding upon the form and the quantum of the sentence, take into account:
-   the victim's need for compensation;
-   any compensation or restitution made by the offender or any genuine effort to that end;

13. In cases where the possibilities open to a court include attaching financial conditions to the award of a deferred or suspended sentence, of a probation order or of any other measure, great importance should be given – among these conditions – to compensation by the offender to the victim;

E. At enforcement stage

14. If compensation is a penal sanction, it should be collected in the same way as fines and take priority over any other financial sanction imposed on the offender. In all other cases, the victim should be assisted in the collection of the money as much as possible;

F. Protection of privacy

15. Information and public relations policies in connection with the investigation and trial of offences should give due consideration to the need to protect the victim from any publicity which will unduly affect his private life or dignity. If the type of offence or the particular status or personal situation and safety of the victim make such special protection necessary, either the trial before the judgment should be held in camera or disclosure or publication of personal information should be restricted to whatever extent is appropriate;

G. Special protection of the victim

16. Whenever this appears necessary, and especially when organised crime is involved, the victim and his family should be given effective protection against intimidation and the risk of retaliation by the offender;

II. Recommends the governments of member states:

1. to examine the possible advantages of mediation and conciliation schemes;

2. to promote and encourage research on the efficacy of provisions affecting victims.

Recommendation No. R (83) 7 of the Committee of Ministers to member states on Participation of the Public in Crime Policy
(Adopted by the Committee of Ministers on 23 June 1983
at the 361st meeting of the Ministers' Deputies)

The Committee of Ministers, under the terms of Article 15.*b* of the Statute of the Council of Europe,

Considering that a crime policy directed towards the prevention of crime, the promotion of alternatives to custodial sentences, the social reintegration of offenders and the provision of assistance to victims should be followed and developed in the Council of Europe member states;

Considering that such a policy is an appropriate response to the crime problems currently facing member states;

Considering that the implementation of the policy presupposes first that this policy is taken up and actively complied with by all professionals directly concerned, in particular judges, magistrates, prison staff and police officers;

Considering, however, that such a policy cannot be effective without a favourable public attitude and even active participation of the public;

Considering that it is important to overcome the indifference, indeed hostility, towards such a policy shown by certain sections of the public and to secure the greatest possible degree of support for the policy's objectives;

Considering that it is essential to involve the public, within the framework of appropriate structures, in the drawing up and implementation of such a policy;

Having regard to the Convention for the Protection of Human Rights and Fundamental Freedoms;

Having regard to Resolution (73) 5 on the Standard Minimum Rules for the Treatment of Prisoners;

Having regard to the proceedings of the 13th Criminological Research Conference (on public opinion in relation to crime and criminal justice, 1978),

Recommends that the governments of member states promote participation of the public in the drawing up and implementation of a crime policy aimed at the prevention of crime, the use of alternatives to custodial sentences and the provision of assistance to victims, particularly in the following ways:

I.   Information and research

1.   Extending the scope and improving the quality of criminal statistics and developing scientific research on crime and criminal justice, including studies on victimisation.

2.   Disseminating the above-mentioned information among the general public in order to counteract prejudice and preconceived ideas concerning both crime and criminal justice.

3.   Incorporating the rudiments of criminal law and criminology in school curricula to this end and generating an awareness of the real problems of crime and criminal justice by the most appropriate means, such as co-operation with the mass media.

II.   Participation of the public in the drawing up of crime policy

4.   Involving the public in the drawing up of crime policy at both local and national level through ad hoc advisory committees, permanent bodies as well as through wide-ranging consultation, in particular by public debates.

5.   Explaining the trends of the crime policy followed by the authorities and trying to obtain the observations of the public on this policy.

III.   Role of the public in the implementation of crime policy

A.   *In general*

6.   Alerting the public by means of appropriate information and structures to the fundamental role it should play in implementing a policy for the prevention of crime and the social reintegration of offenders, notably by involving it in alternatives to custodial sentences and in assistance to victims.

B.   *Social prevention*

7.   Promoting, through courses or advisory services for parents, proper information on the problems of juvenile delinquency, with particular reference to its causes and symptoms and the prevention thereof.

8.   Providing teachers with fuller training in these matters so as to enable them, in the course of their work, to deal with their pupils' adjustment and behaviour problems.

9.   Giving priority to the employment of young people and promoting vocational training for those who have exhibited delinquent behaviour in order to help them to obtain jobs and encourage employers to engage the latter.

10. Encouraging architects and town planners, at national and local level, to give cities a more human face and a layout aimed at crime prevention.

11. Taking account of suggestions by citizens' associations regarding community development in cities and neighbourhoods and giving them opportunities to contribute to town planning in order to improve the quality of life and reduce the criminogenic aspects of urbanisation.

12. Encouraging local authorities to promote a dialogue on these issues with the public in order to strengthen the latter's role in social prevention.

13. Compiling an inventory, in consultation with insurance companies and security specialists in particular, of the elementary precautions and technical means to be taken to prevent opportunities for crime, publicising them widely and encouraging the public to adopt them.

C. General and special crime prevention-application of alternatives to custodial sentences

14. Making the public conscious, through publications and conferences as well as the mass media, of the penal and social consequences of committing various offences, so that a knowledge thereof may act as a deterrent.

15. Encouraging public participation in the reintegration of prisoners by helping them, as far as possible, to contact individuals willing to provide them with assistance.

16. Increasing the involvement of prison staff in the reintegration of prisoners through the provision, for example, of appropriate courses and seminars.

17. Ensuring that prisoners' ties with their families remain unbroken, for example by facilitating contacts between the appropriate staff in the prisons and prisoners' families as far as possible.

18. Making the public conscious of the advantages of non-custodial treatment of offenders from the point of view of their resocialisation.

19. Encouraging the public to play a practical part in the non-custodial treatment of offenders:
- by providing appropriate structures, such as social reintegration boards, welfare associations and committees of assistance for offenders on probation and on conditional release;
- by having increased recourse within these structures to the use of volunteers;
- by making better use of the particular competences of these volunteers; by trying to define their exact role in relation to that of the professional social workers.

20. Urging employers and other persons concerned not to discriminate against offenders on probation and released prisoners.

21. Promoting an appreciation of the policy of alternatives to custodial sentences, among judges, magistrates and police officers, particularly:
- during their initial and further training;
- through their participation in local crime prevention committees, conferences, seminars or round tables;
- through publications intended for specific professional groups.

22. Encouraging by meetings and seminars the families of convicted offenders to prepare the offenders' reintegration.

23. Co-operating with the associations concerned with the social reintegration of offenders by providing them with moral and material support.

24. Establishing contact with associations concerned with protecting the interests of victims in order to secure their support for a crime policy aimed both at fostering the reintegration of offenders, especially through non-custodial treatment, and at making appropriate provision for victims.

D. A *crime policy taking account of the victims' interests*

25. Encouraging the public, through an appeal for solidarity and through the provision of information on the technical facilities available and the appropriate action to be taken, to prevent offences from being committed and assist victims both during and after the perpetration of the offence.

26. Drawing the attention of the police to the need:
- to show consideration for the victims of offences in all circumstances, especially by giving them a sympathetic reception;
- to put victims quickly in contact, if they wish, with local services or associations able to assist them or inform their families;
- to advise victims on measures to be taken to avoid similar occurrences.

27. Setting up services able to provide victims with appropriate psychological, moral or material assistance.

28. Providing, so far as it is practicable, special reception or waiting rooms for victims in police stations or court buildings.

29. Establishing an efficient system of legal aid for victims so that they may have access to justice in all circumstances.

30. Facilitating the compensation of victims by offenders, for example by providing, as an alternative to a custodial sentence, the payment of such compensation.

31. Making state compensation more widely available to victims in the absence of compensation by offenders.

32. Supporting associations that provide the victims with psychological, moral and material assistance and encouraging them to make greater use of volunteers.

Ministerial resolutions

Resolution No. 1 on Victims of Crime
Adopted at the 27th Conference of European Ministers of Justice
(Yerevan, Armenia, 12-13 October 2006)

1.   The Ministers participating in the 27th Conference of the European Ministers of Justice,

2.   Having discussed the topic of "Victims – place, rights and assistance" and, in particular, assistance to categories of vulnerable victims;

3.   Having regard to the extensive standards developed by the Council of Europe in this field and underlining that these standards should be widely disseminated, promoted and concretely implemented;

4.   Welcoming in particular Recommendation Rec(2006)8 on assistance to crime victims, which provides for extensive and effective assistance measures for victims of all types of crime, including victims of terrorism and the most vulnerable victims;

5.   Having regard to the progress report on future areas for the work of the Council of Europe in the fight against terrorism, prepared by the Committee of Experts on Terrorism (CODEXTER) and the decisions of the Committee of Ministers on the basis thereof;

6.   Realising the growing public concern for victims of crime who are in a precarious situation, whether it be from a psychological, social, economic or physical point of view, so that their needs should be more fully taken into account;

7.   Recognising that, in order to receive assistance or to assert their rights victims are obliged to undertake a number of procedures, which, if inappropriate or complex, can contribute to the phenomenon of secondary victimisation;

8.   Convinced of the need to reduce the risk of secondary victimisation, in particular through simplifying procedures and facilitating access to the competent institutions which can help **victims** to obtain assistance;

9.   Considering that, in addition to the measures provided under criminal procedure, civil and, where necessary, administrative or other remedies should be made available;

10.   Underlining that the person committing the crime is the person primarily responsible for its consequences and for compensating the victim;

11.   Underlining further that insurance cover can be provided by both public and private schemes and that subscribing to appropriate optional insurance cover is the responsibility of the individual;

12.   Aware of the important role of compensation schemes in expressing social solidarity towards victims and of the actual and potential role and impact of the insurance industry in covering damage to crime victims and the wide variety of ways in which compensation can be legally and institutionally structured and funded;

13.   Conscious of the need to prevent and treat violence and welcoming the work currently underway to draft a convention against the sexual exploitation of children as well as the launching, in November 2006, of a new Council of Europe campaign to combat violence against women, including domestic violence;

14.   Expressing particular concern about the extent of domestic violence, in particular violence against the partner, as well as concern for members of the family who witness such violence and determined to carry on with the action started by the Council of Europe in order to combat domestic violence, as demonstrated by Recommendation Rec(2002)5;

15.   Concerned to increase the attention paid to the phenomenon of violence against the partner and aware that such violence can be based on discriminating prejudices in terms of inequalities resulting from gender, origins and economic dependency;

16.   Referring to the Declaration and the Action Plan adopted during the Third Summit of Heads of State and Government of the Council of Europe;

17.   Welcoming the national contributions and noting the proposals contained in these contributions;

18.   AGREE that an effective and comprehensive protection of victims, in their role as witnesses, requires a multidisciplinary approach;

19.   DECIDE to promote measures at a national and international level to improve assistance to victims and their protection from repeat and secondary victimisation as well as to ensure, as far as possible, their psychological, social and physical rehabilitation as well as adequate compensation for damage suffered;

20.   RECOMMEND in particular that the Secretary General of the Council of Europe ensures that the activities of the Council of Europe in the field of training of police and personnel involved in the administration of justice include the question of the appropriate ways in which to deal with vulnerable persons, particularly victims;

21.   INVITE the Committee of Ministers to promote further the standards developed by the Council of Europe concerning victims by taking them into account in Council of Europe work, in particular concerning persons and bodies having contact with victims such as judicial and law enforcement agencies;

22.   INVITE the Committee of Ministers to entrust the European Committee on Legal Co-operation (CDCJ), in co-operation with other competent bodies of the Council of Europe, to study the question of civil, administrative and other remedies to be made available to victims of crime with a view to reducing the risk of secondary victimisation and contributing to their rehabilitation from crime suffered and adequate compensation for damage sustained, and to this end identify and analyse the existing best practices:

i) concerning civil and administrative or other remedies, designed to protect the interests of victims, in particular provision of information on procedures, simplified procedures, legal aid and advice before, during and after the completion of criminal, civil administrative or other procedures bearing in mind the needs of categories of particularly vulnerable victims (for example, children, the elderly, disabled persons);

ii) concerning the role of publicly or privately financed insurance schemes in ensuring compensation for damages sustained by victims;

iii). concerning the role of the authorities, organisations and persons dealing with and representing victims, particularly with respect to vulnerable victims;

with a view to making proposals to the Committee of Ministers for possible follow-up action;

23.   INVITE the Committee of Ministers to entrust the European Committee on Crime Problems (CDPC) to:

1° - Assistance to crime victims

examine and promote, in co-operation with other competent bodies of the Council of Europe, the implementation of Recommendation Rec(2006)8 on assistance to crime victims;

2° - Domestic violence, in particular violence against the partner

a. examine, in co-operation with other competent bodies of the Council of Europe, the measures concerning violence against the partner contained notably in the appendix to Recommendation Rec(2002)5 on the protection of women against violence in order to determine the feasibility of and the need for an additional Council of Europe legal instrument on violence against the partner taking into account the discussions of this Conference;

b. report back to the Committee of Ministers on the results of this examination so that it can decide whether there is a need for the Council of Europe to carry out work in this field, possibly in the form of an international normative instrument to combat domestic violence, in particular violence against the partner;

3° - Crime prevention, restorative justice and mediation

taking into account the discussions of this Conference, envisage further activities dealing with the technical and legal aspects of the prevention of crime, in particular crime which targets vulnerable victims, as well as with restorative justice, including mediation (with a view notably to examining the implementation of the 1999 Recommendation on mediation in criminal matters No. R (99) 19);

24.   ASK the Secretary General of the Council of Europe to report on the steps taken to give effect to this Resolution, on the occasion of their next Conference.

Resolution No. 2 on
The Social Mission of the Criminal Justice System –
Restorative Justice
Adopted at the 26th Conference of European Ministers of Justice
(Helsinki, Finland, 7-8 April 2005)

THE MINISTERS participating in the 26th Conference of European Ministers of Justice (Helsinki, 7 and 8 April 2005);

1. Having examined the report of the Minister of Justice of Finland on the social mission of the criminal justice system;

2. Considering that it is of great importance for social peace to promote a criminal policy which focuses also on the prevention of anti-social and criminal behaviour, the development of community sanctions and measures, the victim's needs and offender reintegration;

3. Noting that the use of imprisonment causes a heavy burden on society and causes human suffering;

4. Considering that community sanctions and measures as well as restorative justice measures can have a positive effect on the social costs of crime and crime control;

5. Convinced that by a restorative justice approach the interests of crime victims may often be better served, the possibilities for offenders to achieve a successful integration into society be increased and public confidence in the criminal justice system be thereby enhanced;

6. Bearing in mind that the purpose of restorative justice is also to decrease the number of proceedings before the criminal courts and that alternative non-judicial systems for restorative justice should be developed as far as possible within the national context;

7. Considering that prison sentences cannot always be avoided but that the treatment and management of prisoners can also benefit, inter alia, from the restorative justice approach so as to promote successful reintegration of the offender;

8. Considering that the restorative justice approach should be developed both in the framework of community measures as well as in all stages of criminal justice procedure, including restorative justice measures applied during and after imprisonment;

9. Considering that the prevention of crime, support and compensation for crime victims, and reintegrating sentenced offenders requires a multidisciplinary and/or multi-agency approach;

10. Aware of the need to design particular strategies to address the specific needs of vulnerable groups of victims and offenders;

11. Aware of the particular situation in some countries where the criminal justice system is currently undergoing substantial reforms, and that these countries may be in particular need of technical assistance to carry out these reforms;

12. Bearing in mind the importance of the principles contained in existing relevant international instruments;

13. Recalling the Council of Europe Recommendations of relevance in this field;

14. Recalling the European Convention on Compensation to Victims of Violent Crimes;

15. AGREE on the importance of promoting the restorative justice approach in their criminal justice systems;

16. ENCOURAGE the continuing work of the European Committee for Crime Problems (CDPC) in:

   - updating the European Prison Rules;
   - addressing the needs of victims of crime, including victims of terrorism and of serious violations of international humanitarian law;
   - examining means of enhancing crime prevention policies;

17. FURTHER ENCOURAGE the work of the Council of Europe in conducting a multidisciplinary project on violence and children;

18. INVITE the CDPC to prepare, in accordance with Recommendation Rec(2003)20, an instrument with a view to developing comprehensive standards governing sanctions and measures for dealing with juvenile offenders;

19. INVITE the Committee of Ministers to further entrust the CDPC to examine the issue of probation and post prison assistance with a view to addressing the need to develop the role of probation services;

20. INVITE the Committee of Ministers to ask the CDPC to give further consideration to the possibility of preparing one or more instruments to address the needs of groups of vulnerable victims and/or offenders;

21. FURTHER INVITE the Committee of Ministers to support and develop co-operation programmes put in place to promote the widespread application of restorative justice in the member countries, on the basis of the Council of Europe's Recommendations in this field;

22. ASK the Secretary General of the Council of Europe to report on the steps taken to give effect to this Resolution, on the occasion of their next Conference.

Resolution on the prevention of everyday violence in Europe
*Adopted by the European Ministers responsible for the prevention of
violence in everyday life at their ad hoc conference "Preventing everyday
violence in Europe : responses in a democratic society"
(Oslo, Norway, 7-9 November 2004)*

1. THE MINISTERS participating in the ad hoc Conference of European
    Ministers responsible for the prevention of violence in everyday life
    (Oslo, 7-9 November 2004);

2. Recalling that the Council of Europe aims to promote pluralist
    democracy, the rule of law and fundamental rights and freedoms on the
    European continent;

3. Noting that violence in everyday life is a concern for most citizens of the
    member states of the Council of Europe and may lead to a growing
    sense of insecurity;

4. Deploring the tremendous individual and economic consequences of
    everyday violence;

5. Convinced that a comprehensive and co-ordinated national or regional
    policy to reduce violence in everyday life is most capable of proving
    effective in the long term;

6. Asserting that such a policy must uphold and strengthen human rights
    and the rule of law;

7. Having regard to the work in the field of everyday violence carried out
    within the intergovernmental programme of activities of the Council of
    Europe, by the Parliamentary Assembly and the Congress of Local and
    Regional Authorities of Europe, and, especially, the legal instruments,
    declarations, guidelines, reports, handbooks and examples of good
    practice prepared in connection with the Integrated Project "Responses
    to violence in everyday life in a democratic society" (2002-04) launched
    on the initiative of the Secretary General;

8. Having discussed the conclusions and the twelve policy principles for an
    integrated policy response to violence in everyday life set out in the final
    report of the Integrated Project;

9. Having taken note of the work carried out in this field by other
    international organisations, especially the World Health Organization,
    and the European Union as well as the important work carried out by
    civil society associations;

10. Considering it appropriate to encourage democratic debate on
    responses to everyday violence and strengthen preventive action both in

general as well as in the light of the constitutional framework and the specific priorities of each member state;

11. WELCOME the results of the efforts made by the Council of Europe in connection with the Integrated Project "Responses to violence in everyday life in a democratic society" to improve knowledge of the situation regarding everyday violence and its prevention in Europe and to offer decision-makers and field operators pragmatic instruments and examples of good practice with a view to applying an integrated prevention policy;

12. CALL UPON the member states of the Council of Europe to encourage the development and implementation of national or regional policies to prevent and reduce violence in everyday life inspired by the twelve policy principles summarised in the Appendix to this resolution;

13. CALL UPON the member states of the Council of Europe to improve knowledge of different forms of violence as well as their root causes, interconnections and consequences, and to exchange information about research into these questions;

14. INVITE the Committee of Ministers of the Council of Europe to ensure the widest possible dissemination of the results and conclusions of the Integrated Project and, especially, the legal instruments, policy principles, declarations, guidelines, reports, handbooks and examples of good practice prepared by the Council of Europe in connection with the Project;

15. INVITE the Committee of Ministers to prepare a recommendation to the member states of the Council of Europe on the development of national or regional policies to prevent and reduce violence in everyday life based on the twelve policy principles summarised in the Appendix to this resolution;

16. INVITE the Committee of Ministers to support the initiative of the Congress of Local and Regional Authorities of Europe to set up a European observatory of everyday violence in partnership with other intergovernmental organisations, the European Union and civil society;

17. INVITE the Committee of Ministers to encourage work on issues related to the prevention and reduction of violence in everyday life within its intergovernmental programme of activities (in particular in the fields of legal co-operation, human rights, social cohesion, health, victim support, education, youth, sport and culture) with yet more emphasis on cross-disciplinary action and intersectoral co-ordination;

18. INVITE the Committee of Ministers to support the implementation, within its intergovernmental programme of activities, of an inter-disciplinary

project concerning children and violence, based on the conclusions of the Integrated Project.

Appendix to the Resolution

Summary of principles for an integrated policy response to violence in everyday life[45]

a) *Integrated approach:* violence in everyday life necessitates a comprehensive and co-ordinated response applied through the thematic, horizontal, vertical and strategic integration of national prevention policy and its implementation at all levels.

b) *Systematic reliance on partnerships:* an integrated response to everyday violence should be based on partnerships of all people and institutions involved in preventing and reducing violence in order to pool resources and share responsibility, while respecting the role of all those involved.

c) *Democratic accountability and participation of civil society:* responses to violence should be accountable to citizens' democratically elected representatives at all levels and involve the active participation of civil society.

d) *Preventive approach:* in the first place violence should be prevented before it takes place but if violence occurs its consequences should be minimised. Special attention should be given to educational measures.

e) *Victim-oriented approach:* satisfactory support, care and protection of victims should be used as essential standards for planning, implementing and evaluating responses to violence.

f) *Offender-oriented prevention:* rehabilitation of offenders, their reintegration into society and the prevention of recidivism should be taken as serious aims in a comprehensive prevention policy.

g) *Developing the use of mediation:* mediation as a consensual and restorative means of preventing and solving conflicts should be promoted while its scope of application, methods and ethics should be clarified.

h) *Giving priority to local prevention programmes:* sufficient priority and resources should be given to local partnerships for the prevention of violence.

i) *Planning and continuous evaluation:* responses to violence should be carefully planned based on situational analyses, adequately documented

---

[45] A more detailed version of these principles can be found in the Final Report of the Integrated Project "Responses to violence in everyday life in a democratic Society", Confronting everyday violence in Europe: an integrated approach. Council of Europe, Strasbourg. 2004.

and continuously evaluated through comparable and evidence-based criteria.

j) *Sustainability:* prevention programmes should be designed and resourced for sufficiently long periods of time to ensure that the targeted impact can be reached and sustained.

k) *Training for all partners:* people working in violence prevention partnerships should receive training or guidance to match the skills required in their tasks.

l) *Interdisciplinary research policy:* interdisciplinary research into violence should be supported in order to generate an adequate knowledge base for policy development and practice.

Expert Report

Victims of Terrorism – Policies and Legislation in Europe: an Overview on Victim-Related Assistance and Support[46]

1. Introduction

1.1 Key Issues

Questions related to the compensation and assistance of victims of terrorist acts must be dealt with from a broad perspective that includes general victim related policies, for example compensation, restitution and the role of the victim in criminal proceedings, policies against (transnational) terrorism, legal and political responses to situations of mass violence or war as well as finally racist or, more general, hate violence.

From the 1980ies on the crime victim received particular attention in criminal policy and subsequently also in criminal legislation[47]. This led to legislation that was protective as regards possible averse impacts of criminal proceedings and supportive as regards compensation of material and immaterial losses caused by the victimizing event. National legislation and policies generated amendments of criminal procedural codes and victim support schemes. The Council of Europe and the European Union developed standards and instruments backing up the movement for a better treatment of crime victims. From the seventies on, terrorism, back then mostly in the form of national, separatist and political terrorism, started to trouble European countries. The policy response was more or less restricted to tailoring police and criminal procedural laws to new demands of law enforcement in face of organised violence exerted against individual exponents of economy and politics to put pressure on legitimate governments. A few exceptions can be observed with France and Italy introducing specific victims of terrorism legislation after experiencing terrorist violence in the seventies and eighties. However, it was only after the attack on the World Trade Center (WTC) on 11 September 2001 with its devastating consequences for civil society and the extreme toll for human life that more attention has been devoted to the question of how victims of terrorist attacks can be accommodated better. This process has been accelerated by the terrorist acts of Madrid that claimed almost 200 lives. The policies developing since can be placed alongside such policies that have been adopted in order to respond to the aftermath of mass violence such as state wars or civil wars. The developments may also be considered to be

---

[46] Expert report prepared by Hans-Joerg ALBRECHT and Michael KILCHLING, Max-Planck-Institute for Foreign and International Criminal Law, Freiburg (Germany) for the Group of Specialists on Assistance to Victims and Prevention of Victimisation (PC-S-AV) reporting to the Committee of Experts on Terrorism (CODEXTER) and to the European Committee on Crime Problems (CDPC). The views expressed in this report are those of the authors and do not necessarily reflect the position of the Council of Europe or of its member states.

[47] Declaration of Basic Principles of Justice for Victims of Crime and Abuse of Power, adopted by the UN General Assembly Resolution 40/34 of 29 November 1985.

part of general victim of crime policies that recently tend to branch out into special policies devised to meet the needs of particular groups of victims such as victims of trafficking, victims of sexual violence and abuse or victims of traffic accidents. But, the phenomenon of terrorist violence and its impact on civil society and individuals exhibits also a close relationship to racist or hate violence and ethnic hatred. The latter may be understood as the little brother of international terrorism which feeds on the vulnerability of modern societies and seeks to destroy the very basis of social integration that is social solidarity.

Solidarity with victims (in terms of individual and victimized states) in fact is regularly mentioned in official statements addressing terrorism and the fight against terrorism.

1.2 Terrorism: Legislation after 11 September 2001 and the Victim

Anti-terrorism legislation that has been drafted and enacted after 11 September certainly carries clear signs of co-ordination and convergence. Co-ordination and convergence have been pushed by precise demands voiced by the UN, the security council as well as other international and supra national bodies. Moreover, anti-terrorism legislation after 11 September implements a programme that has been developed in the context of controlling transnational organised crime, money laundering as well as illegal immigration throughout the eighties and nineties. The Madrid bombing has again accelerated the pace of actions against terrorism, in particular in Europe and within the framework of the European Union (EU). Anti-terrorism legislation is of a cross sectional nature as it is headed towards amendments not only of criminal law but also towards amending telecommunication law, immigration law, police law etc. In substantial criminal law we find new offence statutes that penalize support of terrorist organisations and financing terrorism, in procedural law police powers have been widened while telecommunication providers are subject to prolonged periods of keeping data. Co-operation between police and intelligence agencies has been facilitated; the emergence of task force approaches that combine police, intelligence agencies, customs, immigration authorities etc. is pointing also to the convergence of policies of prevention and repression. At large, anti-terrorism legislation demonstrates the transformation of the formerly privileged status of politically and ideologically motivated violence into behaviour deemed to be particularly dangerous and therefore eligible for increased penalties and incapacitation. Such transformation can be also understood as the emergence of an enemy type criminal law which is opposed to the version of criminal law which addresses citizens and with that treasures the salience of civil liberties. The focus of terrorism legislation so far has been and still is on ways to improve prevention and repression of terrorist acts.

The issue of victims of terrorism, however, did not play a significant role in international and national anti-terrorism policies although the US Department of State accounts of global patterns of terrorism show clearly that civilians bear the main toll of terrorist violence. Up to 90% of deaths linked to terrorist violence worldwide are suffered by the civilian population[48].

But, the UN Security Council in its Resolution 1566 (2004)[49] requests the elaboration of recommendations by a working group to establish a fund to compensate victims of terrorism and their families. Funds should be raised by voluntary contributions and through assets seized and forfeited from terrorists and terrorist groups.

2. European Developments in the Field of Support of Victims of Terrorism

2.1 The Council of Europe and Victims of Terrorism

The Council of Europe addressed the issue of compensation to crime victims from public funds already in the early seventies, eventually leading to the establishment of the European Convention on the Compensation of Victims of Violent Crimes in 1983[50]. The Convention entered into force 1988. The aims of the Convention are to introduce or develop schemes for compensation to crime victims and to establish minimum provisions for compensation of material and immaterial losses. The Convention states that compensation shall be paid by the state on whose territory the crime was committed to nationals of the states party to the Convention as well as to nationals of all member states of the Council of Europe who are permanent residents in the state on whose territory the crime was committed. Regarding eligibility, those who have sustained serious bodily injury or impairment of health directly attributable to an intentional crime of violence as well as the dependents of persons who have died as a result of such a crime shall be eligible for compensation. This shall apply also if the offender cannot be prosecuted or punished. Compensation shall cover, at least, loss of earnings, medical and hospitalisation expenses and funeral expenses and, as regards dependants, loss of maintenance. Compensation may be made subsidiary to compensation obtained by the victim from any other source. The Convention obliges the Contracting States to designate a central authority to receive and take action on requests for assistance from any other Party in connection with the matters covered by the Convention. The Council of Europe then issued Recommendations on Assistance to Victims of Persecution and the Prevention of Persecution on 17 September 1987.

Recently the Council of Europe drafted guidelines on the Protection of Victims of Terrorist Acts[51]. Herewith, it was recognised that the suffering of victims of terrorist acts deserves national and international solidarity and

---

[48] US Department of State: Global Patterns of Terrorism 2003. Washington, April 2004.
[49] Adopted by the Security Council at its 5053rd meeting on 8 October 2004.
[50] OJ L 63E, 4 March 1997, p. 2.
[51] Adopted by the Committee of Ministers on 2 March 2005 at the 917th meeting of the Ministers' Deputies.

support. The guidelines underline the states' obligation to take the measures needed to protect the fundamental rights of everyone within their jurisdiction against terrorist violence, in particular the right to life and thus points also to the European Convention on Human Rights as well as decisions of the European Court of Human Rights holding that states are under a strict duty to implement policies devised to provide for effective protection of human life[52]. According to the guidelines states should ensure that persons who have suffered physical or psychological harm as a result of terrorist violence as well as under certain circumstances close relatives can benefit from the services and measures prescribed by these guidelines. A couple of principles are elaborated in the guidelines which reflect fairly well and consistently those principles which have been developed for ordinary victims (of violence). When looking into the victim of terrorist approach we find the principle that the granting of services and support should not depend on the identification, arrest, prosecution or conviction of the perpetrator of the terrorist act and the principle of respect for the dignity, private and family life of victims of terrorism which should be also protected against intrusive media practices. The importance of emergency assistance is stressed as well as long-term medical, psychological, social and material assistance. Then, the duty of effective investigation of terrorist acts is highlighted, a duty which is in line with decisions of the European Court of Human Rights as regards protection of human life[53]. In case of decisions not to prosecute it is recommended that states give victims the right to have this decision re-examined. Effective access to the law and to justice for victims of terrorist acts should be provided and the position of victims of terrorist acts adequately recognised in criminal proceedings. Fair, appropriate and timely compensation for the damages is mentioned not to be affected by national borders. Material compensation should come with support in order to provide for relief as regards other impacts of terrorist acts. Protection of the right to privacy and family life against too intrusive media practices is demanded for as is protection of witnesses against risks for life and health that can come with testifying in terrorist trials. The latter evidently refers to organised crime legislation where victim and witness protection has been recognised as an important issue. The guidelines then address the need for information to be delivered to victims of terrorist activities and which – along the well known information standards of general victim policies – refer to information on criminal proceedings, victim rights and victim support. The guidelines conclude with urging states to establish specific training programmes for officials dealing with victims of terrorism.

The victims of terrorism guidelines insofar reflect general standards of delivering support and granting compensation to crime victims. With focussing on protection in criminal proceedings, safeguarding privacy, fair

---

[52] Guidelines on the Protection of Victims of Terrorist Acts (adopted by the Committee of Ministers on 2 March 2005 at the 917th meeting of the Ministers' Deputies).
[53] European Court of Human Rights, 28 March 2000, Kiliç v. Turkey; 18 May 2000, Velikova v. Bulgaria.

and effective compensation (including advance payments), adequate training of law enforcement staff those focal concerns are raised which have been dealt with by partisans of crime victims for the last three decades.

2.2 The European Union

The European Union has dealt with victims of crime and victims of terrorism in various Green Papers[54], declarations, framework decisions issued by the European Council and the European Parliament. The attention paid to victims of crime became visible in a Council Joint Action (97/154/JHA) which aims at combating trafficking in human beings and sexual exploitation of children[55], in the Vienna Action Plan of the Council and the Commission of 1998 which deals with how to implement with best effects the provisions of the Treaty of Amsterdam on an area of freedom, security and justice (pointing in particular to Articles 19 and 51(c) thereof)[56], in the Commission's communication to the Council, the European Parliament and the European Economic and Social Committee which carries the title "Crime Victims in the European Union Reflections on Standards and Action"[57], in the Resolution of 12 December 2000 on the initiative concerning the Council Framework Decision on the standing of victims in criminal procedure[58] as well as in the final Council Framework Decision of 15 March 2001 on the standing of victims in criminal proceedings[59]. On the other hand, the European Union put the emphasis on combating terrorism with the Resolution of 5 September 2001 on the role of the European Union in combating terrorism[60], the Resolution of 6 February 2002 on the proposal for a Council Framework Decision on combating terrorism[61] and the Council Framework Decision of 13 June 2002 on the definition of terrorist offences. When dealing with terrorism European Union statements also recognise that victims of terrorism must be taken care of in order to respond effectively to terrorist goals that aim at destroying social solidarity.

The establishment of an area of freedom, security and justice must also take account of the needs of crime victims in the EU. The Vienna Action Plan[62] of the Council and the Commission, adopted by the Council 1998, called for addressing the question of victim support by making a comparative survey of victim compensation schemes and assessing the feasibility of taking action

---

[54] Commission of the European Communities: Green Paper. Compensation to crime victims (presented by the Commission) Brussels, COM(2001) 536 final, 28 September 2001.
[55] ETS No. 116.
[56] OJ C 19E, 23 January 1999, p. 1.
[57] OJ C 59E, 23 February 2001, p. 5.
[58] 1 OJ C 232, 17 August 2001, p. 36
[59] OJ L 82, 22 March 2001, p. 1.
[60] OJ C 72E 2002, p.96
[61] Official Journal RR\477381EN.doc 7/18 PE 310.970.
[62] OJ C 19, 23 January 1999, p. 1. Point 51 (c).

within the EU. The Commission presented a Communication[63] on crime victims in 1999, covering not only compensation aspects but also other issues that could be addressed to improve the position of crime victims in the European Union. The conclusions of the European Council in Tampere 1999 called for the drawing up of minimum standards on the protection of the victims of crime, in particular on crime victims' access to justice and on their rights to compensation for damages. It also called for the setting up of national programmes to finance supportive measures, and for effective protection of victims. Since decades the European Parliament has supported firmly improvements of crime victim compensation schemes. The Council adopted a framework decision[64] on the standing of the victim in criminal proceedings on 15 March 2001. The framework decision, based on Title VI of the EU Treaty, includes an obligation for member states to ensure that crime victims can obtain a decision on compensation from the offender in the course of criminal proceedings. An in-depth study[65] of the position of crime victims in the EU covered, among other aspects, the possibilities for crime victims to receive compensation from the state under the national laws of the member states. The results of this study have been published as a Green Paper of the Commission of the European Communities (CEC) on compensation to crime victims[66]. Here, it is stated that recognition of crime victims needs and comparable legal regulation are needed in a common space of free movement, justice and security and referred in particular to the principles of non-discrimination and the right to have a fair hearing as well as decisions by the European Court of Justice that provide for certain basic standards[67]. The study found out that current victim compensation rules cover in principle three groups: direct and indirect victims as well as third parties (victimized through helping the victim or by official interventions aimed at helping the victim. Most systems cover all crime victims independent of nationality and residence, some requiring reciprocal victim support in case of non-EU citizens. In general a violent and/or intentional crime is required. The type of losses that can be recovered through compensation schemes concern first of all medical expenses, partially also compensation for property losses. Permanent disability is recognised by all member states as a ground for compensation. Quite significant differences can be observed as regards compensation for immaterial damages (pain and suffering). Differences are found also with respect to how the principle of subsidiarity is to be applied. A formal complaint is mostly required to be brought to the competent authorities within a defined, though varying, period

[63] Communication from the Commission to the Council, the European Parliament and the Economic and Social Committee. Crime victims in the European Union – reflexions on standards and actions. COM(1999) 349 final, 14 July 1999.
[64] OJ L 82, 22 March 2001, p. 1.
[65] Wergens, A.: Crime victims in the European Union. Brottsoffermyndigheten, Umeå 2000.
[66] Commission of the European Communities: Green Paper. Compensation to crime victims (presented by the Commission) Brussels, COM(2001) 536 final, 28 September 2001.
[67] Case 186/87 Ian William Cowan v. Trésor public [1989] European Court of Human Rights 195; Case Rolf Gustafson v. Sweden, Judgment of 27 May 1997.

of time. Almost all member states allow for advance payments. The basic legitimation for setting up victim compensation legislation throughout the European Union is seen – besides criminal policy rationales - in equity and social solidarity which constitute also the basic principles behind the 1983 European Convention on Compensation of Crime Victims. Other member states connect the need for state compensation schemes to considerations of criminal policy. While it is recognised that the one primarily responsible for compensation should be the offender it is argued everywhere that most crime victims in fact cannot get compensation from those responsible due to various reasons. The Green Paper draws from that the conclusion that the function of state compensation schemes lies in providing a safety net for victims and it is then not surprising that the general approach adopted optimizes the crime victims' rights on compensation with paying no regard at all at costs and problems coming along with such a re-distribution scheme of funds (that are borne after all by civil society through taxes).

The need to adopt a common European Union policy is justified specifically with obstacles stemming from cross border situations and related to information on the possibilities to get state compensation, to make an application for state compensation and to the necessary investigation that must follow the application. Reference is made to judicial co-operation between the member states for service of documents and for taking of evidence[68].

A resolution of the European Parliament[69] welcomes the Green Paper[70] and puts the question of victim compensation and victim support in a perspective that stresses free movement under conditions of security and justice, the heavy toll criminal victimization places on citizens of the EU, the need to recognise indirect victimization, the particular damage to victims caused by terrorism. The need for developing a common EU victim of terrorism policy is grounded on equity, solidarity and a rational crime policy that overcomes differences between the systems of crime victim compensation in the member states.

The Committee on Legal Affairs and the Internal Market for the Committee on Citizens' Freedoms and Rights, Justice and Home Affairs has evenly welcomed the Commission's Green Paper on Compensation to crime victims with declaring that the EU should adopt binding Community provisions in order to create a common area of justice for citizens who are the victims of crime. The Committee adopted the view that in order to be complete and

---

[68] 21 Council Regulation (EC) No. 1348/2000 of 29 May 2000 on the service in the member states of judicial and extrajudicial documents in civil or commercial matters, OJ L 160, 30 June 2000, p. 37. Council Regulation (EC) No. 1206/2001 of 28 May 2001 on co-operation between the courts of the member states of the European Union in the taking of evidence in civil and commercial matters, OJ L 174, 27 June 2001, p. 1.
[69] European Parliament Resolution on the Commission Green Paper on compensation to crime victims (COM(2001) 536). C5-0016/2002. 2002/2022(COS)).
[70] OJ C 125E, 27 May 2002, p. 31.

efficacious, any such compensation must cover both material and non-material damage and called on the Commission to treat as a main priority the issues relating to time-limits for submission of claims for compensation, procedural guarantees and the introduction of harmonised claim forms in all the Community languages. Furthermore, minimum requirements for subsidiary application of the state's responsibility are demanded for as well as making compensation independent from nationality. Finally, the declaration voices the opinion that a mutual assistance system must apply which compensates the problems crime victims experience in case of cross border victimisation.

In line with the preparatory work a Council Directive relating to compensation to crime victims was adopted 29 April 2004. This directive shall ensure that by 1 July 2005, each member state has a national scheme in place which guarantees fair and appropriate compensation to victims of crime. Then, the directive aims at implementing easy access to compensation in practice and regardless of where in the European Union a person becomes the victim of a crime. Implementation of this aim shall be facilitated by creating a system for co-operation between national authorities which should be operational by 1 January 2006.

The approach emerging in particular with the European Union statements and decisions is certainly in line with the traditional concept of a welfare state that tries hard to compensate all the risks individuals are faced with in modern societies and to compensate damages resulting from such risks fully. It goes beyond the conventional welfare approach with pushing compensation towards tort law and a full compensation approach that is normally justified only by a perpetrator being individually responsible for an act that causes damage to another person. Then, this approach is hardly consistent with the fact that the welfare systems in all member states are overburdened and that such systems are cut back in order to allow for new assessments of what should fall within the responsibility of the state and what should fall into the individuals' responsibility. Problems of fraud and exploitation of such compensation schemes are also hardly analyzed.

The statements and declarations consistently refer to solidarity, solidarity with individual victims of terrorist attacks as well as states falling prey to terrorism. In a declaration on Combating Terrorism the European Council responding to the Madrid massacre stresses the need to assist victims of terrorist crimes by way of adopting the Council Directive on compensation to crime victims. The Council demands then that the Commission allocates the funds available in the 2004 budget for supporting victims of terrorism. What is also mentioned concerns the need of effective protection of witnesses in terrorist cases and indirect victimization in terms of minority communities that are at risk of falling prey to a backlash after a terrorist attack[71]. In particular the latter should receive thorough attention as the backlash against minority

---

[71] See also Conclusions and Plan of Action of the Extraordinary European Council Meeting on 21 September 2001, SN 140/01, p. 4.

communities evidently is part of terrorist strategies devised to destroy social solidarity and establish a climate of fear, ethnic and religious hate favourable to the spread of violence.

In the EU Guidelines for a Common Approach to Combating Terrorism larger concepts of protection of victims are introduced with demanding for the enhancement of the capability of member states to deal with the consequences of a terrorist attack on the civilian population in the area of vulnerable infrastructure.

2.3 Experiences with Victim of Terrorism Compensation and Support Outside Europe

2.3.1 Victim of Terrorism Legislation in the United States of America

Specific victim of terrorism legislation and practice are developing in the US since the early eighties. The process is based on the conviction that although victims of terrorism have much in common with other violent crime victims and with disaster victims, they appear to experience higher levels of distress and display also different needs, partially due to the magnitude and scope of specific violent events. What is in particular stressed are those particulars which are due to the cross border or transnational character of both terrorism and victimization leading to new demands for procedure and organisation of victim relief and support schemes. In fact, the US has a rather long history of legislation to the benefit of victims of terrorism. The first law that provided federal assistance to victims of terrorism was the Hostage Relief Act of 1980, which was enacted in response to the Iranian hostage crisis. However, the Bill was enacted also in response of the treaty concluded between the US and Iran which contained a provision that barred victims from seeking tort damages in US courts against Iran. The benefits included hostages loss of income, medical expenses due to captivity, tax exemption of compensation and payments for educational expenses for a partner or a child. In particular medical compensation was accompanied by a subsidiarity clause. A second piece of legislation concerns the Victims of Terrorism Compensation Act 1986. This act applies to government employees only but is not restricted to a specific terrorist act. In addition to the benefits described above the Act awards each victim 50 US-$ for each day of captivity. Another law responded to the bombing of PanAm flight 103 and provided aid and support to all US citizens (United States Response to Terrorism Affecting Americans Abroad, Title 22, Aviation Security Improvement Act of 1990). The Oklahoma City bombing resulted in the Justice for Victims of Terrorism Act (amending Title 42 of the Antiterrorism and Effective Death Penalty Act). With this Act, federal payments to states, public agencies and NGOs for relief for terrorism victims are provided besides offering immediate crisis response efforts to the victims. The amendment provided also for the right of victims to participate in trial proceeding arising from the Oklahoma City bombing. The Antiterrorism and Effective Death Penalty Act of 1996 also contained a provision requiring state crime victim compensation programmes to include in their compensation programmes state residents who are victims of terrorism while outside of the United States.

The most recent Bill relates to the 11 September attacks and its aftermath[72]. The Victims of Terrorism Tax Relief Act provides tax relief to relatives of victims of the 11 September attacks, the Oklahoma City bombing and the anthrax attacks following 11 September. Income tax liability of a deceased victim is waived for both the year of the attack and the previous year, provides other tax exemptions. The Air Transportation Safety and System Stabilization Act of 2001 establishes a Victim Compensation Fund which addresses economic and non-economic losses but seeks also to shield in particular airlines from civil litigation[73]. An eligible claimant can receive an immediate advance payment of $ 50,000 in cases involving death or $ 25,000 in cases involving serious injury. The Act authorizes the head of the Compensation Fund to examine economic and non-economic harm suffered in light of individual circumstances. The noneconomic loss compensation is set for the spouse and each dependent of a deceased victim at $ 100,000 in addition to a $ 250,000 payment awarded on behalf of all decedents. Other payments and sources of compensation, however, are to be deducted with the exception of tax relief, Social Security benefits, workers' compensation benefits and support from charitable donations.

US legislation in the area of victims of terrorism is characterized by responding to specific acts of terrorism. However, US-American law provides also for effective civil legislation which enables victims of terrorism to sue foreign perpetrators in US federal courts and based on US tort law.

In terms of organisation and procedure the Office for Victims of Crime (OVC) plays a decisive role. In 1996, OVC was given the authority to access the Victims of Crime Act emergency reserve fund of $ 50 million to assist victims of terrorism and mass violence.

There are five types of support available from OVC to respond to terrorism and mass violence: (a) Crisis response grants; (b) consequence management grants; (c) criminal justice support grants; (d) compensation grants; and e) technical assistance/training services.

The OVC created the Terrorism and International Victims Unit (TIVU) the task of which is to help victims of terrorism, mass violence, and such international crimes as trafficking of women and children and child abduction. Moreover, the administration of the international terrorism victims compensation programme is entrusted to the unit as is the maintenance of

---

[72] Peck, R.S.: The Victim Compensation Fund: Born from a Unique Confluence of Events Not Likely to Be Duplicated. DePaul Law Review 53(2003), S. 209-30.
[73] Mariani, R.L.: The September 11th Victim Compensation Fund of 2001 and the Protection of the Airline Industry: A Bill for the American People. Journal of Air Law and Commerce 57(2002), S. 141-186; the final rules governing the Victim Compensation Fund of 2001 were published on 6 March 2002 (P.L. 107-42).

an International Crime Victim Compensation Programme Directory in collaboration with the State Department that links victims abroad to available resources and lists crime victim compensation programmes in various foreign countries in an attempt to deal effectively with international terrorism affecting citizens at home and abroad. The OVC has issued guidelines to provide compensation and assistance to victims of acts of terrorism or mass violence within the United States and assistance to US citizens and government employees who are victims of terrorism and mass violence abroad.

The specific victim of terrorism programmes are built on federal and state law – emerging parallel to European developments since the early eighties - that assigns certain responsibilities and duties to agencies involved in investigating and prosecuting crime with respect to crime victims. The rights to be respected and services to be provided concern identifying the victims, providing them with information on the availability of medical, psychological counselling, compensation and restitution, providing information about the status of the criminal investigation and later the prosecution of the criminal case against the suspects, facilitating victim participation in the criminal case through trial attendance, and presenting impact information (Victim impact statements) during the sentencing part of the trial.

The US thus have adopted an individualized approach which is focussed on specific terrorist attacks. With that flexibility is adopted as is the possibility to consider various and differing (political and economic) goals when deciding whether and to what extent victim of terrorism legislation should be enacted to respond to terrorist attacks. The basic problem then concerns control of discretion and implementation of equal treatment[74].

The US approach to compensation to victims of terrorism has not only been criticized because of problems of equal treatment. Critic has been voiced also as regards its guiding principles that tend to be rather close to tort law principles and go away from a support and social welfare approach[75].

2.3.2 Israel

Israel certainly is a country which has experienced mass violence, terrorism and war in abundance over the last four decades. Insofar it does not come as surprise that Israel has collected also vast experiences with legislative and practical efforts to cope with problems of victimization through terrorism and various forms of collective violence. The Israeli legislator has in fact devised comprehensive legislative responses to two of the primary issues arising in the context of compensation for harm caused by terrorism: first, the Victims of Hostile Action (Pensions) Law, 1970 provides compensation for

---

[74] See for example Shapo, M.S.: Compensation for Victims of Terror: A Specialized Jurisprudence of Injuries. Indiana Law Review 36(2003), pp. 237-249.
[75] Diller, M.: Tort and Social Welfare Principles in the Victim Compensation Fund. DePaul Law Review 53(2003), pp. 719-768.

bodily injuries suffered in terrorist attacks, as well as compensation for family members of deceased victims. Second, the Property Tax and Compensation Fund Law, 1961 provides compensation for property damage caused by terrorism[76]. The Israeli system is a permanent compensation system emerging out of the political will that damages caused by war shall be borne by the whole public respectively public funds and not by individuals suffering such damages. This approach was then expanded to cover victims of terrorism. The compensation system therefore is justified with the principle of solidarity and the recognition that general risks such as war, collective violence and terrorism must be borne by the general public. While historically risks stemming from war were considered to be restricted to members of military forces or warring factions such differences cannot play a role anymore since World War II and subsequent wars which have shown drastically that the main toll of losses in human life and property will be borne by civil society and not by the military. Terrorism - when drawing a parallel to war – targets and drags random civilians into violence and makes them (and the whole of civil society) involuntary draftees in a war that has been called small or private war. Israeli law makes no distinction between civilians harmed by war and civilians harmed by terrorism. Both are addressed as suffering from "enemy-inflicted injury" (which encompasses also losses due to "friendly fire"). As do specific US laws Israeli law covers Israeli citizens falling prey to terrorism at home and abroad. Foreign nationals (having entered Israeli territory legally) are covered when victimized on Israel territory. Providing evidence is facilitated through a presumption of a hostile act given a reasonable basis to assume such act. Benefits drawn from compensation and support schemes are administered by The National Insurance Institute. Compensation includes costs incurred for medical care as well as living stipends while in medical treatment. Financial support is calculated on the basis of the victims' pre-victimization income. Besides medical expenses the law compensates for a range of other Family members of victims are treated as are treated family members of military forces who died in the line of duty. In case several options for compensation are available the victim has the choice. The compensation for property loss is also seen as an extension to compensation schemes established for losses due to war. The system applicable to property damage underwent changes from an insurance model to a social support system. The law covers direct and indirect damages to property (excluding, however, those damages that are general consequences of an economy deteriorating after major terrorist attacks). Difficulties may arise out of distinctions to be made between hostile acts and mere acts of violence (or property crime). The applicant has to provide for evidence as regards a hostile motive.

---

[76] Sommer, H.: Providing Compensation for Harm Caused by Terrorism: Lessons Learned in the Israeli Experience. Indiana Law Review 335 (2003).

3. Country reports

3.1 Introductory notes

The country reports have been structured along information on specific regulation relating to victims of terrorism and particular regimes established for victims of terrorism. Protection and assistance (including judicial procedure) should be covered as well as compensation rules and information on national victim support associations or services. In case no particular regime was available for victims of terrorism information should be provided as regards the situation and practice in the field of protection and assistance outside the context of the judicial procedure on compensation and support for terrorism victims. The research for information was based on the five questions set by the Group of Specialists.

Due to the short time given for the preparation of this survey, no – or no reliable – information could be obtained from the following six Council of Europe member states: Albania, Andorra, Latvia, Monaco, San Marino and "The former Yugoslav Republic of Macedonia".

3.2 Member states of the Council of Europe

3.2.1 Armenia

Specific legislation related to victims of terrorism does not exist. According to the Armenian Code of Criminal Procedure (Section 20, Articles 154-164) victims of terrorism can apply for compensation of damages caused by a criminal act.

3.2.2 Austria

The Austrian system of crime victim compensation does not provide for particular rules or regimes for victims of terrorism. However, the general system that is in place to provide relief, support and protection for victims of violent crime covers also terrorist acts and their consequences. In addition, Austria has a public crime victim compensation programme, based on the Victim Support Act (VOG)[77] which provides financial compensation to victims of serious (violent) crime who have suffered physical/mental injuries. Family members are eligible for compensation in case of violence resulting in murder as are citizens of other EU countries (if Austrian citizens are covered by the respective states compensation scheme, too). There are no statutory maximum limits to compensation. Benefits drawn from the programme cover medical expenses, lost income, lost maintenance (in case of relatives of murder victims). As a result of the 2004 amendment to the Pension and Maintenance Act[78], the costs for psychotherapy will be covered in the future

---

[77] *Verbrechensopfergesetz über die Gewährung von Hilfeleistungen an Opfer von Verbrechen (VOG)* of 9 June 1972, Bundesgesetzblatt [official journal] No. 288.
[78] *Versorgungsrechtsänderungsgesetz*, 2004 (VRÄG 2004).

as well. Advance compensation to victims of crime was introduced 1978 in the Code of Criminal Procedure. Conditions for advance payment are so strict that in practice virtually no use is made of advance benefits. The programme is funded through criminal fines and other (public) sources.

The compensation programme is administered by the Federal Social Welfare Office (*Bundessozialamt*) which receives applications by victims and reviews the applications.

In terms of NGOs, the "*Weisser Ring*" is the most important victim support organisation which is engaged in compensation but also in providing for legal advice and general information.

As regards the position in criminal proceedings the crime victim under certain conditions has the right to actively participate in criminal proceedings and to be represented by a lawyer (Sec. 50-1 Criminal Procedural Code). Costs for legal representation, however, must be borne by the victim. Criminal procedure amendments of 1987 and 1993 introduced statutory duties of criminal justice agencies to provide for information on victims rights (rights to participate, date and place of trial, compensation) and protective devices for vulnerable witnesses in the form of video transmitted witness interrogation (in case in particular of vulnerable victims of sexual crimes and abuse) and the anonymous witness (to be protected against intimidation and violent retaliation). Compensation within the framework of criminal proceedings is dependent on a victim joining criminal proceedings in an active role (as a civil claimant).

3.2.3 Azerbaijan

Azerbaijan has enacted legislation as regards terrorism which includes compensation for victims of terrorism. According to the Law Against Terrorism of 18 June 1999, social rehabilitation measures are provided for victims of terrorist acts. Social rehabilitation comprises judicial assistance, medical and psychological support and assistance in finding employment and accommodation. The cost for social rehabilitation are borne by the federal budget of the Republic of Azerbaijan.

3.2.4 Belgium

In the Belgium justice system a special programme for victims of terrorist acts has not been established. A general statutory crime victim regime applies (Victim of Violent Crime Compensation Act of 1985) which offers compensation to victims of (intentional) violent crime that has been committed on Belgium territory. There are exemptions from eligibility for negligent manslaughter, property crime and traffic offences. Foreign citizens are covered by the programme if they are legal residents. The compensation programme covers medical expenses, income loss, disability benefits (also to relatives taking care of victims of violence or dependent relatives of deceased victims) but does not award advance payments. The programme's sources are public (partially criminal fines collected by the state).

As regards NGOs, private victim support groups started to receive public funding from the eighties on. In the Flemish-speaking part of Belgium it is the organisation "Victim Support Flanders" (*Slachtofferhulp Vlaanderen*) which is providing for support for victims. In the French-speaking region victim support groups are integrated into the existing services for offenders (*aide sociale aux justiciables*). At the level of municipal police victim units exist through which police should provide information and practical aid. Furthermore victims must be referred by such police units to victim support or social service organisations. Within the prosecutor's offices and the courts 'reception and information services for victims' (*slachtofferonthaal op de parketten en rechtbanken, accueil des victimes dans les tribunaux et parquets*) have been established. Moreover, a National Forum on Victim Policy (*Nationaal Forum voor Slachtofferbeleid*) was founded in 16 June 1994, which has the task of co-ordinating the community-based victim policies and making recommendations to the Minister of Justice.

A 1998 procedural code amendment demands that victims of crimes must be dealt with respect and provided with information on victim support and compensation. Victims have now the right to have themselves registered as injured persons which results in the right to be informed on certain aspects of criminal proceedings as well as the right to demand for additional investigation. A 1992 amendment to the Police Act requires that police has to inform crime victims about their rights and available victim support. The Victim of Violence Compensation Act of 1985 has been amended in 1997 and 2003. Application procedures have been facilitated and maximum benefits have been increased. Financial compensation is dependent on the victim joining criminal proceedings as a civil claimant and is excluded if the victim receives compensation by the offender or insurance. Compensation covers permanent or temporary disability, immaterial damages, medical expenses, loss of income, costs stemming from the trial itself. Compensation is finally dependent on the financial situation of the victim.

Privacy protection is mainly achieved through holding the trial in camera. A strict ban on publication introduced through the 1989 Act on Sexual Offences is restricted to the identity of victims of sexual crimes.

3.2.5 Bosnia and Herzegovina

In Bosnia and Herzegovina no specific legal provisions related to victims of terrorism exist. The general legal rules related to compensation are applicable for victims of terrorism as for victims of crime in general.

When it comes to protection and assistance outside of the context of judicial procedure, it should be noted that in post-war ages, the NGO sector has been developing in two main directions. Firstly, due to the 1992-1995 war, the population of Bosnia and Herzegovina has been seriously victimized as a consequence of numerous war crimes. This caused direct as well as indirect victims among which men as well as women and children could be found. In order to get organised on local or regional level the forming of very specific NGOs came up on a sector being pretty much focused on coping with traumas from the war. The second direction was caused by democratization processes and a need for fight for the human rights of specific categories of population, such as disabled persons, children, women etc.

On the other side, despite the fact that during the last 10 years Bosnia and Herzegovina had experienced some criminal events that were at the time characterized as terrorist attacks of a local scale (without an international dimension) there is no specific NGO that within its mission statement focuses specially on victims of terrorism. Nevertheless all kinds of support, counselling etc. are provided also for victims of terrorism by the existing NGOs.

Regarding compensational matters, the procedure in Bosnia and Herzegovina is defined within The Laws on Obligations (entity level[79]) and within the Civil Procedure Codes (entity levels) and Criminal Procedure Laws (on both state and entity level).

According to these laws, a victim, or any other authorized (entitled) person, can submit a request for compensation within a criminal or a civil procedure. However, due to the fact that the procedure is clearly defined within the Laws on Obligations, the request will be discussed and decided upon based on the provisions of that law, regardless whether the request is submitted to a criminal or to a civil court. If the request is submitted to a criminal court, that court can, but does not have to, decide about the compensation request. If the court decides not to discuss about the request in the course of criminal proceedings (because discussing about it would unnecessarily prolong the criminal proceedings e.g.) the criminal court is obliged to inform the victim that the request can be submitted to a civil court as a civil claim.

The law of Bosnia and Herzegovina provides for compensation with regard to material (funeral costs, medical care and other treatments related to medical treatment, loss of income) as well as non-material damage (fear, physical or psychological pain).

In case of the death of the victim compensation can be awarded to the marital partner, the children and parents for psychological pain they suffered; brothers and sisters and the victim's life partner (even if they were not formally married) can apply under the condition that they lived together with the deceased victim in the same household. The same provision applies to the legal successors but only as far as it is clearly stated within a court's decision.

---

[79] Federation of Bosnia and Herzegovina, Republica Srpska and Brcko District of Bosnia and Herzegovina.

The victim itself will be compensated by the offender. The state represented by its official institutions and organs can be obliged to compensate a victim only if victimization is the result of a misconduct from the state.

Special funds for compensation, that could be used in cases where an offender is not known or where an offender does not have resources to compensate a victim, do not exist in Bosnia and Herzegovina.

3.2.6 Bulgaria

Under Bulgarian criminal legislation no specific regimes concerning victims of terrorism exist. The Code of Criminal Procedure allows for the anonymous witness (Article 97a) and witness protection programmes. The crime victim in general has the right to join criminal proceedings with a civil law suit against the accused.

Establishing a compensation scheme is evidently seen as resulting in an economic burden too heavy in face of the poor economic situation of the country. Furthermore, a working group has been established in the Ministry of Justice which deals with adjusting legislation to the needs coming with entering the European Union. The working group will discuss also the victim related European Union framework decisions.

3.2.7 Croatia

In 2003 Croatia has adopted a Law on the responsibility for Damage caused by Terrorist Acts and Public Demonstrations[80]. This act regulates the responsibility for damages caused by terrorist acts and other acts of violence which is exerted with the aim to disturb seriously public order by intimidating and spreading the feeling of insecurity among the public and during demonstrations or riots in public places. Croatia with this act has accepted to be liable for damages caused by terrorism and public demonstrations on the basis of social solidarity, an equal distribution of a public burden and the principle of fair and prompt compensation. Compensation is not dependent on identification, prosecution or conviction of the offender. Victims eligible for compensation include direct victims of terrorist violence as well as those who suffered losses as a consequence of preventing or helping the victim of violence.

Croatia has enacted legislation aiming at protection of vulnerable witnesses[81]. The law puts into force a witness protection programme designed to counter intimidation and retaliation coming with organised crime or other serious crime (including terrorism). Inclusion in the programme is made dependent on the willingness of the witness and an assessment of the

---

[80] Official Journal No. 117/03.
[81] Witness Protection Act, Official Journal, No. 163/03, in force since 1st January 2004.

specific vulnerability. Moreover, the criminal procedural act was amended several times in order to allow for protection of vulnerable witnesses and victims during trial proceedings. This includes anonymity of witnesses and testimony through a video link.

Private victim support organisations exist.

3.2.8 Cyprus

Cyprus has no specific regulations as regards victims of terrorism. Moreover, compensation of crime victims is not well developed. Compensation is available within criminal proceedings as a penal sanction and can be imposed by the court. In practice, victims are evidently rarely compensated. Police have no special duties as regards, e.g., information of crime victims. Victims, however, can sue the offender before a civil court. Legal aid provisions do not exist for victims of crime, nor exist state compensation schemes.

National victim support services are not available in Cyprus.

Particular rules devised to protect the victim during trial proceedings have been enacted as part of conventional criminal procedural provisions that allow under certain circumstances to hold trials in camera.

Witness protection programmes have not been introduced until now. Protective measures as regards victims so far are restricted to victims of domestic violence.

3.2.9 Czech Republic

The Czech Republic has a statutory crime victim compensation programme to provide financial compensation to victims of violent crime. Victims of terrorist acts are not mentioned but they fall under the rules of compensation as far as violent victimization is concerned. Victims of violent crime who have suffered physical injury and family members of murder victims are eligible for benefits awarded according to the Compensation Act[82]Law. Applicants must be either citizens of the Czech Republic or foreigners authorized to stay permanently in the territory of the Czech Republic. Foreign nationals are eligible for compensation only if this is provided for by an international agreement. Following submission of the application and appropriate documentation of the case and the damages resulting from violence the Ministry of Justice must decide on compensation with a period of three months. The law does not set maximum limits to compensation. Medical expenses and loss of maintenance are covered.

---

[82] Act No. 209/1997 Coll., on Provision of Financial Aid to Victims of Crimes and on Amendments of Some Other Related Acts.

Further rights and protection measures for victims of crime are provided in Sec. 43 et seq. of the Code of Criminal Procedure[83].

In terms of victim support associations, a partner organisation of the "*Weisser Ring*", named *Bily Kruh Bezpeci*, operates nationwide.

3.2.10 Denmark

Denmark has not enacted specific legislation as regards compensation of victims of terrorist acts. Denmark, however, has a crime victim compensation programme to provide financial compensation to victims of violent crime. Eligible for compensation are victims of crime themselves, dependents of homicide victims, foreign citizens victimized in Denmark and Danish citizens victimized abroad. There is no maximum award limit for compensation which covers medical expenses (including mental health and rehabilitation costs), income losses due to disability resulting from the crime. Other damage may be compensated but is restricted to some 1000 Danish Kroner. Advance payments are not available. The programme is funded through the state budget. Decisions on applications are taken by a special compensation board which is chaired by a judge.

The National Association for the Support of Victims of Violence (LHV) offers assistance and support throughout the country.

3.2.11 Estonia

Estonia has no specific legislation related to victims of terrorism. On 1st February 2004, a (general) Victim Support Act (VSA) was enacted in Estonia which provides for state compensation to victims of crime. According to Article 8 of the VSA, victims of terrorism and their dependants, as any victim of a violent crime, are entitled to protection, assistance and compensation. According to Article 7 of the VSA, compensation shall be paid to Estonian citizens and citizens of the European Union or a state which is a party to the European Convention on Compensation of Victims of Violent Crimes, or to a refugee. Compensation under the VSA is restricted to violent acts being committed within the territory of Estonia. It covers expenses for medical treatment, damage arising from incapacity for work, all medical expenses and funeral costs. Furthermore, up to ten sessions of psychological counselling and up to fifteen sessions of psychotherapy are paid as well.

The amount of compensation shall be 70 % of the material damage and not exceed a total of 50,000 kroons (~3,200 EUR). The compensation for dependents of a victim who dies as a result of a crime of violence shall receive compensation based on the victim's previous income: 75 % of the income in the case of one dependent; 85 % in the case of two dependents; 100 % in the case of three or more dependents.

---

[83] Act No. 141/1961 Coll., on Proceeding in Courts of Justice, as amended.

According to the § 3 of the VSA, public victim support service is aiming at maintaining or enhancing the coping ability of persons who have fallen victim to negligence, mistreatment or physical, mental or sexual abuse. Victim support services consist of providing counselling and assistance to victims (including indirect victims) in communicating with state and local government authorities and legal persons, providing information and necessary aid (e.g., taking the person to psychologist). A network of victim support services was created at the beginning of 2005. Currently, 35 specially trained officials hired in the police prefectures are providing help and information to the victims of crime. Besides they need to develop the network including rescue officials, social and health care workers, child care workers, volunteers etc. The victim support services shall be regional-based. The Ministry of Social Affairs, in co-operation with state and local government authorities and legal persons is in charge for providing victim support services and for the supervision of the victim support volunteers and the organisation of training for such volunteers.

3.2.12 Finland

Finland has not enacted victim of terrorism compensation legislation. Finland operates a crime victim compensation programme which responds to victims of violent crime. Terrorist offences and victimization due to terrorism thus fall under the rule of the Finnish compensation programme. Those eligible concern crime victims, descendents/dependents of deceased victims of violence, foreign nationals victimized in Finland and Finnish citizens victimized abroad.

The programme is administered by the Treasury and Social Insurance organisations. There exist limits for the maximum amounts awarded under the programme for different damages. Compensation covers medical expenses, income loss due to disability, maintenance for dependents, items destroyed by the crime itself and legal aid costs (arising out of the attempt to sue the offender). Advance payments can be made under restrictive conditions. The programme is funded by tax money.

3.2.13 France

France has created specific legislation as regards compensation of victims of terrorism. It is justified with a need of "national solidarity" as well as needs of victims to experience moral support and material compensation. Besides that France has established also a crime victim compensation programme to provide financial compensation to victims of general crimes.

For victims of terrorism the Law of 1990 amending the terrorism Act of 1986 assigns victims of terrorism the status of victims of war and draws with that conclusions about the character of national (and international) terrorism[84]. In 1986 the FGTI (*indemnisation intégrale des victimes du terrorisme par un "Fonds de Garantie"*[85] was founded which allows for compensation of victims of terrorism on the basis of funds collected through property insurance taxes. The Fund succeeds into the rights of the victim against the perpetrator with compensating the victim.

Through enactment of a law of 30 December 1986 terrorist acts from 1st January 1985 on are covered by this type of compensation. With the amendment of 23 January 1990 all victims of terrorism are assigned the status of civil war victims (Article 26). The status is assigned retroactively to all victims of terrorism since 1st January 1982.

Full compensation is the consequence of personal injury or death caused by an act of terrorism which occurred either on French territory or, in the case of French nationals, outside France. Victims of crime, dependents of victims, foreign citizen (when violence occurred in France and the foreigner stayed legally in France) are eligible for compensation. Compensation (which is not statutorily limited) covers medical expenses, pain and suffering, income losses, rehabilitation, maintenance, vocational training and rehabilitation. Advance payments are possible.

The procedure is dependent on whether the case involves a victim of terrorism or a victim of other crimes.

In case of a victim of terrorism the "*Fond de Garantie*" is the addressee of an application which will be handled in amicable proceedings. The assignment of a civil victim of war result in some privileges that are available also for descendents of deceased victims and their partners (Widow of war).

In case of a victim of ordinary crime a formal (judicial) procedure is to be followed starting with an application for compensation at the Commission for Compensation of Crime Victims. Almost all crimes may be compensated, however, acts of terrorism, acts committed during hunting and traffic accidents are excluded from this type of procedure. The applicant has to provide evidence of the act itself. The conditions under which property crime can be compensated are restrictive (requiring, e.g., low monthly income etc.).

In 2004, the *Fond de Garantie* has paid approximately 200 million € compensating victims of crime and terrorism and has recovered some 32 million € from perpetrators.

There are NGOs which deal with crime victims. It is in particular *S.O.S. Attentats* which plays an important role. This organisation has also the right

---

[84] Law No. 90-589 of 6 July 1990, Articles 13, 14 and 18, *Journal Officiel* of 11 July 1990, in force 1st January 1991.
[85] Law of 9 September 1986.

to participate in trials against terrorists as a civil party (*partie civile*) alongside the victim (Article 2-9 of the Criminal Procedural Code). *S.O.S Attentats* lobbies for an International Compensation Fund for Victims of Terrorism.

3.2.14 Georgia

The national law has no specific provisions, neither in relation to victims of terrorism nor to victims in general. Decisions on possible assistance and compensation are made in every particular case according to the available means.

3.2.15 Germany

Germany has not enacted special legislation on compensation for victims of terrorism. However, a crime victim compensation programme to provide financial compensation to victims of violent crime exists which covers also victims of violent terrorist offences. The Crime Victims Compensation Act (*Opferentschädigungsgesetz*)[86] was enacted in 1976 and is restricted to crimes of violence. Beneficiaries are victims of violent crime (in case of foreign nationals who have no legal status of residence in Germany, reciprocal agreements or laws are required) and – if victims are deceased – dependent family members. No maximum award limits are established by the Compensation Law which allows for covering medical expenses, vocational rehabilitation, loss of income or maintenance. The Compensation Act makes reference to the Federal Maintenance Law (*Bundesversorgungsgesetz*)[87] which has been created to accommodate victims of war (and their dependents). Compensation of victims of violent crime is state funded; advance payments are not available.

There is one serious practical problem which may arise when a compensation claim is filed: the allocation of evidence. Following a general principle within social law, the claimant has to provide all necessary evidence for all facts that found the claim. This includes the precondition that the crime has to be committed intentionally. Court practise has shown a certain restrictive tendency to affirm this fact in cases where an offender remained unknown[88]. However, as regards at least terrorist attack cases, it is hardly imaginable that authorities or courts would deny a claim for compensation based on the ground that the intentional character of such a crime cannot be established – even if no particular offender(s) responsible for that crime has been identified.

---

[86] *Opferentschädigungsgesetz (OEG)* of 15 May 1976 (BGBl. I, p. 1181) as amended by the first Amendment Act of 7 January 1985 (BGBl. I, p. 2)), the second Amendment Act of 21 July 1993 (BGBl. I, p. 1262) and the Immigrations Act of 30 July 2004 (BGBl. I, p. 1950).

[87] *Bundesversorgungsgesetz* of 20 December 1950, BGBl. I, p.791.

[88] For further details on this problem, compare Kilchling, M. & Kaiser, M.: Germany, in: D. Greer (ed.), Compensating Crime Victims. A European Survey, Freiburg i. Br. 1996, pp. 255-297.

In principle, state compensation under the Crime Victim Compensation Act is limited to violent offences committed within the German territory (including ships and aircrafts). Damages resulting from a terrorist attack abroad are, therefore, not covered. At the occasion of the *Djerba* attack of 2002 which killed and wounded seriously some 20 German citizens the Federal Government provided for support and compensation (although there was no statutory duty to do so). The generous intervention of the government can rather be explained by the publicity such acts of compensation most likely draw. They are evidently subject to problems of equal treatment.

Recent amendments of the criminal procedural code introduced the anonymous witness, protection of vulnerable witnesses (in particular victims of sexual crimes and children) as well as a witness protection programme (as part of action taken against transnational organised crime).

There exists a range of some 400-500 NGOs dealing with crime victims, most of them small groups of voluntaries operating on the regional or local level. The most important nationwide association is the so-called "*Weisser Ring*" which in the meantime has partner organisations in several other EU countries.

3.2.16 Greece

A general crime victim compensation programme does not exist in Greece. Although the country has signed the respective European Convention on the Compensation of Victims of Violent Crimes it was not yet ratified. Currently, new legislation on the establishment of a general victim compensation programme is under preparation. In deviance from this general situation, victims of terrorism enjoy significant legal protection. Law no. 2928/2001 provides the possibility to take extraordinary measures in order to keep the victims appearing as witnesses away from revenge or intimidation by terrorists. Also in terms of state compensation, several laws offer a great variety of possibilities how victims are being supported. A state fund for victims of terrorism was established as well as a special victim support service for victims of terrorism.

In concrete terms, Law No. 1897/1990 provides that public officials and employees within the public service are granted a full pension as far as they have become completely or partially disabled to work by a terrorist attack (Article 1). In case of their death the entitlement to a pension is transferred to the widow and the children (Article 2). Furthermore, other forms of financial support are guaranteed for the victim as well as for the spouse and the children. The state also covers the costs for medical treatment and care. Article 10, finally, grants certain preferences and privileges for the children whose parents have died or become to 100 percent disabled as a result of a terrorist attack; these include, in particular, registration at a university nearby their place of residence, and the option to enter the public service as an employee. These options are unique and unparalleled among all Council of

Europe member states; they were made applicable retrospectively for all terrorist events since 24 July 1974[89].

In the subsequent years, the option to join the public service has been further extended. Spouses and children of a Greek citizen who has died or become unable to work by a terrorist attack have to be employed in the public service. The only precondition is that they have to pass a written test. Access is, in principle, independent from the budgeted and available number of jobs. If there exists no vacant position such a position related to the person is either to be created[90] or the candidates are to be ranked with a priority-scale in the waiting list of people who are to be employed next[91].

By several amendments, the rules for pensions were improved for victims of terrorism as well. The pension of persons disabled to work is calculated at a base wage of 35 years of employment[92]. And since 1993, the family members who receive survivors' pension must no longer be financially dependent on the deceased victim of terrorism in order to receive such a pension[93]. Apart from these payments, all kinds of material damage is being compensated as well[94]. In this context, not only material loss but also any kind of medical treatment and health care is covered by the state. Self-employees and entrepreneurs being victims of a terrorist crime enjoy social assurance premiums[95] and better conditions if they need a credit for loss caused by the terrorist crime[96].

General legal protection for witnesses or victims has not been enacted yet. However, some conventional instruments such as, e.g., the possibility of a victim to participate as a civil party in criminal proceedings, are available. Furthermore, there are also no nationwide operating victim support services in existence. However, local initiatives take care of domestic violence and victims of terrorism and torture. In addition to these groups, a private association of victims of terrorism named *Thanos Axarlian* exists.

3.2.17 Hungary

Hungary to date has not enacted formal legislation on the compensation of victims of crime. In fact, however, victims of violent crime – including terrorist acts – can apply for compensation which is being granted based on a governmental ordinance[97]. It provides for compensation in the case of death or grave injuries. Eligible for application are the victims themselves as well

---

[89] Compare Article 32 of Law No. 1968/1991, through which Law No. 1897/1990 was extended accordingly.
[90] Article 20 s. 21 of Law No. 27/1999.
[91] Article 9 s. 2 of Law No. 3189/2003.
[92] Law No. 1977/1991.
[93] Article 10 of Law No. 2163/1993.
[94] Article 18 of Law No. 2093/1992.
[95] E.g., through Article 15 of Law No. 2042/1992.
[96] Ministerial decision No. 2042120/7361/0025 (1991) of the Ministry of Finances.
[97] Governmental ordinance No. 209/2001 (X.31).

as relatives in the direct line (plus foster children and foster parents as well as life partners) who have been living in the victim's household. It includes Hungarian citizens as well as EU citizens and immigrants and refugees with a legal status. The compensation, however, is restricted to offences that have been committed later than 7 July 1999 on Hungarian territory. Not enough, the compensation under the present rules underlies the principle of social need that is granted to persons with low income and wealth. The application has to be filed to the National Fund for Victims of Crime.

The present situation regarding victim compensation is deemed insufficient. In order to improve the legal options for compensation and to comply with the Council of Europe and European Union standards, a general victim protection act is under parliamentary preparation. Currently there is still a dispute between the Minister of Justice of the Minister of Home Affairs about the political and legislative responsibility.

Unlike in the field of compensation, protection of victims of crime has been comprehensively regulated in the criminal procedural code[98], a special ordinance on witness protection[99] and an additional law on the participation in criminal proceedings[100]. By this so-called 'triad' of regulation, a complex system of regulations has been enacted which provides for an effective protection of victims and indirect victims during their role as witnesses.

Also in terms of victim support associations, Hungary has quite a number of NGOs who are providing help for victims of crime. Most of these are working on the local level. There is also a nationwide acting national branch of the "*Weisser Ring*" which is named *Fehér Gyürü* in Hungary.

3.2.18 Iceland

Iceland has established a statutory compensation programme for victims of violent crime in 1995, but has no legislation in the field of victims of terrorism. According to this act compensation claims are dealt with by a "Committee on Criminal Damages" (whose members are appointed by the Minister of Justice). The statute restricts compensation to damages suffered from violent crime (including immaterial damage and – to a limited extent – property damage resulting from the offence). Damage to property is compensated if the perpetrator was under care or supervision of the state at the time when the offence was committed. All types of compensation are limited.

NGOs which provide support for all crime victims do not exist. There are specialized services for victims of sexual crimes.

---

[98] Articles 81-82 and 95-98 of the code of criminal procedure: Be. 1998. évi XIX. törvény.
[99] Governmental ordinance No. 34/1999 (II.26).
[100] Law No. 2001. évi LXXXV. Törvény.

The crime victim can join criminal proceedings as a civil party. Victims of sexual crimes and violent crimes have the right to free legal assistance. However, no rules provide for general duties to inform, advise etc. victims of crime nor do rules exist that provide for protection of witnesses or victims.

3.2.19 Ireland

Ireland has no specific legislation or programmes for victims of terrorism but covers such victims by a general compensation scheme for victims of violent crimes. The programme is not based on a statute and is administered by the Criminal Injuries Compensation Tribunal (which deals also with compensation of police and prison officers who had been victimized in the line of duty). Victims of violent crime (including foreign nationals) or – in case of a deceased victim – the dependents may apply for state compensation. No compensation is paid for pain and suffering. Compensation covers medical expenses, loss of income, loss of maintenance (for dependents), rehabilitation in case of disability. No maximum limit applies. Advance payments are not available.

Ireland has adopted a (non-statutory) Charter for Victims of Crime which contains standards for the treatment of victims in legal proceedings and crime investigation. However, several pieces of legislation introduced protective devices such as CCTV transmission of interrogations of vulnerable witnesses.

3.2.20 Italy

Italy has had special provisions for the compensation of victims of terrorism for several decades. In 1990, a special compensation programme for victims of terrorism and organised crime was established by Act No. 302 (*"Norme a favore della vittime del terrorismo e della criminalità organizzata"*)[101] through which earlier decrees and laws issued in the 1970s and 80s were amended and partly replaced. In 1998[102] and 2000[103], further provisions were introduced. Compensation covered personal injuries leading to disability that reduces the capacity to work by at least 25% and support for dependents if the act has resulted in the death of the victim.

In 2004, the state compensation was significantly extended with special regard to victims of terrorism and related assassinating acts by Act No. 206 (*"Nuove norme in favore della vittime del terrorismo e delle stragi di tale matrice"*)[104]. Now, any degree of disability whatsoever is sufficient for a disability pension. Based on the principle according to which an annual pension of 2,000 € is granted per one percent of disability, victims can

---

[101] Act No. 302 of 20 October 1990, Gazzetta ufficiale of 25 October, No. 250.
[102] Act No. 407 of 23 November 1998, Gazzetta uffiziale of 26 November, No. 277.
[103] Article 82 of Act No. 388 of 23 December 2000.
[104] Act No. 206 of 3 August 2004, Gazzetta ufficiale of 11 August, No. 187.

receive a maximum pension of 200,000 € per year[105]; if the victim is disabled to 80 percent or more, the pension is transferred to the relatives without reduction in case of the death of the victim. The relatives of the victim receive an additional personal subsidy of 1,033 € per month each[106]. In the case of the death of the victim, the spouse and any descendent who has been living in the victim's household get their additional subsidies for another 2 years[107]. It has to be noted in this context that, according to the general principles, an additional 13th regular instalment is being remitted per year. Furthermore, the pension is income tax-free for the victim, and the pensions of the relatives are 'tax-neutral', i.e., it is not counted in the calculation of the individual tax rate according to the progressive income tax table.

Victims of terrorism and their relatives are, finally, exempt from all major types of further taxes and fees[108]; this includes all taxes for administrative acts (such as stamp tax and transaction tax) and fees for civil, administrative and criminal trials in connection with matters resulting from the original injury. And they enjoy medical care (including psychotherapy), medicine and other medical aid and instruments free of charge.

The decision on compensation is prepared by a medical and a compensation committee; the final decision is made by the ministry of the interior. It has to be issued no later than 4 months after the application was made[109]. Advance payments can be granted by the Compensation Committee. Such advance payments must not be paid back in case compensation is ultimately not awarded. Foreign nationals are eligible in case the crime occurred on Italian territory. Italian nationals may be compensated for terrorist or organised crime that occurred outside the territory. The extended provisions for victims of terrorism introduced by the 2004 Act, however, retrospectively apply only for those terrorist events abroad that took place since 1st January 2003 (which, by the way, has the effect that these improvements would not apply for victims of the 11 September attacks of 2001); terrorist events inside Italy are retrospectively included in the extended state compensation since 1961[110]. And with regard to this retrospective scope of application, earlier determined cases are subject to be adjusted according to the new rules.

Italy also provides for particular protection in case of organised crime. Such measures amount to full blown witness protection programmes.

General victim support organisations do not exist on a national level. However, a range of local and regional organisations provide for support and help for victims. A special association named *"Associazione vittime del*

---

[105] Article 5-1 of Act No. 206 of 2004.
[106] Article 5-3 of Act No. 206.
[107] Article 5-4 of Act No. 206.
[108] Article 8 to 10 of Act No. 206.
[109] Article 14 of Act No. 206.
[110] Article 15-1 of Act No. 206.

terrorismo" cares especially for the interests of the victims of terrorism. Apart from their role as political interest groups, such NGOs may join criminal proceedings in specific cases as civil party or as simple participants.

3.2.21 Liechtenstein

Liechtenstein has not implemented yet explicit legislation that provides for support, protection or compensation, neither for victims of terrorism nor for victims of ordinary crime.

Currently, a general victim compensation act is under legislation[111]. It aims at granting, on a subsidiary basis, state compensation to all victims of intentional committed violent crimes. That would include victims of terrorist acts as well. The principles of compensation as well as the procedural rules according to which compensation claims shall be handled in the future, are rather similar to the system enacted in Switzerland.

NGOs in the area of victim support are restricted to specific victims groups such as victims of domestic violence.

3.2.22 Lithuania

Lithuania has not enacted specific provisions related to victims of terrorism. However, several national laws determine rights and grounds for relief to victims, in general. They have the same legal status as provided in the code of criminal procedure for victims of crime in general. Additionally, article 107 allows for voluntary compensation at any stage of prosecution by the offender (suspect or accused) for any loss of the victim. If the damage is not voluntarily compensated, Article 110 provides that the victim can charge the offender with a civil suit for material and non-material harm, be it a direct or an indirect consequence.

Article 118 stipulates that, if the offender is not able to reimburse the damage suffered by the victim, the state can provide for compensation in advance. This provision does, however, not grant an original claim against the state. A new piece of legislation that will provide for independent state compensation for victims of violent crimes, is presently in preparation.

In 1996 the Parliament of Lithuania (*Seimas*) had adopted a law on the protection of officers of justice and parties during criminal investigations and the penal process. This law is applicable to victims and their close relatives. The law provides for special measures of protection against criminal detriment, including terrorism.

The "Crime Victim Care Association of Lithuania" offers help to all victims of crime. In addition, manifold organisations are in existence which assist

---

[111] Explanatory report for the Parliamentary hearing [*Vernehmlassungsbericht*], issued by the Department of Justice on 15 October 2004.

specific groups of victims such as, e.g., women suffering from violence, victims of human trafficking, violence against disabled persons and violence against children and many other kinds of organisations. However, no NGO has been founded so far that would particularly care for victims of terrorism.

3.2.23 Luxembourg

Luxembourg has established a crime victim compensation programme on the basis of the State Compensation Act (SCA) of March 12th 1984. There exists no special programme for victims of terrorist acts. However, victims of terrorist acts fall under the general programme if conditions of eligibility are fulfilled. Compensation on the basis of this programme is restricted by the application of subsidiarity. Compensation can only be obtained if no other sources of compensation are available to the victim. Eligible are victims of Luxembourg nationality and dependents of homicide victims. Luxembourg nationals are eligible also if the were victimized abroad. Maximum limits apply to compensation which may cover medical expenses, lost income, maintenance for dependents and home aid for disabled victims. Advance payments are possible on application and prove of urgency.

No particular protective rules have been introduced to the advantage of victims or witnesses.

An act of 1994 introduced a victim support service as part of the criminal justice system.

There are several NGOs which support victims of crime, the most important among them the "*Weisser Ring*".

3.2.24 Malta

Malta has adopted legislation aimed at protecting crime victims. But, there is no specific legislation which would deal with victims of terrorism nor is there legislation which would allow for state compensation of crime victims[112]. In 1987 a non-statutory crime victim compensation programme was introduced in order to provide for assistance to selected groups of victims of violent crime. Eligibility is dependent on violence resulting from a breakdown of law and order. Illegal force by police and violence suffered in the line of duty concern other situations which may result in compensation. This of course does not amount to a full victim compensation programme.

There are no national NGOs or NGOs that would deal with victims of crime in general.[113] Victim needs are partially addressed by probation services

---

[112] Caruana, E.: Compensation and restitution to victims of crime. Unpublished thesis, University of Malta 1989; Saliba, E.: Victims' rights: contemporary approach to criminal justice. Unpublished Thesis, University of Malta 2001.
[113] Note of the Secretariat of the Council of Europe: On 23 October 2006, the Secretariat received a submission on behalf of Victim Support Malta (VSM) stating

when investigating a case in order to write a pre-sentence report or social inquiry reports. Pre-sentence reports may include a recommendation for court ordered compensation to the crime victim. Specific victim support is delivered by Women Associations.

Policy debates relate in particular to domestic violence and violence against women. Recently, the problem of victims of trafficking (of women and children) has found attention.

Sec. 75-80 of the Police Act provides for protection of vulnerable or intimidated victims and witnesses through establishing a witness protection programme and allowing under certain conditions the giving of testimony through a live video link.

3.2.25 Moldova

Moldova has not yet enacted explicit legal provisions that would formally grant assistance or compensation to victims of crime in general or to victims of terrorism in particular. In 2002, however, the parliament passed a resolution that envisages measures concerning the social rehabilitation of victims of terrorist acts[114]. The social rehabilitation comprises judicial assistance, medical and psychological help and assistance in employment and accommodations.

The costs for social rehabilitation of these persons are recovered from the budget of the subject or from the federal budget of the Republic.

3.2.26 Netherlands

There are no specific provisions relating to victims of terrorism in Dutch law. Victims of terrorism, as other victims of crime, can profit from general victim-oriented provisions that have been implemented in the Penal Code, the Code of Criminal Procedure and a couple of further laws since the mid-90s. Most important are the so-called Victim Act *Terwee*[115], the Act on Legal Aid and the State Fund for Victims of Violent Crime, and the Witness Protection Act. Further safeguard for the victim rights comes from victim guidelines and directives which have also binding legal character what makes them not only internally but also externally binding for the prosecution authorities. And the Legal Aid Act offers the possibility to victims with limited resources to enjoy state subsidized legal aid, provided either by so-called legal aid centers or by legal practitioners who are subsidized by contractual agreements with the

---

that assistance to victims in Malta is given by VSM, an NGO (foundation) which works in collaboration with other institutions, including the police (see www.victimsupportmalta.org).

[114] Resolution on assistance for victims of terrorist acts, of 8 July 2002.

[115] Victim Act Terwee of 1st April 1995 (Act to amend the Penal Code, the Code of Criminal Procedure, the Act on the State fund for victims of violent crime and other acts containing provisions for the benefit of victims), accompanied by the so-called Guideline Terwee of 22 March 1995.

Ministry of Justice. All these regulations provide a comprehensive system of protection and assistance to all victims of crime. In practice, the compliance of the official institutions with all these rules falls under the monitoring power of the National Ombudsman[116]; victims have the possibility to complain to the Ombudsman if they think that a victim-related rule was not correctly applied to.

Apart from several options to obtain compensation directly from an offender through a civil action in the context of a criminal trial or by means of a compensation order – these possibilities were also improved by the afore-mentioned Act Terwee – the Netherlands have also a scheme for state compensation (*Schadefonds Geweldsmisdrijven*) which was institutionalised already in 1974[117]. It offers a 'one-off' payment to everyone who has suffered injuries or serious material and immaterial losses due to an intentional violent crime committed on Dutch territory. Compensation for such a crime committed on Dutch ships or aircrafts is restricted to EU citizens only. Surviving relatives can apply as well. The compensation is determined by the Committee of the State Fund according to the principles of reasonableness and fairness. Maximum limits apply; they are set at 22,700 € for material loss (including costs caused by injuries such as, e.g., medical care, loss of income, household aid, etc., and costs caused by a victim's death) and 9,100 € for immaterial damages, e.g, emotional damage such as sorrow, pain and loss of pleasure in life. Provisional payments can be granted. The State Fund subrogates in the rights of the victim against the offender.

In the Netherlands there exist numerous NGOs that are caring for particular groups of victims or victims in general. Most of them operate on the local level. There exists also a nationwide agency specialized in giving aid to victims of crime, '*Slachtofferhulp*'. This agency is partly funded by the government and provides emotional support, practical advice and might even give judicial advice.

3.2.27 Norway

Norway has a crime victim compensation programme to provide financial compensation to victims of violent or personal crime. The Crime Victim Compensation Act 2001 determines the conditions under which compensation is awarded. There are no special rules dealing with victims of terrorist crime. But, the general victim compensation rules cover also victims of terrorism. Persons victimized by violent crime in Norway (and in selected other cases, Norwegian citizens victimized abroad) are to be compensated for medical expenses, income loss and other material damage (including compensation for persistent disability in case disability is above 15%). Compensation includes also awards for pain and suffering as well as maintenance for dependents of homicide victims. Compensation is limited to

---

[116] Compare the Act on the National Ombudsman of 4 February 1981.
[117] Act on the State Fund for Victims of Violent Crime.

a sum calculated on the basis of the National Insurance Law and furthermore subject to the principle of subsidiarity. The application is made to the county governor whose decision may be appealed at the Compensation Board for Victims of Violent Crime. Advance payments are possible. The programme is funded by the state and tax money.

NGOs that cater to victims needs have been founded in Norway. Although there is as yet no well-established, national victim support movement in Norway, there have been several individual enterprises aiming to help victims cope with their situation. Most of these cater for victims of sexual offences and/or violence. There are 19 Support Centres against Incest (*Støttecenter mot incest*). These centres are self-help groups offering support to women who are victims of incest or who are mother to a child who is a victim of incest, with the exception of one centre which deals exclusively with male victims. In addition to the Support Centres against Incest, there are approximately 50 Crisis Centres (*Krise Senter*) around the country offering support to battered and raped women. The Crisis Centres offer victims and their children temporary housing, counselling and help in contacting the police, legal aid, social welfare, medical services, and so on.

The State Recovery Agency is responsible for collecting any compensation that the injured person has been awarded during a criminal trial.

The Criminal Procedural Act gives the victim (of sexual crimes) the right to have a legal council (remunerated by the state). Investigating authorities when interviewing the victim the first time shall ask whether the victim wishes to claim compensation from the perpetrator and advise accordingly. Section 456 of the Criminal Procedure Act states that a compensation claim ordered to be paid to a victim, takes priority over a criminal fine. The victim may be given protection against intimidation and retaliation by the offender through a protection order or by testimony given through a video link.

3.2.28 Poland

Polish legal system does not know any specific regulations relating to victims of terrorism, assistance to them (including in the judicial procedure), or compensation. There are also no national victim support associations or services (public or NGO), concentrating exclusively on victims of terrorist acts. This may be mainly due to the fact that Poland has practically no experience with the phenomenon of terrorism, neither historical nor current. Terrorism remains still something quite distant.

However, there are several associations, having mainly non-governmental character, active in the general area of victim support and victims' rights, independently of the character and type of victimization. It seems that the only type of non-governmental associations and organisations concentrating on specific type of victimization constitute various organisations dealing with issues and consequences of domestic violence, sexual exploitation of women and sexual abuse of children. Other victim organisations do not narrow the scope of their activities in any way. These NGOs started to mushroom during the 90s, as a result of growing dissatisfaction with the position of the victim in criminal procedure, and the way victims are handled by criminal justice agencies. They concentrate on two main types of activities. Firstly, they constitute lobbying for victims rights in legislative process and promoting victims' rights (also through the media), secondly, they engage routinely on counselling and help in concrete cases.

Protection and assistance to victims of crime in Poland takes place first of all within the framework of criminal procedure and activities of institutions involved in this type of procedure (police, public prosecution system, courts). An injured person[118] enjoys in criminal procedure several rights, first of all the right to participate in proceedings as a party. In this way an injured person may influence the course of proceedings and try to guarantee its final outcome satisfactory from the point of view of the victim's interests. The same applies to court proceedings. The criminal procedural code provides for protection in case of vulnerable witnesses through a live video link and the anonymous witness. Moreover, during this phase an injured person may participate as a party to the proceeding either as the so called subsidiary prosecutor, or as civil plaintiff, or both. The code of criminal procedure regulates in a detailed way rights of both, subsidiary prosecutor and civil plaintiff, and their possibilities of influencing the course of proceedings. There is, however, no special state system of assistance and support to victims of crime. All state agencies, first of all police and prosecutors, but also courts, have only the duty to inform victims of all their rights and to assist them in eventual implementation of these rights.

There exists also no state system or fund for compensating victims of crime in Poland. However, victims have some legal possibilities to obtain compensation in a criminal process. The first possibility, used in fact rather seldom, is to participate in court proceedings as a civil plaintiff[119]. In such cases the victim demands the decision on compensation (damages) according to the rules of civil responsibility, to be taken by the court deciding the issue of criminal responsibility. Due to a variety of limitations and evidentiary problems criminal courts in Poland were never very eager to decide issues of eventual civil damages resulting from an offence. They preferred always to leave for the victims the way of civil litigation to satisfy their eventual demands. The other possibility to obtain compensation by the victim is provided by Article 46 of the criminal Code of 1997. Under this provision, the criminal court, on the motion of the injured person or public prosecutor, may impose on the perpetrator the duty to restore in part or in the whole the damage caused by the offence (what is quite different from formal civil law claim as civil plaintiff). This provision is applicable only in cases of certain offences mentioned in this provision, first of all offences

---

[118] Under Article 49 § 1 of the code of criminal procedure of the year 1997 an injured person is a natural or legal person; this goes beyond the traditional definition of a victim in victimology which usually is limited to natural persons.

[119] Articles 62-70 of the code of criminal procedure.

resulting in death or bodily injury, including road traffic offences. This provision was intended as introduction of elements of restorative justice into Polish criminal law. This form of compensation should make it easier for the victim to obtain compensation in criminal process, as certain rules and limitations applicable in case of suing for civil damages do not apply here. This measure may be imposed in two forms. It may either accompany penalties and other penal measures, or it may be imposed as a sole penal measure of restorative character. Recent changes in criminal procedure were intended to clarify certain problems regarding application of these measures and to make it easier to use them.

From the point of view of compensating victims, including victims of terrorism, the main issue may constitute the fact that all these measures may be used only during the criminal procedure. This means that for the victim to enjoy their benefits the case has to be cleared (i.e. the perpetrator has to be identified), and he/she/they have to be brought to trial and convicted. Without a criminal conviction, it is impossible to issue a decision on victim compensation, neither in form of civil damages nor in form of restoration. Due to the absence of a state system or any other fund for compensating victims, all victims of offences which were not cleared or perpetrators of which were not brought to justice cannot profit from the existing options for compensation. In such cases, the general rules of civil law, insurance law and various disability schemes may apply. But here of course all regular preconditions have to be fulfilled.

Further limitation is constituted by the definition of an "injured person" in Polish law, meaning that as such may be treated only a person whose legal rights were *directly* violated or threatened by an offence. This excludes from making eventual use of these rights those who were only indirectly injured or threatened by an offence. They just are not considered as victims in the formal meaning of the term. The only exception applies in case of a victim's death; his/her rights may be enjoyed by close relatives then.

All rights of the victims of crime in Poland are to a certain extent codified in a document called "Polish Charter of Victims Rights" (*Polska Karta Praw Ofiar*)[120]. This document was prepared in 1999 and signed by the Minister of Justice. However, it does not per se constitute a source of law in the formal meaning, as it does not have legislative character. It gathers only in one document all provisions and regulations of the Polish (and international) legal system relevant from the point of view of victim rights. It refers to provisions of both, international and domestic law, in the last case first of all penal and civil law. It is relevant first of all from the point of view of providing information to the victims on their rights.

---

[120] See: http://www.ms.gov.pl/prawa_ofiary/karta.shtml.

3.2.29 Portugal

The Portuguese legal system does not provide specific legislation. Victims of terrorism benefit from the general rules applicable to victims of all other types of crimes[121]. This includes special measures of victim protection[122] which join the general standards as provided in most other EU member states. Victims of terrorism may apply to the general crime victim compensation procedures, which in general has to be made through a civil claim within the criminal procedure; in some exceptional cases, the claim may be lodged separately, i.e., without an individual offender being prosecuted. In any case, however, it is a pure civil liability claim, which can only be enforced against the respective defendant and his or her assets.

Of greater relevance for victims of terrorism is state compensation which is provided for victims of violent crimes[123]. Under this statute, victims of "violent crimes", as defined by law, who have failed to enforce their civil compensation award against the respective defendant, may be, under certain criteria, entitled to receive compensation from the Portuguese state. If an individual offender cannot be identified or an identified offender cannot be sued – a situation that is of high relevance, in particular in cases of attacks in the context of international terrorism – state compensation as available as well. The same principle applies if an individual offender has been killed in the course of the crime (suicide attack) or later on. Only material damages, including income, maintenance or alimony, are covered by the State compensation whereas psychological damages are not attended. Payments are granted to direct and indirect victims of any nationality if they were victimized on Portuguese territory (including aircrafts and ships); compensation for victimizations abroad can be applied by Portuguese nationals only. Article 113 provides a definition of the different classes of eligible persons and legal criteria concerning indirect victims. Maximum limits apply. The application is to be made to the State Compensation Committee which can also award advance payments. Civil pensions are being granted based on civil law principles only. It requires for permanent or temporary but incapacitating disability to work for at least 30 days or the death of the victim; in the latter case, indirect victims are also eligible.

In addition, victims of terrorism have access to the general benefits ruled by the Portuguese social security system which provides benefits in cases of, e.g., extreme poverty, homelessness, physical or psychic injuries. In case of emergency the so-called "Emergency Social Network" provides further help.

---

[121] See the Portuguese Criminal Code: Decree Law N°. 400/82 of 23 September 1982, the Portuguese Criminal Procedure Code: Law No. 5/98 of 25 August 1998.

[122] Witness protection is regulated through Law No. 93/99 of 14 July 1999, Decree Law No. 190/2003 of 22 August 03.

[123] State compensation for victims of violent crimes: Decree Law No. 423/91 of 30 October 1991 (modified by Law No. 136/99 of 28 August 1999 and Decree Law No. 62/2004 of 22 March 2004).

It has, however, only a limited scope of application. It is further noteworthy that non-Portuguese victims of terrorism, if the general legal criteria are fulfilled, are entitled to seek for asylum in Portugal.

An integrated victim protection scheme is available through the nationwide NGO called APAV ("*Associação de Apoio à Vítima*"). The scope of activity of this victim support association is to provide emotional, psychic and legal support to victims of all types of crime, including terrorist victimizations. This entity, although well acknowledged as a public interest prosecution association and with good relations with the key institutional players, has no public powers of intervention. Its intervention is limited to consultation, advice and logistic assistance to victims, including indirect victims.

3.2.30 Romania

As many other countries, Romania has enacted special legislation on the prevention and combat of terrorism[124]. It provides, however, no specific victim-related matters. Victims of terrorism can profit from the general rules enacted for the protection, assistance and compensation of victims of serious crime. The relevant provisions are codified in the Witness Protection Act of 2002[125] and in the Victim Protection and Compensation Act of 2004[126]. After having enacted these two pieces of legislation, Romania also signed the European Convention on Compensation of Victims of Violent Crimes in April 2005.

Under the regime of the Victim Protection and Compensation Act which came into force on 1st January 2005, victims of terrorism, like victims of other types of serious crimes, can profit from the new rules on information, psychological counselling, free legal assistance and state compensation[127].

Protection and assistance are provided on request, but only in relation with some judicial procedure. Psychological counselling is provided through the court services of probation and victim protection, for a maximum period of three months for adult and up to six months for juvenile victims. Psychological counselling is free of charge to the victims of a catalogue of crimes causing serious harm and to the family members of victims of murder[128]. Legal assistance is provided to persons who have been victims of similar crimes and to some indirect victims (spouse, children and dependents who had been supported and cared for by the direct victim) in the case of murder or other offences that resulted in the death of the direct victim[129].

---

[124] Law No. 535/2004 of 25 November 2004 on the prevention and combat of terrorism, OJ No. 1161 of 8 December 2004.

[125] Law No. 682/2002 on witness protection, OJ of 28 December 2002.

[126] Law No. 211/2004 of 27 May 2004 on certain measures to ensure the protection of victims of crime, OJ No. 505 of 4 June 2004.

[127] Article 1 of Law No. 21/2004.

[128] Article 8 of Law No. 21/2004.

[129] Article 14 of Law No. 21/2004.

Financial compensation is granted under the same preconditions as free legal assistance. It covers only crimes committed in Romanian territory. Eligible to apply are Romanian nationals, foreigners with a legal status and foreigners on the grounds of international conventions.

The Romanian State grants compensation for hospitalisation costs and all other medical expenses, material damage and loss of income. For family members, funeral expenses as well as maintenance and alimony are covered. The compensation of material damage is limited to the value of 10 minimum gross salaries. Advance payments can be granted under certain circumstances; applications have to be rendered within 30 days. The state compensation is, in principle, not subsidiary. It does not depend on the existence of an identified perpetrator. The state is subrogated to probable victim claims against the perpetrator. And payments to the victim resulting from civil damages by the perpetrator or insurance payments shall be deduced.

All requests have to be addressed to the competent tribunal of second instance of the victim's legal domicile. At each such tribunal, a Service for Probation and Victim Protection has been established who are in charge for all matters of information, protection, assistance and counselling. Compensation is awarded and managed by the Crime Victims Financial Compensation Board which operates within each tribunal as well.

3.2.31 Russian Federation

With the Law on Property, adopted 1990, Russia provides for a general system of crime victim compensation. Compensation for victims of terrorism is specifically addressed in the Anti-Terrorism Act of 1998[130] which created general rules on compensation but evidently also came under heavy criticism when implemented. According to the 1998 law, the duty to compensate victims of terrorist acts lies with the federal districts where the terrorist act occurred. Security forces responding to terrorist acts and damages resulting from such responses to bystanders or third parties are exempt from compensation. A demand for compensation has to be filed to the local court which then has to determinate the amount of compensation to be paid. Article 18 of the Anti-Terrorism Act provides for measures for the social rehabilitation of victims of terrorist acts. These measures include judicial assistance, medical and psychological rehabilitation, as well as assistance in (re-) gaining employment and accommodation. The costs for social rehabilitation of these persons are recovered from the federal budget of the Russian Federation or the budget of the subject of the Russian Federation, on which territory the terrorist act took place. In addition, a number of parliamentary resolutions focus on the assistance for victims of particular terrorist acts; such resolutions were passed, e.g., with regard to

---

[130] Law against Terrorism of 25 July 1998.

the attacks in *Budenovsk* (19 June 1995), *Dagestan* (23 January 1996) and *Vladikavkas* (22 March 1999).

Court decisions following law suits after the siege of the Moscow musical theatre 'NORTH-EAST' in 2002 held that the city of Moscow was not liable to pay for moral damages (pain and suffering), because only terrorists themselves could be made liable for such damages and that the compensation offered by the Moscow administration was sufficient. The local courts decisions were upheld by the Russian Supreme Court in 2004 and ultimately by the Russian Constitutional Court in 2005 which argued that a new law against terrorism currently under review of the *Duma* will change profoundly the compensation scheme in case of terrorist acts. Claims for compensation (in addition to the compensation sums determined by the Moscow city administration) of foreign nationals were thrown out by local courts.

As a general rule, state compensation is granted in case of death or injury of victims or indirect victims of terrorist acts on a 'one-off' basis only, according to a fix tariff system according to which the relatives of a victim who came to death receive an amount of 500 minimum salaries, persons who become invalid receive compensation equating 100 minimal salaries (invalidity of first and second degree) or 50 minimal salaries (invalids of the third degree). Victims who suffered serious injuries are compensated by an amount of 30 minimal salaries, those who were slightly injured an amount of 15 minimal salaries. Regular pensions solely based on the fact of a terrorist victimization, are not paid.

Concrete figures can be drawn from several cases that came to public attention in recent years. Families of the victims of the two passenger jet crashes of 2004 receive 100,000 Rubles (approximately 2,800 €) from the federal government. Additional compensation was provided by other federal districts. Victims injured by a terrorist bombing in Moscow in 2004 received 50,000 (serious injuries) respectively 3,000 Rubles (light injuries) on the basis of a decree signed by the Moscow mayor. Survivors of the North-East theatre siege received some 2,700 US-$ while families or relatives of those who died received approximately 9,500 US-$. The state compensation practice according to decisions made over the last years means that families of deceased victims will receive some 100,000 Rubles (in addition to limited compensation for burial costs and sometimes maintenance payments: a local Moscow court in 2004 awarded a widow of a victim of the theatre siege some 5,700 Rubles in monthly payments; this equates to approximately 160 €) and those seriously injured some 50,000 Rubles.

There exists no nationwide association for victims of crime in general. However, the Ombudsman for Human Rights of the Russian Federation also cares for victim issues. In March 2003, his office published the first report on the situation of and the protection measures for victims of terrorism and other violent crimes.[131]

There are also several NGOs who are in care for special victim groups such as, e.g., regional centres for female victims of violence or trafficking. In the aftermath of terrorist attacks loosely organised associations of victims of terrorism emerged which pressed for fair compensation and for thorough investigation into the state's responsibilities for the damage linked to rescue operations. One of these associations who particularly represent the interests of victims of terrorism is called "NORTH EAST"; it was founded by victims of the fatal terrorist massacre in the musical theatre North East in 2002. A further one was initiated by victims of the *Beslan* school hostage of 2004.

3.2.32 Serbia and Montenegro[132]

In the Federal Republic of Serbia and Montenegro, no specific legislation has been enacted so far that provides support, protection or compensation for victims of terrorism. There is also no special legislation in force that cares for victims of crime in general.

However, many victims can profit from a general rule for state compensation that is part of the so-called 'Code of Obligations'[133]. This special type of law which similarly exists also in other States which were formerly part of the Yugoslav Federation (compare, e.g., the situation in Croatia or Slovenia) regulates all kinds of public obligations and liabilities. Article 180 of the Code of Obligations provides that the state is liable for all damage resulting from death, bodily harm or material loss suffered as a consequence of a violent or terrorist act (or any other act in the course of public demonstrations or manifestations). It is a general option for state compensation, based on the assumption that the state failed in preventing the criminal act. As a consequence of this underlying principle of liability, this type of compensation is limited to damages resulting from inner-territorial events only. Criminal acts outside Serbia and Montenegro are not covered.

3.2.33 Slovak Republic

A state compensation programme does not exist nor exists legislation which would grant crime victims the right to state compensation. Neither does specific legislation for victims of terrorist violence exist. Crime victims who have suffered damage may (under certain circumstances join criminal proceedings (adhesion trial) and pursue their civil claims.

---

[131] See http://www.ombudsmanrf.ru.
[132] At the time of preparing this publication, Serbia and Montenegro have become two independent States.
[133] Federal Law Journal SFRJ 29/78, 39/85, 57/89 and SRJ 31/93; see also the decision of the Constitutional Court of Yugoslavia No. 363/86, published in the Federal Law Journal SFRJ 45/89.

In 1998 a law on the protection of witnesses[134] went into force which establishes a witness protection programme and which foresees testimony during trial given through a closed circuit television link.

A national crime victim association does exist. Moreover, local crime victim support groups have been founded which provide advice, assistance and support. Victim Support Slovakia is a national non-governmental organisation which supports and assists victims of crime.

3.2.34 Slovenia

Slovenia has not enacted legislation which would enable crime victims to seek state compensation. Neither do exist specific legislation or programmes for victims of terrorism. There are also no general public funds available for compensation of victims of crime.

However, there is a relevant specific provision in the Code of Obligations (*Obligacijski zakonik*). Namely, Article 156 of that code provides that in case of damage resulting from death or bodily harm as a consequence of a terrorist act or other act in the course of public demonstrations or manifestations, the liability for that damage lies upon the state or upon other organisation that should have prevented such act to occur. This covers only crimes committed within the territory of Slovenia.

NGOs that provide services to victims of crime on a general basis have not been founded so far in Slovenia. There exists, however, a Crime Victim Assistance Service (*Zavod za vzpodbujanje in razvijanje kvalitete življenja*) named PAPILOT which provides crisis intervention in Ljubljana and other mayor cities.

3.2.35 Spain

In 1995 a law went into force which gives victims of violence the possibility to apply for state compensation in case of serious violent offences. Victims of crime are eligible as are dependents of homicide victims and foreign nationals (if reciprocity is guaranteed).

With regard to the threat of terrorism by ETA, victims of terrorism enjoy special attention of the Spanish legislators. In 1979 already, a state compensation scheme for victims of terrorist crimes was established; compensation is to be awarded for physical and psychological injuries as well as property damage that are the result of crimes committed by an armed gang or a terrorist organisation. Eligible are direct victims and, in case of his or her death, the legal successor(s) or the spouse or life partner and descendents. Second degree successors can be eligible as well.

---

[134] Act No. 256 of 8 July 1998 on the protection of the witness and on the modification and amendment of certain laws.

Compensation covers medical expenses and mental health expenses of the victim; psychological and psycho-therapeutic expenses and cost for funerals are covered for indirect victims (family members). Advance payments can be made. In addition, financial support is granted for income loss of disabled victims and maintenance for dependents of homicide victims. The payments are based on a fixed tariff system[135]. In case of death, 138,232.78 € are granted to the successor(s), the victim him/herself receives 390,657.87 € in case of total invalidity, 96,161.94 € in case of total incapacity to work or 48,080.97 € for partial or 36,060.73 € for temporal incapacity. These are so-called 'solidarity' payments which are granted once. Pensions based on the ground of permanent invalidity are being paid in addition, according to the regular pension legislation. Furthermore, for terrorist crimes that occurred since 1 January 1987, extraordinary pensions are being granted that differ from the regular pensions[136].

Victims of kidnapping or hijacking receive an extra support which is granted according to a fixed tariff system, too[137]. The State grants a basic compensation of 12,020.24 € for the victimization itself plus an extra 180.30 € per day of duration of the crime. The maximum amount is set at 36,060.73 €. This support is also payable in addition to the other types of compensation or financial support.

All victims of terrorism, their spouses and children are exempt from any administration fees within the educational system including universities. And, similar to the situation in Italy, all payments of compensation and financial support are tax-free.

In principle, state compensation and financial support is granted only for terrorist crimes within the Spanish territory. With regard to the 11 September attacks in the US Law No. 32/1999 was amended. It provides the possibility that the compensation and support provided by that law can be retrospectively grated also to victims of extraterritorial events that occurred later than 1st September 2001[138].

This comprehensive set of national regulations in favour for victims of terrorism is further supplemented by additional regulation enacted by the regional entities[139].

With the 1979 Law, a National Commission on Aid and Assistance to Victims of Violent Crimes and Crimes against Sexual Freedom was established. Applications for assistance will be filed with the Ministry of Economy and

---

[135] See the appendix to Law No. 32/1999.

[136] Improvements introduced by Royal Decree No. 1576/1990 of 7 December 1990.

[137] See also the appendix to Law No. 32/1999.

[138] Amendment introduced by Law No. 2/2003 of 12 March 2003.

[139] For more details, see CODEXTER Report No. (2004) 15 on the protection and compensation of victims of terrorism, submitted by the Managing Director of the Spanish Foundation for Victims of Terrorism.

Finance. The decision on compensation is made after a hearing and introducing the report of the governmental Legal Services. The decision of the Ministry of Economics may be appealed at the National Commission for Assistance to Victims (*Comisión Nacional de Ayuda y Assistencia a las Víctimas de Delitos Violentos y contra la Libertad Sexual*). In 2004, the position of a High Commissioner for Victims of Terrorism (*Alto Comisionado par alas Víctimas del Terrorismo*) was established who has the duty to co-ordinate all national, regional and local political and administrative initiatives for victims of terrorism.

In terms of NGOs, several associations for assistance and support of victims and victims of terrorism exist. They are supported by the State Office for Victim Support (*Oficina de Atención a las Victimas*). The so-called Association of the Victims of Terrorism (*Asociación Víctimas del Terrorismo - AVT*) cares for the interests of these victims. And by the end of 2004, finally, the Association of the Victims of 11 March 2004, (*Asociación Víctimas del 11m*) was established in order to ameliorate the assistance to victims of terrorism. This move was a response to critics who argued that the governmental response was not co-ordinated and in some aspects also dysfunctional.

3.2.36 Sweden

Sweden has a crime victim compensation programme to provide financial compensation to victims of violent or personal crime. State compensation was made available with the Criminal Injuries Compensation Act (*Brottsskadelag*) 1978. Victims of crime, dependents of homicide victims, foreign nationals and Swedish nationals victimized abroad may apply for compensation that covers medical expenses (including psychotherapy) and property damages, pain and suffering, lost income in case of disability, lost maintenance for dependents, rehabilitation measures and other side expenses. Compensation for losses due to property crime is limited to offences that are committed by prisoners or other (selected) institutionalized persons. An application is to be sent to the Criminal Victim Compensation and Support Authority which is a central agency. Advance payments are available. The programme is funded by tax money.

Selected crime victims have a right to a legal council. A victim protection order exists as does a victim protection programme, however, no special rules have been introduced that would protect victim witnesses in case of organised or terrorist crime procedures except conventional rules that for example allow for the accused to be ordered out of the courtroom while the witness is interrogated.

In Sweden a national victim support organisation exists. The National Victim Support Organisation (*Brottsofferjourernas Riksförbund*) was founded in 1988. Other NGOs such as the National Association of Relatives of Homicide Victims care for special victim groups.

3.2.37 Switzerland

Article 124 of the Swiss Federal Constitution demands that victims of violence and sexual crimes have to be compensated fairly if they need such compensation. In October 1991, the Federal Law on Crime Victims Assistance went into force. The law was implemented at the Cantonal (State) level and amended in 2002[140]. Victims of terrorism are not specifically addressed; they are, however, covered by the rules of compensation. The federal law contains general guidelines for crime victim assistance (in terms of counselling, protection during criminal proceedings, and compensation) and requires the establishment of local counselling centres. Crime victims (including dependents of crime victims) may seek compensation and assistance through the counselling centre in the canton (state) where the crime has been committed. Swiss nationals may apply also in case they have been victimized abroad and did not receive adequate compensation there. Each state then established guidelines as to the amount and kind of compensation to be made available to victims of crime. According to the law victims of violence (including sexual offences) may apply for state compensation which covers material damages and (in most serious cases) pain and suffering. Compensation and the amount of compensation for material damages is dependent on the victim's income and subject to the principle of subsidiarity; compensation for pain and suffering is awarded independent of the victim's financial situation.

The Federal Law on Crime Victims Assistance regulates also the protection of victims and witnesses during criminal proceedings. It contains rules that oblige police and prosecution services to inform the victim properly and rules that provide protection for vulnerable victims, in particular child victims, by way of allowing testimony through video links.

The draft Federal Procedural Law contains comprehensive regulations that provide for protection of vulnerable and intimidated witnesses.

Besides a national victim assistance organisation with branches in all cantons there exist also NGOs that deal with crime victims on a regional and local level. The most important one is called "*Weisser Ring*" which was founded subsequent to the foundation of the German "*Weisser Ring*".

3.2.38 Turkey

In absence of a general scheme for victim compensation, the Turkish Parliament passed a special compensation act for victims of terrorism in 2004[141]. In the course of the same year, the government issued further guidelines which regulate the procedural details[142]. In each of the

---

[140] Kunz, K.-L., Keller, P.: Die Rechtsprechung zum Opferhilfegesetz in den Jahren 1993 bis 1998. Eine Studie im Auftrage des Bundesamtes für Justiz. Bern 1999.
[141] Law No. 5233 of 17 July 2004.
[142] Ordinance No. 7955 of 4 October 2004.

81 provinces, a victim compensation committee has been established which is responsible for the compensation procedure. The committee is headed by the Deputy Governor; one of the five additional members is an elected member of the local bar association. Eligible for application are victims or, in case of death, relatives who are inherited. In the latter case, the committee has to meet and to open the case within ten days. The nationality of the victim does not play a role. Legal entities are eligible as well.

Based on the information filed by the applicant, it has to determine the concrete amount of the damage and to make a concrete proposal on the amount of compensation. Compensable are any kind of material damage, loss of income and maintenance, loss of use of real estate and farmland, bodily injury, temporal and permanent disability, medical care and funeral costs. In legal terms, the final proposal of the committee has the character of a settlement offer. If the applicant does not agree he can file a complaint to court.

The funds for this new compensation programme are borne by the Federal Ministry of the Interior which provides a special budget for this purpose. If the expenses exceed the budget the additional means are recovered by the general budget of the federal government.

3.2.39 Ukraine

There are no general provisions available that would provide for protection or compensation of victims of crime in general.

In 2003, the Ukraine has enacted a Law against Terrorism which provides also measures concerning the social rehabilitation of victims of terrorist acts[143]. According to Article 20 of that Law, social rehabilitation comprises judicial assistance, medical and psychological help and assistance in employment and accommodations. The costs for social rehabilitation of these persons are recovered from the federal budget of the Ukraine.

3.2.40 United Kingdom

3.2.40.1 England/Wales

In England/Wales the Criminal Injuries Compensation Authority has jurisdiction over compensation for being victimized by violent crime. Compensation is footed on a statute that was amended in 2001 and provides for a tariff like system of compensation for criminal injuries. Victims of terrorism are not covered explicitly but they fall, when falling prey to terrorist violence, under the compensation law. The state compensation system goes back to the sixties.

---

[143] Law against Terrorism, of 20 March 2003.

All persons are eligible who are victims of a violent crime in England/Wales. There are restrictions that give discretionary power for excluding for example persons with a criminal record or members of criminal or terrorist organisations.

After the Criminal Injuries Compensation Act went into force in 1995 awards for criminal violence are based on a system of tariffs. Compensation covers pain and suffering, loss of income (after a period of 28 weeks), costs of care, reasonable funeral expenses. A dependency award, a loss of parental service award or a "fatal injury" award (max. 11.000 GBP) may be claimed by (dependent) relatives of a victim killed in a violent crime. Foreign nationals are to be compensated as are British nationals, however, the latter are not compensated when victimized abroad. Minimum and maximum limits apply to awards as well as tariffs; the minimum is 1000 the maximum for the same injury is 500.000 GBP. With respect to compensation for injuries 25 tariffs respectively levels from a minimum of 1000 GBP up to 250.000 GBP[144] are assigned to various types of injuries.

Any compensation paid for the same injury will be deducted from sum awardable according to the Compensation Act.

The Criminal Injuries Compensation Authority will decide on the application. The decision may be reviewed by the Authority and – if reviewing does not lead to the expected result – may be appealed at the Criminal Injuries Compensation Appeals Panel. The compensation scheme has developed in an important field of law suits. In 2004, 4,434 appeal cases have been received by the Appeals Panel while approximately 5,000 appeal cases were pending[145]. Specialized law services have emerged with a focus on compensation[146]. Total compensation paid per year goes beyond 200 million GBP.

In 2004, the Domestic Violence Crime and Victims Act went into force. According to that new law the Secretary of State must appoint a Commissioner for Victims and Witnesses whose task is to promote the interests of victims and witnesses. The Secretary of State must appoint also members to a Victims' Advisory Panel. The law provides then for the creation of a Victims' Code of Practice[147], which currently is in a consultation process and will describe precisely the services which victims must receive from each criminal justice organisation.

As regards compensation for damage that results from other crime, compensation schemes do not exist. However, in the United Kingdom a well

---

[144] The Criminal Injuries Compensation Scheme 2001.

[145] Criminal injuries compensation appeals panel eighth annual report and accounts for the year ended 31 March 2004.

[146] See, e.g., http://www.criminal-injuries.co.uk.

[147] Minister of State for the Criminal Justice System: Victims' Code of Practice. Consultation. London, March 2005.

established system of compensation orders (which is an element within the system of criminal sanctions) exists which is used extensively and provides for compensation for all types of crime by the perpetrator of the offence.

English procedural law provides for protection of witnesses (and victims). Interrogation by way of CCTV and other protective devices is available as is (restricted though) available the anonymous witness (in case of threats to the life of the witness).

Various NGOs exist that cater to crime victims at large or specific groups of victims. Support offered ranges from lobbying, initiating new programmes, giving advise to accompanying victims or witnesses during the trial.

3.2.40.2 Northern Ireland

For Northern Ireland, a system of compensation was established along the Criminal Injuries Compensation Act 1995. However, the system differs in some aspects from the one established in England/Wales and Scotland. The Criminal Injuries (Compensation) (NI) Order 1988 for example excludes those who had been at any stage "engaged in the commission, preparation or instigation of acts of terrorism at any time whatsoever". In 2001, a commission presented a report on the criminal injury compensation scheme[148]. The commission advised to introduce into the Northern Ireland compensation system a "bereavement support payment" and wider recognition of psychological injuries. Furthermore it recommended to exclude considering a criminal record of the victim when deciding on an application and to abolish total exclusion of victims that had been involved in acts of terrorism[149].

A Compensation Statute went into force 2002 (No. 796 (NI.1)) which established the Northern Ireland Criminal Injuries Compensation Scheme. It provides for a standard amount of compensation, determined by reference to the nature of the injury and covers also loss of earnings; a bereavement support payment can be awarded to survivors of homicide victims. Excluded remain those who are or were members of unlawful associations or those who were ever involved in acts of terrorism[150].

For Northern Ireland specific victims of terrorism compensation legislation was introduced with the Terrorism Act 2000 which reformed and extended existing legislation to counter terrorism in the United Kingdom. Part VII and Schedules 10-13 of the Act relate specifically to Northern Ireland. Schedule 12 allows for compensation for damage to property to be claimed from the

---

[148] Ad Hoc Committee: Report on the Proposal for a Draft Criminal Injuries Compensation (NI) Order 2001.

[149] Ad Hoc Committee: Report on the Proposal for a Draft Criminal Injuries Compensation (NI) Order 2001.

[150] For details see The Compensation Agency: Annual Report and Accounts 2001-2002.

Secretary of State in case counter terrorism activities have led to property damage. The 2000 Terrorism Act covers property which was taken, occupied, destroyed, or damaged, or any other private property rights which are interfered with as a consequence of action taken under Part VII of the Act. However, restrictions apply which include those established for criminal injury compensation.

The Northern Ireland Peace Agreement reached in the multi-party negotiations mentions victims of violence explicitly and stresses the importance to provide support for victims of (terrorist) violence. The Peace Agreement states that: "The provision of services that are supportive and sensitive to the needs of victims will also be a critical element and that support will need to be channelled through both statutory and community-based voluntary organisations facilitating locally-based self-help and support networks. This will require the allocation of sufficient resources, including statutory funding as necessary, to meet the needs of victims and to provide for community-based support programmes"[151].

NGOs exist that cover crime victims needs among them those with a focus of victims of terrorism.

3.2.40.3 Scotland

Scotland has adopted legislation, covering also England/Wales, that allows for compensation of crime victims; but, terrorist violence and victims of terrorism are not dealt with separately in Scotland. Victims of terrorism fall, however, under the general compensation scheme. The Criminal Injuries Compensation Act 1995 was passed on 12 November 1995. State compensation for victims of violent crime is arranged on the level of the United Kingdom. From 1964 until 1990 compensation was awarded by the Criminal Injuries Compensation Board on an ex gratia basis and on the basis of common law tort principles. Under the new Compensation Act a victim of a violent crime - as was elaborated earlier - can be compensated for personal pain and suffering, loss of earnings, and costs of care. Injuries and losses resulting from domestic violence are covered. However, restrictions apply. Claims amounting to less than 1,000 GBP are not accepted. The tariff scheme sets a maximum of 500,000 GBP.

Scottish criminal law allows for a compensation order to the benefit of the victim of crime.

Scottish criminal procedural law allows for the protection of vulnerable witnesses, in particular child victims by way of introducing testimony through a closed circuit television link. Police operate a witness protection programme.

---

[151] For a report on victims of terrorism needs see also Bloomfield, K.: Report of the Northern Ireland Victims Commissioner, April 1998.

As regards the victim and mass media, a statutory offence is established with publicizing the name of a victim of a sexual offence.

Recent law amendments to the advantage of victims concern the Criminal Justice (Scotland) Act 2003 which improved the anonymity of children in Children's Hearings, the Vulnerable Witnesses (Scotland) Act 2004 which allows child and adult vulnerable witnesses to benefit from a number of special measures and the Criminal Procedure (Amendment) (Scotland) Act 2004 that gives witness more certainty about when they will give evidence in court.

The Scottish Strategy for Victims, launched in January 2001, set out in clear terms the action needed to fulfil that promise. A progress report of 2004 provides for detailed insight into Scottish policies of victim support[152].

There are several NGOs that provide support to victims of crime. Victim Support Scotland is a national organisation.

4. Summary and Conclusions

4.1 What is Particular in the Compensation of Victims of Terrorism?

Large scale terrorist violence and its consequences for victims in the last decades provide for some lessons about the particulars that have to be considered when discussing if victims of terrorist violence should be dealt separately and how compensation of victims of terrorism should be regulated.

Research has shown that victims of violent crime experience a wide range of needs – physical, financial, emotional, and legal – which include also long-term mental health services for posttraumatic responses to the criminal event. But, in general victims of terrorism are not different as regards the impact of violence and the needs following the victimizing event when comparing them to victims of serious (individual) violence. The impact of terrorist acts creates a sense of vulnerability, trauma, disruption of everyday life, destruction of the future and financial problems that come with loosing parents, being disabled etc. This kind of impact is comparable to that of ordinary violence. It is arguable whether compensation of victims of terrorism is needed because a lack of compensation would lead to a growth of fear of terrorist violence and thus would contribute significantly to achieving terrorist goals[153]. There are differences though; however, such differences are rather

[152] Scottish Executive: Scottish Strategy for Victims. Progress Report 2004.
[153] Sommer, H.: Providing Compensation for Harm Caused by Terrorism: Lessons Learned in the Israeli Experience. Indiana Law Review 335 (2003), pp. 335-365, p. 364.

located in the areas of planning, organisation and co-ordination of the response to victimization as for example US experiences demonstrate[154].

Such differences will also be dependent on the type of administrative system that is in place to respond in particular to situations of mass victimization. The preference of terrorists for soft and symbolic targets and the aim to provoke a maximum of public attention will most likely lead to many casualties (in few cases) in a single act of violence and will also result in the need to accommodate for more victims of foreign nationalities (as became visible in the 11 September attacks or in the Moscow musical theatre siege). This calls for systems that are capable to deliver in a short period of time a maximum of integrated assistance and to avoid problems of delivering support and assistance across national borders and under differing systems of support and compensation[155].

The victim related responses to the 11 September attacks have been summarized as indicating that it is of utmost importance to provide for emergency training for staff involved in victim support and assistance, to integrate compensation and assistance personnel in emergency centres, to integrate compensation and mental health with legal assistance and support with financial and daily concerns of victims and to prepare for a high volume of claimants to be dealt with within a short period of time[156].

What is creating differences between victims of ordinary violence and victims of terrorism concerns the particular attention terrorist acts draw upon themselves in the media and in the political system. This, of course is feeding the perception that there is inequality in the response to ordinary violence when comparing such approaches to the attention received by victims of terrorist violence. Another outcome could be symbolic (and sometimes pathetic) legislation which has as main goal the expression of the state´s capacity to act in face of dramatic threats to the safety of its citizens.

When looking at the reasons given for compensation of victims of ordinary violence and victims of terrorist violence we find the same type of legitimation. The basic ground to provide state compensation and assistance to victims of violence and victims of terrorism is seen in the need to express social solidarity and to compensate for risks the state could not prevent to turn into damage and injury. But, there are competing models of victim compensation as the survey has shown.

---

[154] US Department of Justice Office of Justice Programs: Responding to Terrorism Victims: Oklahoma City and Beyond. Washington, October 2000.
[155] US Department of Justice: New Directions from the Field: Victims Rights and Services for the 21st Century. Washington 1998.
[156] Gonzales, A.R., Henke, T.A., Gillis, J.W.: Responding to September 11 Victims: Lessons Learned from the States. www.ovcttac.org.

4.2 Varying Models and Practices of Compensation of Victims of Violence and Victims of Terrorism

Member states of the Council of Europe legislation in the area of victim of violence compensation can roughly be divided into three groups:

- States that have enacted specific victim of terrorism legislation and specific programmes. Such specific legislation is modelled along the precursor of compensating military and civil victims of war. The German law on compensating victims of violence is evenly referring to a structure of compensation which is derived from a statute that organises support for losses due to war. With the reference to war an analogy is created between victimization through terrorist acts and victimization through war. This becomes evident for example when civil victims of terrorist violence are conceptualised as "soldiers" drawn involuntarily into a violent conflict between terrorist groups and the state[157]. The analogy is also driven by the understanding of modern terrorism as small or private wars (and of course by declaring war on terrorism). Specific victims of terrorism legislation was found in France, Italy, Greece, Spain and Russia. The outcomes of the systems are evidently quite different. While France and Spain have set up separate administrative bodies of victim of terrorism support Russia responds by ordinary courts assessing applications on the basis of rules that evidently much discretion in deciding on whom and what to compensate. Most of the countries that have created specific victims of terrorism legislation have suffered during the last forty years under extended periods of terrorist attacks which had or have either separatist or ideologist, but mostly local, roots.

- States that have elaborated crime victim compensation and protection programmes which cover also victims of terrorism but do not mention victims of terrorism specifically.

- And finally, states that have until now not at all or only very limited created legislation in the area of compensation of victims of crime and/or have, due to various reasons, not implemented compensation laws or victim assistance and support schemes. These reasons are found in restricted public funds that can be made available for victim compensation and/or the adoption of the view that other areas of social policy require a higher priority when deciding on where public investments should be made.

---

[157] Sommer, H.: Providing Compensation for Harm Caused by Terrorism: Lessons Learned in the Israeli Experience. Indiana Law Review 335 (2003), pp. 335-365.

The compensation legislation states then can be subdivided into models that

- tend to provide full compensation (in particular for pain and suffering and with that adopt tort law as a basic approach);

- find a basic legitimation in a social welfare approach which responds to a financial crisis and special psychological and other support needs as a consequence of violence (or other damaging behaviour), is subject fully to the principle of subsidiarity and prevents that the state and society step in to replace an offender who is either not identified, dead or financially not capable to compensate fully the victim.

When adopting a principled approach it seems clear that a full compensation model (following civil tort law) cannot be justified. The full compensation model as it developed in the US and as it seems to find some support in Europe is based on the concept of punitive damages and with that on blame. Such an approach puts rather pressure on social solidarity because of evident problems of unequal treatment than adding to social integration as the US example today demonstrates clearly. The Moscow law suits following the theatre siege and (unsuccessfully) claiming millions of US-$ as compensation in a country where the average monthly income does not exceed 200 US-$ demonstrate the type of problems that come with expectations and promises of broad and full compensation.

Then, convincing arguments speak in favour of adopting a statutory basis for compensating victims of violence instead of adopting an event compensation model that responds to specific acts of terrorism (or mass violence). Although event based compensation is flexible it is at the same time generating inequality and tends to be influenced by varying political and economic objectives.

Variation can be observed in the extent to which NGOs have been founded for catering to the needs of victims. This is, however, not surprising because such variation follows evidently differences in the status of private participation in community related tasks.

Protection of victims and witnesses during criminal proceedings and during trial has been put rather high on legislators agendas when transnational, organised crime emerged as an eminent criminal problem in the nineties and sexual abuse in particular child victims of sexual abuse fuelled demands to reduce secondary traumatisation by way of providing for introduction of evidence through video tapes or live video links. In many European countries it is now victims of human trafficking that receive attention in this regard[158]. Victims of terrorism, however, fall under the rules that have been enacted to protect intimidated victims or victims under the threat of violent

---

[158] See, e.g., Council of Europe, Commissioner for Human Rights, Berlin Declaration as of November 2004.

revenge. Witness protection schemes vary also, in particular as regards the type of crime victims that are eligible for protective measures.

4.3 Conclusions

Issues to be covered when trying to elaborate a legitimate and just scheme of compensating victims of terrorism are certainly the problem of rare events. It is clear that full blown terrorist attacks with scores of victims will remain rare events in the core of Europe in the future. An exception is the Russian Federation where the pace of terrorist attacks will continue to be determined by the armed conflict in Chechnya.

Insofar it seems reasonable to suggest to make compensation of victims of terrorism part of general victim compensation legislation and to abstain from developing a support and compensation scheme exclusively for terrorist victimization.

As regards emergency relief and general support and assistance, it seems preferable to make co-ordination of support and assistance, emergency relief etc. part of general civil and public disaster response schemes that are in place in most of European countries.

Then, indirect victimization in terms of minority communities that are at risk of falling prey to a backlash after a terrorist attack should be made part of response plans. A significant backlash against minority communities evidently is part of terrorist strategies devised to destroy social solidarity and establish a climate of fear, ethnic and religious hate favourable to the spread of violence.

The compensation of victims of violence should have a statutory basis. Event based compensation and ad hoc programming of compensation and assistance does not meet requirements set by principles of predictability and equal treatment.

Compensation of victims of violent crime is justified by social solidarity which in turn justifies a social welfare approach which makes the type and the amount of compensation dependent on the financial needs that are due to falling prey to violence.

Variation in legislation and practices in the area of victim compensation is large in Europe. What could be envisaged is the development of good practices in both victim compensation, NGO based victim support and witness (victim) protection based on evaluation of systems.

Contacts

Institutions and organisations responsible for victims

Albania

Ministria e Drejtesise
Department of Codification
Blv. Zogu I
Tirana
Albania
Tel.: +355-42-32704

Andorra

Ministeri de Justícia i d'Interior
Edifici Serveis de l'Obac
Escaldes-engordany
Tel.: +376-872080
Fax: +376-869250
www.govern.ad

Minsiteri de Salut i Benestar
Av. Princep Benlloch, 30, 4rt
Edifici Clara Rabassa
Andorra la Vella
Tel.: +376-829346
Fax: +376-825838
min.sanitat@andorra.ad
www.salutibenestar.ad

Armenia

Ministry of Justice
3 Vazgen Sargsyan street
Yerevan
Tel.: +3741 58 17 24

Austria

Bundesministerium für Justiz
Museumstr. 7
1070 Vienna
Tel.: +43-1-52 1 52-0
www.bmj.gv.at

Weisser Ring
Marokkanergasse 3
1030 Vienna
Tel.: +43-1-712 14 05
Fax: +43-1-718 83 74

office@weisser-ring.at
www.weisser-ring.at

Azerbaijan

Ministry of Justice
Inshaatchilar ave. 1
Baku
Tel.: +99-412-492 06 48

Belgium

Ministry of Justice
Service 'Justitiehuizen' Victim
support
115, Bld. de Waterloo
1000 Brussels
Tel.: +32-2-542.65.11

Ministry of the Interior
Dept. Security and Prevention
Policy
Tel.: +32-2-500 25 15

Commissie voor financiële hulp
aan slachtoffers van opzettelijke
gewelddaden
Waterloolaan 115
1000 Brussels
Tel.: +32-2-542 65 11
commissie.slachtoffers@just.fgov.be

Bosnia and Herzegovina

Ministry of Justice / Ministarstvo
pravde BiH
Trg Bosne i Hercegovine 1
71000 Sarajevo
Tel.: +387-33-223 501; 223 503
Fax: +387-33-223 504
kontakt@mpr.gov.ba

Ministry for Human Rights and
Refugees / Ministarstvo za ljudska
prava i izbjeglice BiH
Trg Bosne i Hercegovine 1
71000 Sarajevo

Tel.:+387-33-206 273 or 655;
+387-33-445 122
Fax: +387-33-206 140
ljudprav@mhrr.gov.ba

Victimology Society
Ulica Patriotskc ligc 30
Sarajevo
Tel.: 071/663-947
Fax: 071/617-257

Bulgaria

Ministry of Justice / Ministerstwo
Prawosjdieto
Yl. Slawjanska1
1040 Sofia
Tel.: +359-2-98 74 398
pr@justice.government.bg
www.justice.government.bg

Croatia

Ministry of Justice, Department of
international co-operation and
human rights / Ministarstvo
pravosuđa Republike Hrvatske,
Uprava za međunarodnu pomoć,
suradnju i ljudska prava
Pomoćnica ministrice gđa Ljiljana
Vodopija-Čengić
Republike Austrije 14
10000 Zagreb
Fax: +385-1-3710 672

Croatian Society of Victimology /
Hrvatsko Zrtvoslovno Drustvo
Sveuciliste u Zagrebu
Pravni Fakultet
Trg. M. Tita 14
10000 Zagreb
Tel.: +385-1-456 4317

Cyprus

Ministry of Justice and Public
Order
125 Athalassas Ave.

1461 Nicosia
Tel.: +357-22-808 915
Fax: +357-22-305 115
cuipcd@police.gov.cy
www.police.gov.cy

Czech Republic

Ministry of Justice
Vyšehradská 16
128 10 Prague 2
Tel.: +420-2-21 997 111
posta@msp.justice.cz
www.portal.justice.cz

Supreme Prosecutors Office
Vrchni statni zastupitelstvi
Nam. Hrdinu 1300
140 65 Prague 4
Tel.: +420-2-61 196 402
Fax: +420-2-41 409 339

Weisser Ring / Bily Kruh Bezpeci
Duskovo 20
150 00 Prague 5
Tel.: +420-2- 57 317 110
Fax: +420-2-51 512 299
bkb@volny.cz
www.donalinka.cz

Denmark

Ministry of Justice, Law
Department, Criminal Law Division
Slotsholmsgade 10
1216 Copenhagen K.
Tel.: +45-33-92 33 40
Fax: +45-33-93 35 10
jm@jm.dk
www.jm.dk

Ministry of Social Affairs
Holmens Kanal 22
1060 Copenhagen K
Tel.: +45-33-92 93 00
Fax: +45-33-93 25 18
sm@sm.dk
www.social.dk

National Association for the
Support of Victims of Violence /
Landsforeningen Hjælp Voldsofre
(LHV)
Rådhusstræde 7, 1.
8900 Randers
Tel.: +45-86-41 59 00
Fax: +45-86-41 59 88
lhv@voldsofre.dk
www.voldsofre.dk

Estonia

Ministry of Justice,
Department of Criminal Policy
Tõnismägi 5a
15191 Tallinn
Tel.: +372-6208 223
info@just.ee
www.just.ee

Ministry of Social Affairs
Social Security Department
Gonsiori 29
15027 Tallinn
www.sm.ee

Finland

Ministry of Justice:

Central Administration and Law,
Drafting Departments
Korkeavuorenkatu 37
Helsinki
Tel.: +358-9-1606 7658

Criminal Policy Department
Mannerheimintie 4
Helsinki
Tel.: +358-9-1606 7900
www.om.fi

Victim Support Finland
Central office
PL 168
00141 Helsinki
Tel.: +358-9-6123232
www.rikosuhripaivystys.fi

France

Ministry of Justice /
Ministère de la Justice
13, place Vendôme
75042 Paris Cedex
Tel.: +33-1-44 77 60 60
www.justice.gouv.fr

Institut National d'aide aux
Victimes et de Médiation -
INAVEM
1, rue du Pré Saint Gervais
93691 Pantin Cedex
Tel.: +33-8-10 09 86 09
administration@inavem.org
www.inavem.org

Guarantee Fund for the Victims of
Acts of Terrorism and other
Offences (FGTI)
contact@fgti.fr
Forms for compensation claims
can be downloaded at:
www.fgti.fr

S.O.S. attentats,
S.O.S. terrorisme
Hôtel National des Invalides
75700 Paris Cedex 07
Tel.: +33-1-45 55 41 41
Fax: +33-1-45 55 55 55
contact@sos-attentats.org
www.sos-attentats.org

Georgia

Ministry of Justice
30 Rustaveli Ave.
0146 Tbilisi
Tel.: +99-532-758 276
justice@justice.gov.ge

Germany

Ministry of Justice /
Bundesministerium der Justiz
Mohrenstraße 37
10117 Berlin

Tel.: +49-1888-580 9030
Fax: +49-1888-580 9046
www.bmj.bund.de

Ministry of Social Affairs /
Bundesministerium für Gesundheit
und Soziale Sicherung,
Postfach 500
53108 Bonn,
Fax: +49-180-51 51 511
www.bmgs.bund.de
www.bmgs.bund.de/download/bros
chueren/A719.pdf

Weisser Ring e.V.
Bundesgeschäftsstelle
Weberstraße 16
55130 Mainz
Tel.: +49-6131-83 03-0
Fax: +49-6131-83 03-45
info@weisser-ring.de
www.weisser-ring.de

Association of German Victim
Support Organisations /
Arbeitskreis der Opferhilfen in der
Bundesrepublik Deutschland e.V.
Perleberger Str. 27
10559 Berlin
Tel.: +49-30-39 407 780
Fax: +49-30-39 407 795
info@opferhilfen.de
www.opferhilfen.de
www.opferhilfe-
hamburg.de/ado.html

Greece

Ministry of Justice,
Department for legal affairs in
European Union and international
organisations matters
Messogeion 96
115-27 Athens
Tel.: +30-2107767310
www.ministryofjustice.gr
Greek Society of Victimology
3, Gladstonos str.
10677 Athens

Hungary

Ministry of Justice, Department for
Penal Legislation / Igazságügyi
Minisztérium
Büntetőjogi Kodifikációs Főosztály
Kossuth sq. 4
1055 Budapest

National Fund for Victims of Crime
Németvölgyi u. 41
P.O.Box 640
1539 Budapest
Tel.: +36-1-441-1353
b-m-k.hu@axelero.hu
www.b-m-k.hu
www.b-m-k.hu/europa.htm

Weisser Ring / Fehér Gyürü
Közhasznu Egyesület
Szt. István krt. 1
1055 Budapest
Tel.: +36-1-3122287
Fax: +36-1-4721162
fehergyuru@axelero.hu

Iceland

Ministry of Justice and
Ecclesiastical Affairs / Dóms- og
kirkjumálaráðuneyti, lagaskrifstofa
Skuggasundi
150 Reykjavik
Tel.: +354-545-9000
Fax: +354-552-7340

Ireland

Department of Justice, Equality
and Law Reform,
Criminal Law Reform Division
Old Faculty Building
Shelbourne Road
Dublin 4
Tel.: +353-1-6028202
Fax: +353-1-6785786
criminal_law_reform_inbox@justice.ie

Victim Support Ireland
Haliday House
32 Arran Quay
Dublin 7
Tel.: +353-1-8780870
Fax: +353-1-8780944
info@victimsupport.ie

Italy

Ministry of Justice, Department of
Legislation / Ministero della
giustizia, Ufficio legislativo
Via Arenula, 70
00186 Rome
Tel.: +39-06-68851
www.giustizia.it

Ministry of Home Affairs / Ministero
dell'Interno
P.le Viminale
00186 Rome
Tel.: +39-06-4651
www.mininterno.it

Italian Association for Victims of
Terrorism / Associazione Italiana
Vittime del Terrorismo
Via Maria Vittoria, 12
10123 Torino
Tel.: +39-011-8125406
Fax: +39-011-8122488
info@vittimeterrorismo.it
www.vittimeterrorismo.it

Latvia

Latvijas Republikas Tieslietu
ministrija
Kanceleja
Brivibas blvd 36
1536 Riga
Tel.: +371-2-7036 716 or 721
tm.kancelejae@simbolstm.gov.lv
www.tm.gov.lv

Liechtenstein

Liechtensteinische
Landesverwaltung
Ressort Justiz
Städtle 49
9490 Vaduz
Tel.: +423-236-61 11
www.llv.li

Lithuania

Ministry of Justice
Gedimino g. 30
011004 Vilnius
Tel.: +370-5-266 29 33
Fax: +370-5-262 59 40
tminfo@tic.lt
www.tm.lt

State Security Department
Tel. +370-5-266 31 88
Tel. +370-5-266 32 65

Crime Victim Care Association
Valakupių g. 5
2016 Vilnius
Tel: +370-8-5-274 06 37

Luxembourg

Ministry of Justice
13, rue Erasme
bâtiment Pierre Werner
1468 Luxemburg
Tel.: +352-478-1
Fax: +352-2668 48 61
info@mj.public.lu
www.mj.public.lu

Weisser Ring – Luxemburg /
Wäisse Rank – Lëtzeburg
Hëllef fir Affer vu Verbriechen
84, rue Adolphe Fischer
1521 Luxembourg
Tel.: +352-402040
Fax: +352-499880

Malta

Ministry for Justice and Home
Affairs
House of Catalunja
Marsamxetto road
Valetta – CMR 02
Tel.:+356-22957127
www.mjha.gov.mt
www.justice.gov.mt

Probation Service
www.mjha.gov.mt/departments/cor
radino/probation.html

National Council of Women of
Malta
www.ncwmalta.com

Moldova

Ministry of Justice
82, 31 August 1989 St.
2012 Chisinau
Tel.: +373-22-20 14 64

Monaco

Ministère d'Etat
Direction des Affaires Législatives
1, Avenue des Castelans
98014 Monaco
www.monaco.gouv.mc

Netherlands

Ministry of Justice / Ministerie van
Justitie
Nationaal Coördinator
Terrorismebestrijding
Postbus 16950
2500 BZ The Hague
Tel.: +31-70-3150 423
Fax: +31-70-3150 320
www.justitie.nl

State Fund for Victims of Crime /
Schadefonds Geweldsmisdrijven

Postbus 1947
2280 DX Rijswijk
Tel.: +31-70-414 2000
Fax: +31-70-414 2001
info@schadefonds.nl
www.schadefonds.nl

National Victim Support
Organisation / Slachtofferhulp
Nederland
Maliesingel 38
3581 BK Utrecht
Tel.: +31-30-2340116
Fax: +31-30-2317655
www.slachtofferhulp.nl

Norway

Ministry of Justice and the Police
Akersgt 42
PO. Box 8005 Dep
0030 Oslo
Tel.: +47-22-24 90 90
postmottak@jd.dep.no

The Norwegian criminal Injuries
Compensation Authority / Kontoret
for voldsoffererstatning
Postboks 253
9951 Vardø
Tel.: +47-78-98 95 00
Fax: +47-78-98 95 10
post@voldsoffererstatning.no
www.voldsoffererstatning.no

National Association for the
Support of Victims of Violence /
Landsforeningen for Voldsofre
Ensjøsvingen 10 b
0661 Oslo
Tel.: +47-22-65 54 55
Fax: +47-22-67 88 43
www.voldsoffer.no

Norwegian center for violence and
traumatic stress studies /
Norsk Forbund for Voldsofre (NFV)
Solberglivn. 94 A
0683 Oslo

Tel.: +47-22-26 76 41
www.nkvts.no

Poland

Ministry of Justice / Ministerstwo
Sprawiedliwości
Al. Ujazdowskie 11,
00-950 Warsaw
Tel.: +48-22-521 23 81
www.ms.gov.pl

Ministry of the Interior and
Administration
ul. Stefana Batorego 5
02-591 Warsaw
Tel.: +48-22-601 44 27
www.mswia.gov.pl

The Office of the Commissioner for
Civil Rights Protection
(Ombudsman)
Al. Solidarności 77
00-090 Warsaw
Tel.: +48-22-551 77 00
www.brpo.gov.pl

Polish Society of Victimology
Ulica Listopadowa 49 # 9
Warsaw
Fax: +48-22-267 853

Polskiej Akademia Nauk
ul. Nowy Swiat 72
Palace Staszica
00-330 Warsaw

The Foundation of Assistance to
Crime Victims
Ul. Wisniowa 50
02-520 Warsaw
Tel.: +48-22-482890

Portugal

Ministry of Justice
Praça do Comércio
1149-019 Lisbon
Tel.: +21-3222 300

Fax: +21-3479 208
gmj@mj.gov.pt
www.mj.gov.pt

Ministry of Home Affairs
Praça do Comércio
1149-015 Lisbon
Tel.: +21-3233 000
Fax: +21-3423 448
www.mai.gov.pt

Ministry of Social Affairs
Praça de Londres, 2 - 16°
1049-056 Lisbon
Tel.: +21-8441 700
Fax: +21-8424 110
gmtss@mtss.gov.pt
www.mssfc.gov.pt

National Victim Support
Association / Associação de Apoio
à Vítima (APAV)
Serviços centrais de Sede
Rua do Comércio, 56 - 5°
1100-150 Lisbon
Tel.: +21-885 40 90
Fax: +21-887 63 51
apav.sede@apav.pt
www.apav.pt

Romania

Ministry of Justice / Ministerul de
Justiție
Directorate for Probation and
Victim Protection
Apolodor str. 17, sector 5
Bucharest
Tel.: +40-21-314 44 00
www.just.ro

Russian Federation

Ministry of Justice
Vorontsovo Pole 4
109 830 Moscou
Tel.: +7-095-955 59 99

The Ombudsman for Human
Rights
Mjasnizkaja str. 47
107084 Moscow
Tel.: +7-095-207 53 37
www.ombudsmanrf.ru

Association 'North-East' of Victims
of Terrorism
Tel.: +7-095-202 22 24
zpch@mail.ru

San Marino

Ministry of Home Affairs and
Justice / Affari Interni e Giustizia
Parva Domus
Piazza della Libertà
47890 San Marino
Tel.: +39-0549-882318
segr.aff.int@omniway.sm
www.interni.segreteria.sm

Serbia

Ministry of Justice
Nemanjina 22-26
11000 Belgrade
Tel.: +381-11-3616-548/549
Fax: +381-11-3616-419
kabinet@mpravde.sr.gov.yu
www.mpravde.sr.gov.yu

Victimology Society of Serbia
(VSS) / Viktimolosko drustvo Srbije
Kolarceva 4/III
11000 Belgrade
Tel./Fax: +381-11-621 797
vds@eunet.yu
www.vds.org.yu/indexe.html

Slovak Republic

Ministry of Justice / Ministerstvo
spravodlivosti Slovenskej republiky
Odbor rehabilitácií a
odškodňovania
Župné námestie 13
813 11 Bratislava

Tel.: +421-2-59 353 281
Fax: +421-2-59 353 203
www.justice.sk

Victim Support Slovakia / Pomoc
obetiam násilia
P.O.Box 83
820 05 Bratislava 25
Tel.: +421-2-5464 7141
info@pomocobetiam.sk
www.pomocobetiam.sk

Slovenia

Ministry of Justice / Ministrstvo za
Pravosodje
Župančičeva 3
1000 Ljubljana
Tel.: +386-1-639 52 00
Fax: +386-1-369-57 83
gp.mp@gov.si
www.gov.si

Crime Victim Assistance /
Zavod za vzpodbujanje in
razvijanje kvalitete življenja
PAPILOT
Grablovičeva 1
1000 Ljubljana
Tel.: +386-1-231 27 42
Fax: +386-1-133 96 39
www.zod-lj.si

Spain

Ministry of Justice /
Ministerio de Justicia
Dirección
San Bernardo, 45
28015 Madrid
Tel.: +34-91-390 45 00
www.justicia.es

Association of the Victims pf
Terrorism / Asociación Víctimas
del Terrorismo (AVT)
Apdo de correos 53.195
28080 Madrid

avt@avt.org
www.avt.org

Association of the Victims of 11
March 2004 / Asociación Víctimas
del 11m
C/ Puentelarra, 7 - locales 3 y 4
28031 Madrid
Tel.: +34-91-332 04 44
Fax: +34-91-331 93 82
buzon@asociacion11m.org
www.lapalabramagica.com/11m/as
ociacion11m.htm

Sweden

Ministry of Justice
Rosenbad 4
103 33 Stockholm
Tel.: +46-8-405 10 00
Fax: +46-8-20 27 34
registrator@justice.ministry.se
www.sweden.gov.se/sb/d/584

Crime Victim Compensation and
Support Authority /
Brottsoffermyndigheten
Box 470
901 09 UMEÅ
Tel.: +46-90-70 82 00, vx
Fax: +46-90-17 83 53
registrator@brottsoffermyndighete
n.se
www.brottsoffermyndigheten.se

Swedish Association for Victim
Support / Brottsofferjourernas
Riksförbund
Bondegatan 40
Box 110 14
100 61 Stockholm
Tel.: +46-8-644 88 00
Fax: +46-8-644 88 28
boj.riks@boj.se
www.boj.se

The National Association of
Relatives of Homicide Victims
www.rav.se

Switzerland

Federal Department of Justice and
Police / Bundesamt für Justiz
3003 Bern
Tel.: +41-31-322 41 43
Fax: +41-31-322 78 79
info@bj.admin.ch
www.ofj.admin.ch

Weisser Ring / Anneau Blanc /
Anello Bianco
Dufourstr. 95
8008 Zürich
Tel.: +41-44-422 65 62
Fax: +41-44-671 04 06
info@weisser-ring.ch
www.weisser-ring.ch

Regional Victim Support Office
(Canton of Zürich)
Kantonale Opferhilfestelle
Direktion der Justiz und des Innern
des Kantons Zürich
Postfach
8090 Zürich
Tel.: +41-44-259 25 41
Fax: +41-44-259 51 94
kantonale.opferhilfestelle@ji.zh.ch
www.opferhilfe.zh.ch

"The former Yugoslav Republic of Macedonia"

Ministry of the Interior
Dimče Mirčev St bb
Skopje
Tel.: +389-2-311 7222
Fax: +389-2-311 2468
www.moi.gov.mk

Turkey

Ministry of the Interior /
Icisleri Bakanligi
Bakanliklar
Ankara
Tel.: +90-312-425 72 14, +90-505-
466 93 39/466 93 40/466 93 41

Department of European Union
Affairs and International Relations
Tel.: +90-312-425 72 14/425 34 61
www.icisleri.gov.tr

Ukraine

Ministry of Justice
Prov. Rylskiy, 10
01001 Kyiv
Tel.: +38-044-244 15 50

United Kingdom

Home Office
Victims Unit
Room 328
50 Queen Anne's Gate
London SW1H 9AT
www.homeoffice.gov.uk/justice/vict
ims/index.html

Criminal Injuries Compensation
Scheme
www.cica.gov.uk for England,
Wales & Scotland
www.nio.gov.uk for Northern
Ireland

Criminal Injuries Compensation
Appeals Board
www.cicap.gov.uk

Criminal Injuries Compensation
Authority
PO Box 11431
London SW9 6ZH
Tel.: 0845 30 30 900
www.cjsonline.org

Victim Compensation Agency
Royston House
34 Upper Queen Street
Belfast BT1 6FD
Tel.: +44-28-90 54 7323
Fax: +44-28-9054 6956
comp-agency@nics.gov.uk
www.compensationni.gov.uk

Victim Support
National Office
Cranmer House
39 Brixton Road
London SW9 6DZ
Tel.: +44-20-7735 9166
Fax: +44-20-7582 5712
contact@victimsupport.org.uk
www.victimsupport.org

Victim Support Scotland
www.victimsupportsco.demon.co.uk

Victims of Crime in Scotland
www.scottishvictimsofcrime.org.uk

The Network for Surviving Stalking
secure.nss.org.uk

Support After Murder And
Manslaughter SAMM
www.samm.org.uk

The Compassionate Friends
www.tcf.org.uk/

www.crimeconcern.org.uk

www.womensaid.org.uk

Council of Europe Publications
(Order from http://book.coe.int or from specialised bookshops)

The fight against terrorism – Council of Europe standards (2007) – 4th edition

The Council of Europe has drafted a number of international legal instruments and standards reflecting the importance it attaches to combating terrorism and illustrating the underlying message of this Organisation, which is that it is possible to fight against terrorism efficiently while upholding the basic values that are the common heritage of the European continent. This publication contains these texts and is intended to provide a handy, comprehensive reference document.

ISBN: 978-92-871-6277-9, €53 / US$80

« Apologie du Terrorisme » and « Incitement to terrorism » (2004)

The fight against terrorism must never lead to a curtailing of the values and freedoms terrorists intend to destroy: the rule of law and freedom of thought and expression must never be sacrificed in this struggle.

This report analyses the situation in member and observer States of the Council of Europe and their different legal approaches to the phenomenon of public expression of praise, justification and other forms of support for terrorism and terrorists, referred to in this publication as "apologie du terrorisme" and "incitement to terrorism".

ISBN: 978-92-871-5468-2, €19 / US$29

Terrorism: Special investigation techniques (2005)

In order to combat terrorism and serious crime, law enforcement authorities have had to adapt their investigative means and develop special investigation techniques. Since there is a risk that they may infringe individual rights, special investigation techniques must be subject to control.

This publication contains an analytical report, which examines special investigation techniques in relation to law enforcement and prosecution, the control of their implementation, human rights and international co-operation and also contains a survey of national practice.

ISBN: 978-92-871-5655-6, €39 / US$59

Human rights and the fight against terrorism – The Council of Europe Guidelines (2005)

The Council of Europe believes that an effective fight against terrorism fully respecting human rights is possible.

This publication contains the Guidelines on Human Rights and the fight against terrorism, the first international instrument in this area, and the Guidelines on the protection of victims of terrorist acts, together with the reference and supporting texts and relevant case-law of the European Court of Human Rights.

ISBN 978-92-871-5694-5, €8 / US$12

Terrorism: Protection of witnesses and collaborators of justice (2006)

In order to combat terrorism, States often rely on the testimony of people who are closely connected to terrorist groups and who are more vulnerable than others to the use of intimidation against them or against people close to them. This may endanger the success of prosecutions often based on long and complicated investigations. Strengthening international co-operation in this field is also a useful means to ensure the protection of those persons whose protection would prove difficult on a merely national basis, given the conditions in the country where they are located. This publication contains the recently adopted standards in this field, as well as a survey of national laws and practice in Council of Europe member and observer states and an analytical report.

ISBN 978-92-871-5811-6, €39 / US$59

Cyberterrorism - the use of the Internet for terrorist purposes

The new publication in the Terrorism and Law Series looks at the situation in the Council of Europe's member and observer states and gives a comprehensive overview of the issues at stake.

ISBN 978-92-871-6226-7, €28 / US$42

Sales agents for publications of the Council of Europe
Agents de vente des publications du Conseil de l'Europe

BELGIUM/BELGIQUE
La Librairie Européenne -
The European Bookshop
Rue de l'Orme, 1
B-1040 BRUXELLES
Tel.: +32 (0)2 231 04 35
Fax: +32 (0)2 735 08 60
E-mail: order@libeurop.be
http://www.libeurop.be

Jean De Lannoy
Avenue du Roi 202 Koningslaan
B-1190 BRUXELLES
Tel.: +32 (0)2 538 43 08
Fax: +32 (0)2 538 08 41
E-mail: jean.de.lannoy@dl-servi.com
http://www.jean-de-lannoy.be

CANADA
Renouf Publishing Co. Ltd.
1-5369 Canotek Road
OTTAWA, Ontario K1J 9J3, Canada
Tel.: +1 613 745 2665
Fax: +1 613 745 7660
Toll-Free Tel.: (866) 767-6766
E-mail: order.dept@renoufbooks.com
http://www.renoufbooks.com

CZECH REPUBLIC/
RÉPUBLIQUE TCHÈQUE
Suweco CZ, s.r.o.
Klecakova 347
CZ-180 21 PRAHA 9
Tel.: +420 2 424 59 204
Fax: +420 2 848 21 646
E-mail: import@suweco.cz
http://www.suweco.cz

DENMARK/DANEMARK
GAD
Vimmelskaftet 32
DK-1161 KØBENHAVN K
Tel.: +45 77 66 60 00
Fax: +45 77 66 60 01
E-mail: gad@gad.dk
http://www.gad.dk

FINLAND/FINLANDE
Akateeminen Kirjakauppa
PO Box 128
Keskuskatu 1
FIN-00100 HELSINKI
Tel.: +358 (0)9 121 4430
Fax: +358 (0)9 121 4242
E-mail: akatilaus@akateeminen.com
http://www.akateeminen.com

FRANCE
La Documentation française
(diffusion/distribution France entière)
124, rue Henri Barbusse
F-93308 AUBERVILLIERS CEDEX
Tél.: +33 (0)1 40 15 70 00
Fax: +33 (0)1 40 15 68 00
E-mail: commande@ladocumentationfrancaise.fr
http://www.ladocumentationfrancaise.fr

Librairie Kléber
1 rue des Francs Bourgeois
F-67000 STRASBOURG
Tel.: +33 (0)3 88 15 78 88
Fax: +33 (0)3 88 15 78 80
E-mail: francois.wolfermann@librairie-kleber.fr
http://www.librairie-kleber.com

GERMANY/ALLEMAGNE
AUSTRIA/AUTRICHE
UNO Verlag GmbH
August-Bebel-Allee 6
D-53175 BONN
Tel.: +49 (0)228 94 90 20
Fax: +49 (0)228 94 90 222
E-mail: bestellung@uno-verlag.de
http://www.uno-verlag.de

GREECE/GRÈCE
Librairie Kauffmann s.a.
Stadiou 28
GR-105 64 ATHINAI
Tel.: +30 210 32 55 321
Fax.: +30 210 32 30 320
E-mail: ord@otenet.gr
http://www.kauffmann.gr

HUNGARY/HONGRIE
Euro Info Service kft.
1137 Bp. Szent István krt. 12.
H-1137 BUDAPEST
Tel.: +36 (06)1 329 2170
Fax: +36 (06)1 349 2053
E-mail: euroinfo@euroinfo.hu
http://www.euroinfo.hu

ITALY/ITALIE
Licosa SpA
Via Duca di Calabria, 1/1
I-50125 FIRENZE
Tel.: +39 0556 483215
Fax: +39 0556 41257
E-mail: licosa@licosa.com
http://www.licosa.com

MEXICO/MEXIQUE
Mundi-Prensa México, S.A. De C.V.
Río Pánuco, 141 Delegacíon Cuauhtémoc
06500 MÉXICO, D.F.
Tel.: +52 (01)55 55 33 56 58
Fax: +52 (01)55 55 14 67 99
E-mail: mundiprensa@mundiprensa.com.mx
http://www.mundiprensa.com.mx

NETHERLANDS/PAYS-BAS
De Lindeboom Internationale Publicaties b.v.
M.A. de Ruyterstraat 20 A
NL-7482 BZ HAAKSBERGEN
Tel.: +31 (0)53 5740004
Fax: +31 (0)53 5729296
E-mail: books@delindeboom.com
http://www.delindeboom.com

NORWAY/NORVÈGE
Akademika
Postboks 84 Blindern
N-0314 OSLO
Tel.: +47 2 218 8100
Fax: +47 2 218 8103
E-mail: support@akademika.no
http://www.akademika.no

POLAND/POLOGNE
Ars Polona JSC
25 Obroncow Street
PL-03-933 WARSZAWA
Tel.: +48 (0)22 509 86 00
Fax: +48 (0)22 509 86 10
E-mail: arspolona@arspolona.com.pl
http://www.arspolona.com.pl

PORTUGAL
Livraria Portugal
(Dias & Andrade, Lda.)
Rua do Carmo, 70
P-1200-094 LISBOA
Tel.: +351 21 347 42 82 / 85
Fax: +351 21 347 02 64
E-mail: info@livrariaportugal.pt
http://www.livrariaportugal.pt

RUSSIAN FEDERATION/
FÉDÉRATION DE RUSSIE
Ves Mir
9a, Kolpacnhyi per.
RU-101000 MOSCOW
Tel.: +7 (8)495 623 6839
Fax: +7 (8)495 625 4269
E-mail: orders@vesmirbooks.ru
http://www.vesmirbooks.ru

SPAIN/ESPAGNE
Mundi-Prensa Libros, s.a.
Castelló, 37
E-28001 MADRID
Tel.: +34 914 36 37 00
Fax: +34 915 75 39 98
E-mail: libreria@mundiprensa.es
http://www.mundiprensa.com

SWITZERLAND/SUISSE
Van Diermen Editions – ADECO
Chemin du Lacuez 41
CH-1807 BLONAY
Tel.: +41 (0)21 943 26 73
Fax: +41 (0)21 943 36 05
E-mail: info@adeco.org
http://www.adeco.org

UNITED KINGDOM/ROYAUME-UNI
The Stationery Office Ltd
PO Box 29
GB-NORWICH NR3 1GN
Tel.: +44 (0)870 600 5522
Fax: +44 (0)870 600 5533
E-mail: book.enquiries@tso.co.uk
http://www.tsoshop.co.uk

UNITED STATES and CANADA/
ÉTATS-UNIS et CANADA
Manhattan Publishing Company
468 Albany Post Road
CROTTON-ON-HUDSON, NY 10520, USA
Tel.: +1 914 271 5194
Fax: +1 914 271 5856
E-mail: Info@manhattanpublishing.com
http://www.manhattanpublishing.com

Council of Europe Publishing/Editions du Conseil de l'Europe
F-67075 Strasbourg Cedex
Tel.: +33 (0)3 88 41 25 81 – Fax: +33 (0)3 88 41 39 10 – E-mail: publishing@coe.int – Website: http://book.coe.int

RECEIVED

MAR 2 8 2008

Heafey Law Library